Art, Design an

An Intr

Also by Malcolm Barnard

Fashion as Communication

Art, Design and Visual Culture

An Introduction

MALCOLM BARNARD

St. Martin's Press
New York

ART, DESIGN AND VISUAL CULTURE

Copyright © 1998 by Malcolm Barnard

St. Martin's Press, Scholarly and Reference Division,
175 Fifth Avenue, New York, N.Y. 10010

First published in the United States of America in 1998

This book is printed on paper suitable for recycling and made from fully managed and sustained forest sources.

Printed in Hong Kong

ISBN 0–312–21691–2 clothbound
ISBN 0–312–21692–0 paperback

Library of Congress Cataloging-in-Publication Data
Barnard, Malcolm, 1958–
Art, design, and visual culture : an introduction / Malcolm Barnard.
p.   cm.
Includes bibliographical references and index.
ISBN 0–312–21691–2 (cloth). — ISBN 0–312–21692–0 (pbk.)
1. Artists—Psychology.   2. Creation (Literary, artistic, etc.)
3. Visual communication.   4. Art and society.   5. Art patronage.
I. Title.
N71.B32   1998
701—dc21   98–21474
                                                                  CIP

To my parents

Contents

List of Illustrations

Acknowledgements

Many of the ideas and approaches covered in this book were suggested to me during my time as a part-time lecturer in the History and Theory of Art and Design at Leeds Polytechnic (now Leeds Metropolitan University) between 1984 and 1990. My colleagues at that time included Jonathan Harris, Ian Heywood, Wendy Leeks, Richard Tyler and Anita Whittle. I am sure that they will recognise what I learned from them.

Many of these ideas and approaches have been refined and developed during my time at the University of Derby. My colleagues here have included Alan Barnes, Robert Burstow, Gail Day, Steve Edwards, David Heathcote, Stanley Mitchell, Giles Peaker, Josie Walter, Julia Welbourne and Rhiannon Williams. I am grateful to them all, and to my friend Chris Jenks, of Goldsmiths' College, University of London, for a great deal of help and many useful suggestions.

Catherine Gray, the commissioning editor, Houri Alavi, the assistant editor, and Nancy Williams have been of enormous help at Macmillan, as has the anonymous adviser whose maturity and rigour tightened up the work considerably. I am also grateful to Simon Birkett and Sally Edwards at the University of Derby for producing prints suitable for reproduction here from some often unpromising originals.

Finally, acknowledgements must be made to the Research Centre for Cultural History and Critical Theory, in the School of Art and Design at the University of Derby, which enabled me to take some time out from teaching in order to write.

MALCOLM BARNARD

The author and publishers wish to thank the following for permission to use copyright material:

British Museum for Hokusai's *Cuckoo and Azalea*; DMB&B and Fiat for the advertisement of Fiat Bravo/Brava; Gilbert and George for *In the Shit*; Interface RSCG and Citroën for the advertisements of the Citroën ZX; Kunsthistoriches Museum, Vienna, for Brueghel's *Hunters in the Snow*; National Gallery, London, for Gainsborough's *Mr and Mrs Andrews*; Rijksmuseum, Amsterdam, for Rembrandt's *The Night Watch*; Tim O'Sullivan for photograph of tattoos; UPI Newspictures for photograph of men wearing Zoot suits.

Every effort has been made to trace all the copyright-holders, but if any have been inadvertently overlooked the publishers will be pleased to make the necessary arrangement at the first opportunity.

Introduction

Few people today, in the late 1990s, would deny that sight, or vision, is as vital and important a system of human communication and cultural expression as language. Indeed, it has become something of a commonplace in the past thirty or forty years to point out the literal and metaphorical centrality of vision and the visual in western cultures. Guy Debord (1977), writing in the 1960s, has argued that modern society may be described as 'the society of the spectacle'. People passively consume images and representations, spectacles, that are divorced from real life and their real needs. Michel Foucault (1977), writing in the 1970s, also thinks that western societies are organised in such a way as to privilege the visual although he disagrees with Debord, saying that 'our society is not one of spectacle, but of surveillance' (1977: 217). People are not watching, but rather being watched, inspected and recorded all the time; they (we) are reduced to appearances, to be scanned and scrutinised by anonymous and unseen authorities. And the 1988 report, entitled *Humanities in America*, for example, which was produced by the National Endowment for the Humanities, suggested that 'our common culture seems increasingly a product of what we watch' (quoted in W. J. T. Mitchell 1994: 1). Martin Jay has referred precisely to this 'visual turn' that has occurred in the past few years in cultural and critical theory. W. J. T. Mitchell wants to call the latest trend in contemporary cultural theory the 'pictorial turn' (1994: 11). And in *The Mirror of Nature*, Richard Rorty (1980) is so worried by the prevalence of visual and mirroring metaphors in our speech that he wants to rid language of them entirely, something that only confirms for Mitchell that 'a pictorial turn is taking place' (1994: 13).

While it has not perhaps been taken up with quite the same alacrity, there has also been something of a cultural turn in contemporary

1

human sciences. As David Chaney points out in a book entitled *The Cultural Turn*, culture has become 'both the dominant topic and most productive intellectual resource' of late twentieth-century work in the humanities (1994: 1). Chaney argues that the two world wars were followed by a 'profound loss of cultural values', which found expression in such art movements as Dadaism. The doubt entertained by many European intellectuals concerning the possibility of universal cultural values was intensified by their developing awareness that modern mass communication and entertainment technologies would increasingly threaten traditional distinctions between elite and mass forms of culture. The argument is that, as traditional forms of culture and knowledge, which had been the province of intellectuals, are questioned or replaced, so cultural themes become more and more important to those intellectuals. Consequently, culture in any form becomes something that intellectuals are more and more interested in, as one of the few areas that they still have any control over (Chaney 1994: 9).

So, contemporary intellectuals, working in American and European universities and colleges, are increasingly interested in the visual and the cultural. However, it is usually both instructive and revealing to look also at everyday, apparently non-intellectual material, in the attempt to understand something. Paying attention to the popular press, for example, can give away what a society is worried about or thinking about. In the 1990s, *The Sunday Times* called its arts and review section 'The Culture', as if there were just one culture in modern Britain and as if reading this section would furnish its readers with all they could wish to know to keep them culturally informed. It may be unfair to call it a surprise hit, but a programme in which a reclusive nun called Sister Wendy discussed the history of western painting was shown at prime time on British television. It is also a good idea to listen to the things that people say, to listen to everyday phrases and colloquial sayings, in order to get some idea of the place, importance and meaning of a subject. These everyday phrases, often thought of as embodying 'common sense', or communal wisdom, will give away what that community thinks about a matter as surely as what that community's intellectuals say. This is precisely what Rorty is worried about: that embodied or embedded in everyday phrases are entire philosophical theories, or preconceptions, which should be examined explicitly rather than simply taken for granted. There are many colloquialisms in English that play upon the ideas of looking, vision and sight, and which give a clue both to the centrality and to the sense of such ideas in English-speaking communities.

In ordinary, everyday English, sexual desire may be expressed by 'eyeing someone up', or 'giving them the eye'. Of course, one only 'makes eyes' at someone if that person is 'good-looking'. If a person is said to be 'no oil-painting', and especially if they have 'four eyes' (wear glasses), they will receive no passes. Animosity may be described as 'looking daggers' at someone and in certain quarters violence may be offered simply by asking 'what are you looking at?' or 'are you looking at me?' The matter of who looks at whom, and with what consequences, is clearly significant here, as is the question of who has the right to look at whom. In popular vernacular, sight and looking are connected with power, as well as sex and violence; in a recent American presidential campaign, George Bush and Bill Clinton accused each other of 'blinking first' in the macho power-game involving 'staring the other out'. Everyday wisdom already recognises what the philosophers below analyse, that meaning, knowledge and the visual are linked in complicated metaphorical ways; every day, people ask 'Do you see what I mean?' Other people, understanding something for the first time, 'get the picture'. It is not entirely accidental that the everyday phrases here have had to do with sex, gender, violence, knowledge and power: these issues are of great importance and interest to contemporary culture and cultural studies. As Camille Paglia says in her account of western civilisation, these issues are 'deeply tangled; we cannot get one without the others' (1990: 32). They will also be of great importance and interest to the analyses found in the following chapters.

Western philosophical and religious traditions which underlie our everyday habits of thought and much unexamined everyday behaviour are almost completely dependent upon visual metaphors, allegories, and what must, unfortunately, be called 'images', to describe and explain subjects such as life's meaning. The ways in which western cultures understand and experience human knowledge and good and evil, for example, are highly dependent upon visual imagery. Philosophy is full of examples of light, dark, sight, blindness, reflections, shadows, mirrors and other visual phenomena being used to get to grips with the intricacies of such momentous subjects. Were it not for these visual metaphors, it might reasonably be suspected that western philosophy and religion would be unable to say anything at all concerning these matters, such is their dependence on them.

Light is often used as a metaphor for the Christian God, for good, and for knowledge. One speaks of 'enlightenment', as opposed to being kept in the dark. Light is also used as a description of Reason. Light, of course, is necessary for human vision; in the dark, human vision does not work so well.

Plato, writing around 420 BC, used an extended visual metaphor, or allegory, to describe human knowledge. More accurately, Plato used a visual metaphor in the dialogue known as *The Republic* to describe the limitations and difficulties involved in human knowledge. In what has become known as the allegory of the cave, Plato has Socrates describe a complex situation in which human beings live in an underground cave, shackled since birth so that they can see only in front of them. Behind them is a fire. Between the fire and the people is a raised road, on which has been built a low wall. Along the road pass other people, carrying implements, statues and figures of animals and human beings. Socrates' poor companion suggests that this is a strange image and that they are strange prisoners. Socrates replies that, to the contrary, they are 'like us', as they see and know nothing of themselves or the world they inhabit except the shadows cast on the wall by the fire. The translator of the Penguin edition of *The Republic* likens the situation endured by Plato's cave-dwellers to that found in contemporary cinemas and even suggests that the shifting shapes they watch are perhaps more like television (Lee 1955: 316). (The implication that Plato would have disapproved of watching television is an interesting one and one which reproduces the old idea discussed below in Chapter 8 that television viewers are 'cultural dupes', passively receiving the messages transmitted.) The point Socrates is making, of course, is that human knowledge is like the shadows cast on the wall, it consists in shadowy images, passively received and far removed from the true light, which is outside the cave and available only to the philosopher, who is not, necessarily, 'like us' at all (Plato 1961: 747ff.). Plato's explanation of memory and Aristotle's account of thinking are also indebted to visual analogies: both rely on the image of the soul receiving an image, as a wax tablet receives an image from a signet ring.

Earlier in the twentieth century, Wittgenstein used visual examples, including pictures, in his attempt to explain how human knowledge and meaning were possible, arguing that 'a picture is a model of reality' and that 'a proposition is a picture of reality' (1961: 8–9, 19). He argues that a proposition is meaningful because it corresponds to the world in the same way as a picture corresponds to the world.

Human knowledge and meaning are again said to be images, or pictures, but here the truth of that knowledge is a result of the proposition corresponding to reality. Slightly later this century, in a series of philosophical remarks which he describes as 'a number of sketches of landscapes' (1974: vii), Wittgenstein uses various images and pictures to show what is wrong with explaining human knowledge and meaning in terms of pictures (1974: 193ff.). One of these images or pictures is the well-known 'duck-rabbit', a series of lines that may be seen as either a duck or a rabbit, discussed in terms of 'metapictures' by Mitchell (Mitchell 1994: 35–82).

Among the great world religions, Judaism considers the visual to be so powerful that it contains a taboo on visual representation. Christianity considers the visual to be so powerful, and so powerful a source of evil, as to make it the subject of the second commandment. Second only to insisting on having no other god but God, the second commandment precludes idolatry and the making and worshipping of 'graven images' and 'likenesses'. A sin that concerns looking, images and likenesses is apparently more significant to Christianity than murder, adultery and coveting one's neighbour's ass. Richard Sennett goes so far as to say that the early Christian theology

> has had a profound and disturbing effect on the way our culture both believes in and suspects the reality of the senses. On the one hand, the eyes offer evidence of God. On the other hand, up to the moment of illumination most of this evidence is false. (1990: 9)

What Sennett is describing here is the way in which what he calls 'our culture' is ambivalent towards sight and the senses generally, capable of producing sayings like 'seeing is believing' whilst at the same time distrusting and denigrating 'vulgarly' empirical evidence.

The idea that an entire culture may be centred around the visual, that a whole cultural system which celebrates and privileges vision may develop is also to be found in Camille Paglia's work. She suggests in her *Sexual Personae* that 'western culture has a roving eye' and that 'western culture is built on perceptual relations' (1990: 32–3). All the products of western culture, from religion, art and architecture to advertising, fashion and films, she says, are profoundly visual phenomena. They are also masculine, in some way. The 'roving eye' of western culture is a male eye, endlessly and optimistically 'hunting and scanning' the terrain (ibid.). There are clear echoes of Plato's cave in Paglia's characterisation of the twentieth century as the Age of

Hollywood, infinitely fascinated by the light and the dark and captivated by the glittering fantasies projected on to the screen. These Platonic echoes are also 'bounced off' the matter of gender in Paglia's argument: 'cinema is the culmination of the obsessive, mechanistic male drive in western culture', she says (1990: 31). The beam of light, penetrating the darkness, and making images visible, is a result of the male creative drive in Paglia's account.

The way in which the visual and the cultural are entwined may also be seen on a much smaller scale. The broad-brush, or wide-screen, pictures of entire cultures and civilisations being dominated by and built around the visual that are sketched above may be complemented by more closely focused examples. People in everyday life often make instant decisions, regarding really quite important topics, on the basis of how something or someone looks. During the late 1980s, Goths knew immediately, just from looking at what someone was wearing, that that person was a Ragga and thus that the two would not get on (Neustatter 1992: 31). It is significant that, in this example, the visual is intimately connected to the cultural. These Goths and Raggas know instantly, on the basis of what someone else looks like, what sorts of things that person is likely to be interested in. The visual cues, found in fashion here, are instantly meaningful and constitutive of cultural groups, groups of people who might be said to 'get on' together. The differences in shoes, T-shirts and choice of colour, for example, mean things to these Goths and Raggas. What is more, they mean things which will probably remain forever obscure to those who are not of a similar age to these Goths and Raggas. So, the visual cues define and differentiate these cultural groups to themselves and from other such groups.

The visual and the cultural are clearly of great interest. It is equally clear that, however the terms are defined and however the relation between the terms is conceived, something called visual culture is also of great interest. And, in Great Britain and America, educational institutions have begun to cater for this burgeoning interest, devising and devoting named specialist degrees to the subject. In Britain, the so-called 'new universities' have become especially interested in visual cultures. In 1991, for example, the University of Derby started running their BA(Hons) Visual Cultures degree. In 1993, this was still the only degree entitled Visual Cultures, although Falmouth College of Art offered a BA(Hons) in Visual Culture. In 1996, however, the Universities and Colleges Admissions Service (UCAS) reported that there were eleven such degrees, all being offered by the new universities. In America, visual culture is also an area of increasing interest. For example, W. J. T. Mitchell reports that there is a Faculty Working Group on Visual Culture at the University of Chicago (1995b: 207), and the Fall 1995 edition of *Art Journal*, published in America by the College Art Association, contains numerous references to visual cultures modules offered at such institutions as Northwestern University and Harvard University (see Clayson and Leja 1995: 47 and Winter and Zerner 1995: 42–3, for example). The nature of visual culture, the characteristic topics to be studied and the methods and concepts in terms of which they are to be studied are all the subjects of contemporary and continuing debates in institutions as diverse as the universities of Derby and Harvard.

Not surprisingly, publishers have begun to take note of these developments in the delineation and definition of what some claim is a new area of the human sciences. The present volume, for example, is the result of the interests of some parts of the academic community coinciding with the interests of the academic publishing industry in the context of the increasing awareness of the centrality and significance of the visual and the cultural that has been sketched above. It is an attempt to help define the nature, function and importance of visual culture, to suggest which topics might profitably be studied and to propose some ways in which they might be approached. Consequently, Chapter 1 begins the attempt to define visual culture by looking at how visual experience, what is seen and the sense that is made of what is seen, may be defined and conceptualised. Visual culture will be introduced as the study of the social and cultural construction of visual experience. It concerns how one sees what one sees and why what one sees appears as it does. Visual culture will be developed in terms of what Raymond Williams calls the 'signifying system' (the institutions, objects, practices, values and beliefs) by means of which society is visually produced, reproduced and contested.

Chapter 2 will continue the definition of visual culture by considering how it may best be studied. Existing disciplines, such as art history and design history, as well as cultural studies, will be examined. Their characteristic approaches, along with their strengths and weaknesses, will be investigated and assessed. This chapter will also investigate the different topics or subjects in terms of which visual culture may be studied. Approaches which concentrate on formal elements, on expression, or on visual culture as a reflection of the *Zeitgeist*, for example, will be assessed. The chapter will argue that lessons may be learned from such approaches as the social history of art, sociology and cultural studies and it will present the contents of the following six chapters as exemplifying some of the ways in which visual culture may be usefully studied. Consequently, Chapter 3 will begin to look at more concrete and positive matters, the substance of visual culture, as it were. Chapter 3 will consider the different ways in which artists and designers have thought about and described the nature of their activities and the different ways they have organised themselves into groups or institutions. It will also describe the relative status accorded artists and designers and the activities of art and design and show how that status is related to the groups and institutions they are members of.

Chapter 4 is concerned with the many and various relationships which the producers of visual culture enter into with the consumers of visual culture. It is about how artists and designers relate to markets, publics and audiences. It may not be immediately apparent, but the ex-graphic design student who sells T-shirts in the local market has much in common with the Royal Academician who sold paintings to wealthy Victorian industrialists, for example, but very little in common with the brewers who sponsor major art exhibitions. Chapter 4 will introduce these issues by looking at traditional models of audiences and markets and at some contemporary critiques of those models. Chapter 5 concerns visual signs and media; it is about the ways in which cultures are made visible. All cultures must make themselves visible in some way: a culture may make itself visible by means of scars and tattoos made on the body, as well as by oil-paintings, furniture and carrier bags. Visual culture may be described as the many different ways in which a culture may make its values and beliefs visible and Chapter 5 introduces the many different ways in which this may be achieved. Chapter 6 revisits the debates surrounding the definition of art, design and visual culture. It will argue that there are various codes, labelled 'internal' and 'external' codes, which govern what is, and what is not, called art, design and visual culture at any given time and place. Behaviour which might result in arrest and incarceration when it is performed on the street may win awards when it is called a 'performance', for example. Urinals used to be merely urinals until Marcel Duchamp displayed one in a New York art gallery in 1917. Different societies will call different things art and design, then, at different times and for various different reasons. This chapter will explain the working of these codes and provide examples of the ways in which visual culture is coded and understood.

Chapter 7 begins to explain how and why cultural products, such as works of art and design, or visual culture, are produced in different forms or types. It is difficult to think of an area of visual culture which does not offer products in different forms. This proliferation of forms exists in fashion, furniture design, photography and graphic design, in addition to painting, car design and film. There are different types or forms, then, and there are different types within these types. This chapter will begin to explain these different types of cultural product as developing in time and in relation to different social classes or fractions of classes. Different social and cultural groups, at specific times and places, use these different types of art and design to construct and communicate their identities. Chapter 8 will reprise and begin to draw together many of the themes and topics covered in previous chapters. It will do this by explaining the role of visual culture. And it will argue that the role of visual culture is in the production, reproduction and transformation of society; it has an important role in the social process. It will argue, then, that the role of visual culture is to maintain and transform the institutions, practices, media, objects and social classes analysed in previous chapters.

Chapter 1

What is Visual Culture?

Introduction

This chapter must begin the task of introducing and defining the notion of visual culture. It will do this by looking first at the idea of the visual and then at the idea of the cultural. Various definitions of the visual, ranging from the very broad (everything that can be seen, for example) to the very narrow (fine art, or paintings, for example), will be considered. The strengths and weaknesses of each definition for the analysis and explanation of visual culture will be clearly explained. A range of definitions of the cultural, from the elitist to the democratic and from the 'unilinear' to the 'multilinear', will also be considered. Again, the strengths and weaknesses of these definitions for the analysis and explanation of visual culture will be explained.

There is a case here for being very careful with one's definitions of the visual and the cultural. As W. J. T. Mitchell says, 'one cannot simply graft a received notion of visual experience on to a received notion of culture' in order to arrive at a satisfactory conception of visual culture (1995b: 208). It is not a question of simply taking over preexisting conceptions of vision or the visual and of culture and welding them together to begin the study of visual culture: the conceptions and definitions of these terms must be developed in tandem, in terms of their relation to each other in the term 'visual culture'. In view of these problems, this chapter will proceed by looking first at the visual, and second at culture, each in the context of their place in the term 'visual culture'. The next section will consider various conceptions of 'the visual', ranging from the very broad, everything that can be seen, for example, to the very narrow, fine art, for example. The strengths and weaknesses of these conceptions as a basis for the visual in visual culture will be clearly displayed. The section after this will consider various conceptions of 'the cultural', again ranging from very narrow and elitist conceptions to broader, more popular conceptions. The strengths and weaknesses of these conceptions of culture as a basis for the cultural in visual culture will also be clearly demonstrated.

The visual

Everything that can be seen

This is the widest or broadest definition of the visual. Including everything that can be seen, this conception is clearly all-inclusive. It may seem at first that the broadest of the conceptions of the visual in visual culture will be the most useful. One does not, after all, want to leave anything out of an account of visual culture, and the more inclusive a definition one works with, the better the account of visual culture. This may be fair up to a point. The problems arise when one needs to say where that point is. To say that the visual in visual culture is 'everything that can be seen' generates problems concerning the role and interpretation of nature, for example. Everything that can be seen must include nature. It must include naturally occurring phenomena, such as landscapes, and all forms of flora and fauna. The problem with this definition, however, is that nature is precisely that which is not culture. Naturally occurring phenomena are necessarily not the products of culture and while it is possible to cultivate desired strains of plants or animals and while many people earn a living from landscape gardening, these are not natural in quite the same sense of nature found above.

This is not to deny that naturally occurring phenomena are not made culturally meaningful. It is to deny that there can be a non-cultural, or natural, form of seeing. It is not possible to see a landscape, or an animal or a plant *as* a landscape, animal or plant without making it meaningful in some way. There can be no non-cultural, or natural, form of the visual in visual culture. In so far as it is meaningful in some way, it will have been made meaningful according to cultural codes and therefore be culturally meaningful. Nor is it to deny that representations of landscapes and so on are meaningful. John D. Barrow argues in his (1995) book *The Artful*

Universe that certain kinds of landscapes represented in paintings and photographs give people pleasure because these landscapes somehow recall the relatively safe and bountiful environment humans encountered when they first ventured out of the trees and began to live and hunt on savannah grasslands. Similarly, generals, farmers and artists are well-known for interpreting the landscape in terms of whether it is defensible, good for arable crops or melancholy, for example.

It is, however, to deny that landscapes and so on are meaningful in the same ways as representations of landscapes and so on are meaningful. What the generals, farmers and artists are doing when they say a landscape is defensible, good for arable crops or melancholy is making it meaningful in terms of something else. They are representing it in terms of something else, defensibility, arable crops or melancholy. It is argued that the representations which are made of landscapes and so on are produced by humans who have some intentions as to what they are trying to do in those representations, whereas the landscapes themselves are not the product of intentions. Only by applying human, that is cultural, intentions to landscapes are those landscapes made meaningful.

The idea that the visual in visual culture is everything that can be seen needs careful handling. 'Everything that can be seen' cannot be adopted as a definition of the visual in visual culture without considering how things like nature, for example, are made meaningful. It was argued above that some form of intention and representation, in which nature was intentionally represented in terms of something else, made naturally occurring phenomena meaningful. The idea that intention and representation provide a clue to the identity of the visual in visual culture is a useful idea and is taken up in the next two definitions.

Everything produced or created by humans that can be seen

This is a more restricted definition of the visual than that presented above. This definition proposes that the visual is everything that can be seen and which is produced or created by humans. Again, this may sound like a good, common-sense definition of the visual in visual culture. Marcia Pointon presents a version of this kind of definition when she restricts the definition of visual culture to 'man-made' structures and artefacts. She says that 'every "man-made" structure and artefact, from furniture and ceramics to buildings and paintings, from photography and book illustration to textiles and teapots, comes within the province of the art historian' (1994: 28–9). Again, there are problems with this definition. And, again, these problems surround the place of nature and the natural. For example, if the definition is to be taken literally, then the body and natural bodily products will have to count and be explained as visual culture. The problem is that not everyone agrees that presenting the natural products of the human body is art, or visual culture. It is possible to argue that some products of the body, urine, for example, are neither art nor visual culture.

However, some modern art has attempted to draw attention to bodily products and present them as art. Assuming that they count as a bodily product, aborted foetuses have been made into ear-rings, for example, and exhibited in galleries. In the 1950s, Manzoni presented canned excrement in the name of art. Andres Serrano's (1987) photograph entitled *Piss Christ*, which showed a model of the crucified Jesus Christ placed in a urine-filled plastic box, was said to be art and also exhibited in galleries. Gilbert and George present themselves as living sculptures and have also photographed their various bodily products, proposing them as art works (see Ill. 1.1). The artist Helen Chadwick, along with her male partner, urinated in the snow, made casts of the differently patterned holes and called the resulting sculptures *Piss Flowers*. Piss, or urine, is undoubtedly a 'natural' product; everybody makes it but nobody learns how to make it, after all. It is to that extent as 'natural' as a landscape is natural.

As was argued in the previous section, it is the cultural significance of the product, rather than any 'natural' meaning that the product has, which is important in these examples. These products are not presented as 'natural' in these examples; they are used intentionally, to perform some function, and the 'natural' products are in fact culturally meaningful. Piss, or urine, is also given a cultural meaning. Indeed, it is likely that it is the cultural meaning of urine in the west, as something disgusting and offensive (and in Serrano's case, blasphemous), rather than the urine itself (which could have been replaced by many yellow liquids to give the same aesthetic effect), that got some people so angry about Serrano's work. And it is presumably the cultural meaning of urine as something that is not usually thought of as being especially or traditionally beautiful, rather than the use of urine itself (which could also have been replaced by water to achieve the holes in the snow), that so surprises viewers of *Piss Flowers*. The cultural representations of urine as offensive or ugly and the intentional use of those representations are what makes the examples meaningful, not any 'natural' meaning that urine might have.

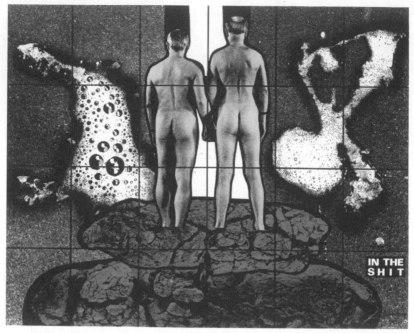

Ill. 1.1   Gilbert and George, *In the Shit*, 1996

Consequently, the idea that the visual in visual culture is everything that is created or produced by humans and which can be seen must also be treated carefully. The argument is as follows. If the meaning of the visual in visual culture is that it is everything that is produced by humans and which may be seen, then it may be objected that urine, for example, is produced by humans but is not necessarily what would be called art, or visual culture. In response to this, it may fairly be proposed that it is the function of the urine, the fact that it has a communicative function, for example, that is what makes it art, or visual culture, not the urine itself. It is not the 'natural' product that is presented as art, or visual culture, in these examples; the art, or visual culture, consists in the treatment afforded those products. Those products are used, intentionally, in terms of what they represent (disgust, ugliness, and so on), not in terms of any 'natural' significance they might possess. It is this idea, the idea of using materials, intentionally, in terms of what they represent and with some functional or communicative intent, that is useful and which is taken up in the next section.

Functional or communicative intent: design

This is the idea that the visual in visual culture is that which can be seen and which possesses some functional or communicative intent. There is a certain plausibility to this definition. This plausibility follows from the implication that the visual in visual culture consists in things which are designed. That is, that which can be seen and which possesses communicative or functional intent is a good definition of design. Both graphic design and product design, for example, are visual and possess communicative or functional intent. It therefore sounds plausible to define the visual as that which possesses communicative or functional intent.

Defining the visual in visual culture as everything that can be seen which also has functional or communicative intent entails certain problems. For example, there are many things that should be accounted for and explained as visual culture that are not primarily produced or created with the intention of being functional or communicative. All the things that usually go under the term 'art' or 'fine art', for example, should be explained as part of visual experience but they are not always things that are produced or created primarily with the intention of being functional or communicative. Many examples of art can be argued as having a decorative function but the appearance, or the aesthetic, of the object takes precedence over the job it is there to do. Coined by the American architect, Louis Sullivan, at the end of the nineteenth century, the phrase 'form follows function' is a basic principle of modern design (Sparke 1986: 17). What it means is that the appearance or the form of the object (or building) is to be subordinated to, or to follow from, the working, or the functioning of that object. All decoration and ornament is seen as unnecessary on this view. Buses and the typefaces used in underground railways are examples of visual culture in which it is possible to see that the appearance, or the aesthetic, of the thing is largely dictated by the job that thing is intended to do. Modern transport systems must move people quickly, efficiently and safely and ornament in design is eschewed in favour of plain, clear styles and forms. They are things that are not necessarily at all beautiful but which to some extent are constrained not to look beautiful because of the job they have to do. Having said that, Edward Johnston's *Railway* typeface of 1916 has been admired for its elegance and is still used to inform passengers on the busy London Underground.

For these reasons, the definition of the visual in visual culture cannot simply be those things that are visible but which also have functional or communicative intent. There is a whole class of artefacts that are created, and visual, which do not have functional or communicative intent as their main, or prime, defining feature. These things are often called art and they are the subject of the next section.

Aesthetic intent: art

The final definition of the visual in visual culture to be dealt with here proposes that it is everything that can be seen which also has aesthetic intent. This is the idea that visual culture is anything that has been created or produced with the intention of having some aesthetic effect. The modern English word 'aesthetic' is derived from the ancient Greek word for perception. One definition of the visual in visual culture, then, would be that it is anything that is produced or created with the intention of being perceived. In this case, it would be anything that was produced or created with the intention of being perceived visually. This is still quite a broad definition of the visual. However, the modern English word 'aesthetic' also carries connotations of something being beautiful. Aesthetics, therefore, has come to have the sense of concerning the perception of the beautiful. On this account, visual culture would be anything that was produced or created with the intention of being beautiful.

Clearly, this is a much less broad definition of the visual, and thus of visual culture. Clive Bell's idea of 'significant form' can help here. Bell suggests that all art possesses 'significant form' and significant form is the way in which line, colour, forms and combinations of forms combine in such a way as to 'stir' or 'provoke our aesthetic emotions' (Bell 1982: 68). It may be a wilful misreading of Bell, who wants to pursue the aesthetic down the path of the beautiful, but it is the case that both art and design stir and provoke 'our' aesthetic emotions. It is also the case that the ugly may be said to thus provoke and stir us. The ugly refrigerators, buses and housing estates of everyday life stir and provoke aesthetic emotions just as surely as do the works of Cézanne and Pissaro, artists who are both highly praised by Bell. Erwin Panofsky's conception of the work of art as 'a man-made object demanding to be experienced aesthetically' (Panofsky 1955: 37) may also be interpreted so widely as to cover both 'art' and 'design' objects.

Defining the visual in visual culture as everything that can be seen that also has aesthetic intention has other problems. First, there are many things that should be accounted for and explained as visual culture that are not primarily produced or created with the intention of being perceived as beautiful. All the things that usually go under the term 'design' or 'industrial design', for example, should be explained as part of visual experience but they are not always things that are produced or created primarily with the intention of being beautiful. Many examples of design and industrial design are there to be seen but the function of the object takes precedence over how it looks. Other design items that go under the term 'design' (fashion, textiles and ceramics, for example) very often are produced with the intention of being beautiful. This definition cannot be considered as the only definition of the visual, then, in that it rules out much of design culture which really ought to be explained and analysed as visual culture.

As noted above, defining the visual as everything that can be seen which also has aesthetic intention comes very close to defining the visual as art. The second problem this raises, then, is the question as to what sorts of art are to be included, and whose definition of art is to be adopted. Different social and cultural groups are well-known for defining art in different ways. The Tate Gallery's purchase of the Carl Andre sculpture *Equivalent VIII* in 1974, for example, was roundly attacked by the British tabloid press for wasting money on 120 fire-bricks, described as 'rubbish' by the *Daily Mirror* (see Walker 1983: 65). The Tate thought that the bricks were art while the tabloid press thought that they were not art. This disagreement may be explained as different social groups, the upper-middle class represented by the Tate, and the working class represented by the tabloids, defining art in different ways. Clearly, where there is conflict, there will be a winner and a loser. The winner's definition of art will be the one that becomes dominant in a society. The fact that these definitions are still in the process of being debated by different social and cultural groups means that they are still available to analysis by visual culture. If different social and cultural groups have different ideas as to the definition of the visual, then visual culture as a discipline must use those differences as part of the explanation of visual culture.

The use which different social and cultural groups make of different definitions of the visual, therefore, is itself a matter to be investigated and explained by the study of visual culture. Having said this, however, a provisional, and as inclusive as possible, definition of the visual in visual culture would be to say that it is anything visual produced, interpreted or created by humans which has, or is given, functional, communicative and/or aesthetic intent.

The cultural

This section might be described as attempting to answer the question 'what conception of culture will enable us to study and explain visual culture?' There are problems involved in defining 'culture' as it appears in the term 'visual culture'; this section must ask what those problems are and what conception of the cultural will best solve them. As with the definition of the visual, it is not the case that a preexisting conception of the cultural can simply be taken over and used in the analysis of visual culture. It is proposed, then, that visual culture is the study of what Raymond Williams calls the 'signifying system' of a society (1981: 13). Williams's formulation may be adapted slightly to suggest that this signifying system may be thought of as the institutions, objects, practices, values and beliefs by means of which a social structure is visually produced, reproduced and contested. A social structure here may be thought of as a social order in which people exist in positions of unequal power and status and visual culture may be thought of as the ways in which that structure of inequalities is first made possible and then either continued or contested. These positions of power and status are the product of a specific economic system, capitalism. In capitalism, one's position in a social order or hierarchy is the result of one's place in that economic system. This aspect of visual culture therefore relates to ideology and politics; it is about the ways in which visual culture produces and reproduces society, as well as the ways in which identities and positions within that society may be contested and challenged.

The term 'visual culture' is ambiguous, then, in that it refers to the system or structure of institutions, objects, practices and so on in which visual experience and the social order are constructed as well as to the ongoing historical and social processes in which those objects, practices and so on construct that experience and order. (It will be noted that it is also being used here as the name for the 'discipline' that studies all these' phenomena.) Following the pattern of the previous section, this section will consider various conceptions of the cultural, ranging from the very broad to the very narrow. The broadest conception or definition of the cultural, as it is to be understood in the term 'visual culture', would be 'the everyday objects and practices of a group of people, or of an entire way of life', or 'anything that is meaningful to more than one person'. The narrowest such conception or definition would be something like 'that which a dominant social group finds meaningful', or 'the serious music and the fine art of a social elite'.

These different conceptions of culture and the cultural will be explored by looking at the different contents and concerns of three books. Rather than give another purely conceptual account of the different forms and functions of culture, this section will look at three books which each approach visual culture with a different set of preconceptions as to what culture is and how it might be presented.

Unilinear elite culture

The first book to be considered is Sir Kenneth Clark's *Civilisation*, first published in 1969. The book is subtitled *A Personal View* and it may therefore be thought legitimate to provide a few biographical details of the person providing that view. Educated at Winchester and Oxford, Clark was keeper of the Department of Fine Art in the Ashmolean Museum (1931–3), Director of the National Gallery (1934–45) and Slade Professor of Fine Art at Oxford (1946–50). He was given a life peerage in 1969, the year in which the television series, *Civilisation*, on which the book is based, was transmitted by the BBC. What is presented here as 'civilisation', as a neutral or innocent term opposing something else called 'barbarism', turns out to be the culture of a specific class group operating at a particular time and place. It is thus not at all neutral or innocent. The argument is that 'civilisation' is presented as a relatively inoffensive term, something to which nobody could reasonably object. Who, after all, will admit to preferring barbarism to civility? What is actually going on in Clark's text, however, is that what has been called 'high culture', the culture of a dominant and elite social group is being presented as the only civilising factor in the whole western world. Other potential civilising factors, such as those that come from the dominated social groups (in this case women, other ethnic groups and the working classes), are ignored, with the implication that they are not culture and thus not civilisation.

The definition of 'civilisation' that the book relies upon is very rarely made explicit. Indeed, Clark is candid enough to confess that at the time of writing he had no clear idea what the word 'civilisation' meant, except that it was preferable to barbarism (1969: xvii). This is not to say, however, that the definition of 'civilisation' is not made perfectly clear in the course of the work. He suggests on page 323, towards the end of the book, that he has tried to define civilisation throughout the book in terms of 'creative power and the enlargement of human faculties'. This enlargement was achieved by means of visual culture, although Clark does not call it that. His definition of the means of civilisation includes almost exclusively painting, sculpture and architecture. There is the odd reference to things which are not what would usually be called 'fine art' – various etching and engraving techniques are represented, as are the Book of Kells and the Sutton Hoo ship burial material. Abbot Suger's porphyry jar and some fourteenth-century ivories are also to be found among the painting, sculpture and architecture, but the products of civilisation are predominantly oil-paintings, architecture and sculpture.

Every once in a while Clark gives a clue as to what he is thinking of when he writes 'civilisation'. In his discussion of de Troy's painting *La Lecture de Molière*, for example, he says that although he has 'tried to go beyond the narrower meaning of the word civilised . . . one can't deny that the de Troy is a picture of civilised life' (1969: 250). Indeed, it is. In the painting, seven aristocrats sit comfortably on superbly upholstered and luxurious furniture, dressed in the latest velvets, silks and embroidered satins, whilst being read to by a character in a huge bow tie, embroidered lapels and lace cuffs. In the background, wallpaper, luxurious drapes and intricately carved wall panels are to be seen to the right of an enormous mirrored fireplace which is decorated with ormolu candle-sconces. The ormolu clock, supported and surrounded by fat cherubs representing Love and Time, shows the time to be half-past three. It is a picture of a certain sort of civilised life. Clark even, once or twice, explicitly asks the question, 'What is civilisation?' He then answers it in an especially obscure fashion. It is, he says, 'a state of mind where it is desirable for a naval hospital to look like . . . [the Royal Hospital at Greenwich] and for the inmates to dine in a splendidly decorated hall' (215). The Royal Hospital at Greenwich is the work of Sir Christopher Wren and Nicholas Hawksmoor. The splendidly decorated hall is, of course, the hall painted by Sir James Thornhill, history painter to King George I, father-in-law of Hogarth, who provided paintings for the dome of St Paul's, Blenheim Palace and Hampton Court. In both cases, it is clearly the culture of the dominant social classes that is presented as civilisation.

These clues also illuminate the cultural institutions presupposed by Clark's account. The institutions are often those he himself is a member of or has been honoured by. The dominant institutions are royalty, the church, Oxford University and the various high-status galleries, such as the Ashmolean and the National. These are representatives of what is often referred to as the Establishment. Again, they are the institutions that are familiar to a certain class or group of people that are presented as the institutions of civilisation.

The book contains few references to women, or 'ladies', as Clark often calls them. Those references which do exist are in general rather patronising. In eighteenth-century France, for example, we are told that 'the influence of women was, on the whole, benevolent' (251). Upper-middle-class and aristocratic women might play the role of 'gifted hostess'; employing the traditionally feminine qualities of tact and sympathy, they established the institution known as the 'salon' and for forty years provided the 'centre . . . of European civilisation' (ibid.). As in that other magisterial and patrician story of art which has been provided by Sir Ernst Gombrich, there is no mention of any women artists. Clark is aware that some of the omissions he has been forced to make as a result of choosing 'civilisation' as his title (rather than 'culture' or 'art', presumably) are 'offensive' (xvii). He is also well-aware that he has omitted everything from Egyptian, Syrian, Chinese, Persian, Indian and Islamic cultures (ibid.). And he says that if civilisation is defined in terms of creative powers and the enlargement of human faculties, then 'slavery is abominable' (323). It is not so abominable, however, that the black servant in Devis's portrait of the modest country gentleman's family is deemed worthy of comment (249–50). The book does touch upon the Industrial Revolution but the social and class upheavals and the new working-class cultures that resulted are ignored. Even the miserable everyday lives of those new working classes are described and illuminated by a Wordsworth poem. The work of Brunel, his tunnels, bridges and railways, finds a place towards the end of the book, only on the grounds that inside such pieces of engineering was 'art' (336).

While this presentation of Clark's work does no justice to the magnificent assurance, the relaxed, witty style and the confident learning of Clark's prose, it is claimed that it is not unfair. The account of culture found in *Civilisation* is unilinear. It presupposes that there is only one proper line of cultural development. It conceives of culture as the development, the maturing and the progressive improvement of the European mind. This is the classic move that this kind of conception of culture enables its proponents to make. If culture is conceived as a line of development, it may be used as a standard, against which other cultures may be compared and judged. Other cultures may be judged either immature or deviant when compared to the one proper line of cultural development. Thus, there are no non-European cultures covered in the work. When Roger Fry's African mask is introduced, it is only to make the point that the Apollo of the Belvedere 'embodies a higher state of civilisation than the mask' (2). As seen above, Clark cheerfully lists the cultures that he has had to omit. Even within Europe, cultures are measured against the standard of the dominant culture. This, after all, is what happens to Spain in Clark's account, despite Spain being a part of Europe. Spanish culture is measured against the general development of European culture and found wanting. This is then made into the reason for excluding Spain, Spanish art and culture, from the account. As Clark says, 'when one asks what Spain has done to enlarge the human mind and pull mankind a few steps up the hill, the answer is less clear' (xvii). The metaphor of the hill clearly shows the conception of culture as a progression to higher things and to a final highest point, that is presupposed here.

Clark's version of culture is also elitist and highly selective. It is elitist in that this conception of culture demands a very high level of a very particular kind of education in order to understand it. This is not to be understood as an argument against people receiving very high levels of particular kinds of education. This book is conceived as contributing to the fairly specialised education of a fortunate minority. It is to point out that not everyone goes to expensive schools and the better universities and becomes learned in the traditions of western art history. Indeed, only a tiny minority of the population enjoys such privileges and consequently the definition of culture cannot be anything but elitist. Unless one knows that history, with its codes and systems of representations, one will simply not feel a part of it and will feel alienated from it. In the same way as Gombrich presents an account of the sort of art that is of interest to a small part of the population and calls it *The Story of Art*, Clark presents the cultural interests of a tiny proportion of the population and calls the *Civilisation*, as if they were the only art, civilisation or culture that ever existed. And it is selective in that not everything from within the European tradition is covered. Only what Clark considers the best of that tradition is selected. Again Clark is quite candid about this; he says 'the Baroque is over-emphasised at the expense of Classicism' (xvi) and he leaves out the German Romantics altogether.

While the definition of the cultural in visual culture should not omit the kind of culture that is presupposed in Clark's work, it should not be limited to that definition. The culture of the dominant European groups of the past four hundred years is no doubt culture. But it is *a* culture, not *the* culture and an elitist, unilinear conception of culture will not be sufficient for the analysis of visual culture. A more democratic and multilinear notion of culture is necessary.

Dominant masculine mass culture

The second book to be dealt with here is Deyan Sudjic's *Cult Objects*, published in 1985. The book is subtitled *The Complete Guide to Having it All*, and it is every bit as much a part of its time and milieu as Clark's book. The differences between the conception of culture presupposed by Clark's work and that presupposed by Sudjic's are immediately obvious. There is nothing that might conceivably be called art in Sudjic's selection of objects. Sudjic has selected a range of designed objects, rather than art objects. These objects include the Porsche 911, an empty Lucky Strike packet and Richard Sapper's anglepoise lamp. They may be relatively inexpensive and therefore available to all, or they may be relatively expensive and to that extent exclusive, but they are all mass-produced. Many of the objects are objects of what might be called mass culture. Strictly, mass culture includes the films and other programmes watched on the all-black Brionvega television, as well as the television itself (1985: 56–7). They are produced in enormous quantities and intended for mass consumption. While a specialised education is necessary to understand or appreciate many of them, this education is not formalised, privileged and associated with an elite social group in the way that the specialised art history-based education necessary to understand the images and sculptures in *Civilisation* is. Indeed, this is one reason why mass culture is often despised or disapproved of by members of those high-status, dominant social groups.

The version of culture found here is a much more 'democratic' version of culture. Almost anyone may purchase a packet of Lucky Strike cigarettes, or a bottle of Coca-Cola. Every self-respecting skinhead and each new generation of students buys a pair of Dr Marten's boots to go with their Levi jeans. However, as Sudjic says, there are high- and low-status cults (Sudjic 1985: 18). Not everyone buys the Porsche 911 or the Le Corbusier *chaise-longue*, and these are clearly high-status cult objects. As noted above, however, all are designed for consumption. As Sudjic's subtitle has it, the book is a guide to possession and consumption, to having and owning things. The guiding principle here is that one defines oneself through what one purchases and owns; this is the sense in which it was said above that the book is every bit as much a part of its times and milieu as Clark's. As Robert Burchfield's article in *The Sunday Times* (Burchfield 1988) implies, the 1980s have entered popular understanding as the decade of designer consumption and Sudjic's book (published in the very middle of that decade) attempts to summarise what designer objects one ought to be consuming in order to communicate the right sorts of things.

Clearly, this is where the book begins to run into cultural trouble. The question immediately springs to mind: whose version of the 'right sorts of things'? The objects collected in *Cult Objects* are not chosen at random or neutrally. They represent the ways in which various social groups constitute themselves as social groups. It is not that one is what was referred to in the 1980s as a 'Yuppy' (1985: 152) and then goes out to buy a Porsche, a Rolex and a Filofax. It is the purchasing of such items that constitutes one as a 'Yuppy' in the first place. Thus, the objects represent the interests of a certain social grouping and are an attempt to differentiate that group from various other groups. They differentiate this group from other, high-culture groups by using mass-produced, if occasionally expensive, items rather than fine art. And they differentiate this group from other lower-culture groups by claiming some kind of designer credibility which furniture that is bought in the high street and Ford Mondeos will obviously lack. This version of culture is no more neutral or innocent than that espoused by Clark's book. It is simply that it creates cultural groups by means of highly designed, mass-produced items which are consumed by being purchased. It is financial capital, rather than what Bourdieu calls cultural capital, which enables these people to participate in and enjoy these objects.

So, some products are exclusive and others are not; it is not that there is ever only one of these products. There is no presupposition that culture has to consist in a series of one-off products, as in Clark's account. That there is nothing in Sudjic's collection that might be called art might be considered a weakness, as far as this chapter is concerned. It is not much of a definition of the cultural in visual culture, after all, that will not admit art. It is also unfortunate that Sudjic's middle-class consumers are all so passive. It is as if these objects always already have meanings which consumers literally buy into. There is no sense of consumers actively creating meanings with these objects, these consumers are completely at the mercy of the objects they buy. When Sudjic writes 'the difference between matt black professionalism and pale pastel playfulness; and why bright yellow is taking over from both' (1985: 155), it is as if the colours have a life of their own, independent of the people who give them these meanings and consume them.

It is worth considering the place of race, ethnicity and gender in the version of culture presupposed here. Race and ethnicity are simply not addressed, as if these objects are equally available to everyone if they have the money. There are four women portrayed in *Cult Objects*. One is standing beside her 'mini Moulton' bicycle being leered at, one is standing beside her Aga cooker, one is holding hands with her boyfriend in the background to his 'phallic' E-type Jaguar (1985: 138) and one is holding her Minox camera. They are hardly the modern, active, career women who confidently fling salads at faithless boyfriends in television adverts for Clark's shoes. Three out of the four are defined in terms of either masculinity or domesticity. Although Eileen Gray is mentioned (106), there is no explicit mention of sex or gender in the entire book, and no attempt made to explain Gray's conspicuous lack of success in the design world of the 1920s. Sudjic seems not to have noticed that the objects chosen are predominantly traditionally masculine objects. They are cars, guns, aluminium briefcases and bottles of Newcastle Brown Ale, for example: all traditionally 'masculine' objects. The context is often business, for example: another traditionally 'masculine' domain. Here, in the businessman's office, we are told that 'keyboards are obviously low status' (91). This is presumably because the people who use them, one's secretary, for example, are also 'obviously low status'. The last example of culture will show some of the limitations of this conception of culture.

The cultural institutions by means of which this form of culture is produced and disseminated are predominantly those of capitalism. To this extent, they may be described as dominant culture. They are commercial institutions, multinational businesses and international markets, as well as car dealerships and other forms of shops. The office, the world of work, of employment, is also represented in Sudjic's account. Many of the contexts in which the objects are discussed, for example, are business contexts. The telephone, the calculator and the Rolodex are all objects with connotations of business. When the institutions are not those of business, they are of expensive, conspicuous leisure and of the home. Unsurprisingly, even the home is treated in terms of impressing one's friends and in terms of male control. The Charles Eames chair, for example, is described as a 'command post from which the master could keep control of his home' (109). The leisure is expensive leisure, involving Barbours, green Uniroyals and a bespoke shotgun from Holland & Holland.

Again, while the definition of the cultural in visual culture should not omit the kind of culture that is presupposed in Sudjic's work, it should not be limited to that definition. The products of the dominant masculine mass culture of the second half of the twentieth century are no doubt culture. But, again it is *a* culture, not *the* culture, and a masculinist conception of culture, even if it is slightly more democratic than that found in Clark's work, will not be sufficient for the analysis of visual culture. A still more democratic and multilinear notion of culture is necessary.

Multilinear popular (sub)culture

The third version of culture is found in Ted Polhemus's book *Streetstyle*, published in 1994 to 'coincide' with the 'streetstyle' exhibition at the Victoria and Albert Museum. This book is also subtitled in such a way as to inform one of its characteristic concerns: the subtitle is *From Sidewalk to Catwalk*. This work demonstrates an even more democratic version of culture than Sudjic's. The subtitle gives the game away; the book concerns the ways in which fashions which originated on the streets, in genuine subcultures, in happenings, festivals, discos, raves and so on, make it into the mainstream of commercially available fashion. These cultures have sometimes been called 'low culture' or 'subculture' as they have been ranked below the high cultures of the social elites.

The book also demonstrates a multilinear version of culture. There are many different cultures, each with its own equally interesting and valid line of development. In Polhemus's book, these numerous lines are even represented in the lines of a complex family tree, or flow diagram (1994: 136–7). The way in which Mods split into Hard Mods and Psychedelics, in which the Hard Mods eventually became Skinheads and in which the Northern Soulies took over the music of the Mods is charted here. The New Romantics of the early 1980s are also shown to owe a debt to the Punks of the 1970s and between them to prepare the way for Goths. Also, at any one time, there are a number of subcultural groups coexisting. Famously, Mods coexisted, not always happily, with Rockers. Casuals, Psychobillies and Pervs all shared the stage with Posers and New Romantics in the 1980s. There is no 'proper' line of development for these cultures. They will revive a style that had been discarded and laid dormant for many years, for example, and are as likely to incorporate expensive Lyle & Scott woollens (Casuals) as safety pins (Punk and Versace) or army surplus (Mods and Technos).

The cultural groups which Clark ignores are well-documented in Polhemus's book. Black cultures are represented by Rastas, Zooties and rude boys, for example. Working-class cultures, whether they survived for long as working-class or not, are found in the styles and attitudes of Skinheads, Oi! and Casuals, for example. And the place of women is filled by flygirls, cuties and riot-grrrls. These groups are not and would not be considered cultural groups in Clark's book; they are marginalised, patronised or simply ignored. Sudjic's book also makes no reference to how such cult objects are received by consumers who are not white, male and middle-class. While there is no explicit mention of gender, the objects he deals with are resolutely masculine. Polhemus's conception of culture is thus able to include or incorporate what have been called different ways of life. It conceives of cultures as different ways of life. Not only are groups that were previously ignored now taken seriously as cultural groups, but the things which those groups do, wear and listen to are also deemed to be cultural phenomena. Although they are not strictly visual, none of the musical styles (from Cab Calloway to Kid Creole) that are associated with these subcultures would have counted as cultural on Clark's account. 'Serious' classical music, part of the culture of the dominant social groups, is all that Clark is interested in. Similarly, the things that these subcultural groups wear (from the military caps and chains of the Greasers to the berets favoured by Acid Jazz fans) would not have counted as culture on Clark's account. Clothing and fashion are never mentioned in Clark's account of 'civilisation', because they are not part of the 'high culture' that he is concerned with.

These subcultural groups will use materials and styles that are explicitly not those of the dominant classes. They are oppositional in this sense and do not always simply reproduce the social order in the way that culture in *Civilisation* and *Cult Objects* often does. The people in *Streetstyle* are more often than not actively producing culture and cultural artefacts, rather than consuming those artefacts, as in Clark's and Sudjic's versions of culture. Little of the visual culture here is bought from Top Shop, or even Brooks Brothers whose conservative suits may be seen in Ill. 1.2. And, even if it is, it has often been 'customised' in some way, as Desmond Dekker 'customised' the suit bought for him by his record company (Polhemus 1994: 59). Punk is probably the best-known and most exhaustively documented way in which alternative, oppositional styles, materials and modes of adornment were created and adopted. Dick Hebdige (1979) chronicles the ways in which 'cheap, trashy fabrics' like PVC, lurex and plastics, along with objects such as tampons, razor blades and safety pins, materials and objects which the dominant cultures of the time considered worthless or ugly, or both, were used as clothing and 'jewellery' (Hebdige 1979: 107; see also Barnard 1996: 130–2). Punks, then, were giving these materials and objects their own interpretations, rather than simply accepting those of the dominant culture. They were actively consuming these objects and materials, rather than passively consuming them. Neither Clark nor Sudjic includes any such conception of active consumption in their accounts of visual culture.

In terms of cultural institutions, leisure and the music business, along with the various forms of clubs, discos, raves, festivals and parties, loom largest. Where other, more traditional or 'establishment' institutions are present, as in the business suit still recognisable in Zoot suits and as worn by many Mods, it is as parody or reinvention. As Polhemus points out, the establishment business suit was intended as an emblem of 'conformity, compliance with the work ethic and conservatism' (1994: 18). When the Zooties got hold of it, it was barely recognisable and had become a 'showy, extrovert garment', a 'refusal' of subservience and a way of creating and negotiating an identity (ibid.). Almost all of the institutions, however, are connected with leisure and with the music business. It is these institutions that most of the styles and fashions spring from. These are underground, unofficial and, although often highly organised, highly informal institutions. While these are evidently cultural institutions, they are about as far from the establishment institutions of church, royalty and university that are found in Clark's work as it is possible to get. And, while it is clear that many of these subcultures are opposed in many ways to the dominant cultures that surround them, it is not clear that Polhemus's conception of culture would rule out or disallow the fact that those dominant cultures *are* cultures.

Ill. 1.2   Business suits, Brooks Brothers, 1996

These, then, are three ways of defining and approaching culture. There is a version in which culture is 'high' culture, the culture of an elite social group. There is a version in which culture is 'low' or 'popular' culture, produced by marginalised or subordinate social groups. And there are versions of culture which exist somewhere between 'high' and 'low' cultures. Each of these definitions of culture proposed its own particular set of cultural objects, practices and institutions. In each of these conceptions, different objects, practices and institutions were involved in the production and reproduction of those cultural groups. And in each of these conceptions, different cultural groups were accorded high or low status. Clark's conception of culture was criticised for being elitist and unilinear. Sudjic's conception was criticised for being masculinist and dominant. And Polhemus's might be criticised if it ruled out cultures that did not originate from 'the street' – if it disallowed Clark's version of culture, for example.

Each of these conceptions of the cultural, then, was 'interested' and 'partial'; none was 'neutral' or 'impartial' in the sense that it did not privilege a set of practices, institutions and objects above another set. This 'interestedness' and 'partiality', however, indicates that they are active. The fact that these definitions are continuously being debated by different social and cultural groups means that they must be continuously studied by visual culture. If different social and cultural groups have different ideas as to the definition of the cultural, then visual culture as a discipline must use those differences as part of the explanation of visual culture.

Conclusion

This chapter set out to introduce and begin to define the notion of visual culture. It proposed to do this by looking first at different conceptions of the visual and second at different conceptions of the cultural, explaining the strengths and weaknesses of all these conceptions. It has proved to be the case that these conceptions cannot be simply accepted or rejected on the basis of their strengths and weaknesses as they are culturally specific. Different cultural and social groups will have different conceptions of the visual and the cultural, which are used to constitute those groups as groups in distinction from other groups. Consequently, while each of the definitions and conceptions may have strengths and weaknesses when considered as potential explanations of the visual and the cultural, they are also the ways in which different groups identify and represent themselves culturally. These different conceptions are therefore part of the explanation of visual culture.

For example, where an elitist and unilinear conception of visual culture may have weaknesses and strengths when considered as a general explanation of visual culture, it may well be the conception that is shared by an elite social or cultural group. It may well form part of that group's self-understanding and it may have the function of constituting that group as a group, in distinction from other groups. That conception is a part of that group's set of beliefs and practices by means of which it produces and attempts to reproduce itself in a social order. Consequently, the explanation of that conception of culture must form part of the analysis and explanation of that group's visual culture. For these reasons, it is not possible for this chapter to provide one definition of the visual or the cultural in visual culture. Each has strengths and weaknesses when considered as a general explanation of visual culture, and all of them are used by social and cultural groups to represent themselves as cultural groups.

Having made some proposals as to what visual culture might be, the next chapter must begin the task of investigating how visual culture may best be studied. It will consider the various methods, disciplines and concepts which are available to the explanation and analysis of visual culture. Formal, expressionist and semiotic methods will be assessed, as will the disciplines of art history, design history and cultural studies.

Chapter 2

How May It Be Studied?

Introduction

The Introduction, above, established that there has been both a cultural and a visual turn in recent work in the humanities. Chapter 1 established that there is indeed a field of study, a system of institutions, objects, practices, values and beliefs in terms of which visual experience is constructed, which might be called visual culture. As W. J. T. Mitchell says, however, 'while the general study of visual culture may seem like an idea whose time has come, it is by no means self-evident how it ought to proceed' (1995b: 208).

This chapter will develop the definition of visual culture introduced in Chapter 1 by looking at the disciplines or subjects by means of which it is possible to study art and design, as well as the characteristic areas or topics into which visual culture has been divided. The point of examining these disciplines and topics here is to begin an explanation of why items of visual culture look the way they do. Why do things as diverse as mobile phones, street furniture and Flemish altarpieces look like they do? These various approaches and disciplines should be assessed in the light of how successfully they enable the analysis and explanation of visual culture, how well they explain why an example of visual culture looks the way it does. We shall see that some traditional ways of studying art and design are simply inadequate when it comes to looking at visual culture. This inadequacy is sometimes a result of visual culture being a slightly different kind of thing to art and design and sometimes a result of the fact that the traditional disciplines are interested in different things. This chapter will also develop the definition of visual culture by looking at the themes and topics in terms of which art and design have been studied. It will propose a set of themes and topics that will be central to any sustained and critical study of visual culture, some of which will be taken up by later chapters.

This chapter will look at different approaches, themes and topics as ways of explaining why pieces of visual culture look or appear the way they do. It will then look at various disciplines, such as art history, design history, cultural studies and sociology, as ways of combining the themes and topics necessary to explain visual culture and argue that only some form of interdisciplinary strategy will be sufficient to the task of explaining visual culture. The next section of this chapter will outline and critique materialist and idealist approaches to the history of art and design as well as showing what is to be gained and lost by following social or formal accounts. It will be argued that any satisfactory account of visual cultures must be historical and sociological in nature and that it must pay close attention to visual production as a set of signifying systems.

Approaches, methods, topics and themes

Many different approaches, methods, topics and themes have been proposed as explaining why things look the way they do. This section will consider some of them.

In a book aimed at potential and existing students of the history of art, Marcia Pointon divides art history, the documentation, analysis and evaluation of visual material, into two distinct approaches (1994: 28ff.). One is a traditional, object-based approach. The other is what might be called a structure-based approach. The object-based approach encompasses three or four main themes or topics. One of the central tenets of such an object-based account is that the object itself proposes ways in which it may be understood, independently of, or unmediated by, the economic, political and social structures that form the structure-based approaches. One version of this approach, for example, holds that by 'responding to purely visual characteristics (form, colour, composition, brushwork) we may . . . gain access to the essential genius of the artist and thence to an understanding of the summary characteristics . . . of an artist, a school or a whole period' (30). This kind of approach may be labelled a 'formalist' approach as it looks only at the formal characteristics of works. It is concerned only with shapes, lines, colours and other formal characteristics like the nature of the brushstrokes or pencil marks.

Perhaps the most extreme, or the clearest, example of such an approach is provided by the work of Clive Bell. Writing in 1914, Bell suggested that 'to appreciate a work of art we need bring with us nothing from life, no knowledge of its ideas and affairs, no familiarity with its emotions . . . nothing but a sense of form and colour and a knowledge of three-dimensional space' (Bell in Frascina and Harrison (1982: 72–3). It is difficult to make much sense of this kind of approach. Even if by 'appreciate' Bell only means 'recognise as a work of art', or 'tell apart from a frock, or St Pancras station', then he is probably mistaken. If, as seems more likely, he means something like 'feel an aesthetic emotion for a combination of forms' (1982: 72), then one might reasonably object that a three-year-old will react emotionally to a combination of forms. But if he intends anything like 'understand', 'analyse' or 'explain', then he is most certainly mistaken. The way a piece of visual culture looks simply cannot be explained by referring to the way that piece of visual culture looks. This is clearly a circular argument and only moves the problem one step back.

Such an object-based approach is also associated with the name of Heinrich Wölfflin in art history. Wölfflin went so far in stressing the formal characteristics of pieces of art that he wanted to do without the notion of the named artist as part of the explanation of art altogether and proposed 'an art history without names'. It was Wölfflin who introduced the practice of 'double projection' into art history lectures. Double projection, in which two slide projectors are used to show two paintings or sculptures side by side is held to be especially useful for highlighting stylistic or formal similarities and differences between works of art. This method is immediately apparent in Wölfflin's *Principles of Art History*, written in 1915. Botticelli's Venus is compared and contrasted with that of Lorenzo di Credi. Botticelli's work is impetuous and endowed with 'verve and animation', while Credi's work is deliberate and in 'repose' (Wölfflin 1960: 2). These differences in style are a product of the artist's individual temperament, according to Wölfflin's account. However, as individuals are inevitably members of larger groups, the individual's style may be supplemented by the style of the school that artist is a member of, the style of the country that artist is a native of and the style of the race that artist is a member of (6). However, it is hardly an explanation of why a painting looks the way it does to appeal to the way it looks, or its style. The argument is circular, again, and of little help to visual culture.

Unfortunately, as John A. Walker points out, some writers of design history have taken Wölfflin's proposal concerning an art history without names literally and applied it to design history. Seigfried Giedion is probably the best-known example of the application of some of Wölfflin's ideas to design history. His book *Mechanisation Takes Control*, published in 1948, is even subtitled *A Contribution to Anonymous History*. Rather than study the style of designed objects, Geidion looks at types of objects, and his approach is subsequently known as typological. He looks at everyday objects, like the Yale lock, the bath, assembly lines in slaughterhouses and so on, and he begins what might be called a kind of social history of design. Rudofsky is mentioned by Walker as a historian who has concentrated upon anonymous builders (which is possibly to miss the point of an art history without names) in his books *Architecture Without Architects* and *The Prodigious Builders*. The method of 'double projection', introduced by Wölfflin into art history lectures, is also a part of the kind of design history which Walker labels 'the comparative method'. This method or approach, is interested in showing the similarities and differences between designed objects. This method, or approach, also known as a formalist approach, is heavily dependent upon notions of style, and thus upon comparing and contrasting different styles. The idea is that one may see quickly and easily the differences or similarities between the objects and images and the styles they exhibit. Walker cites Pugin as an example of this method in design history. Pugin's work *Contrasts*, published in 1836, juxtaposed two images to illustrate the differences between what he saw as the 'virtues of Gothic architecture' and the 'barbarity' of the architecture of his own times (Walker 1989: 103–4).

Among the problems that such approaches encounter is the objection that they are often not sensitive enough to the social and historical context in which these types and styles are found. Such an approach can often neglect the social context of styles, studying them in isolation from the class groups that consumed them, for example, and apart from the uses and meanings that those groups gave them. It can also fall down when it comes to explaining the historical development of styles and types of objects, as if there were some natural force compelling them to change in time. Indeed, there is a further, and stronger, objection that, rather than being placed in an already existing social and historical context, it is these very types and styles that first provide those social and historical contexts. This is the objection that it is not simply a case of looking for the social and historical context, but of looking at the ways in which any idea of social and historical context is only produced by those styles and types of objects in the first place.

This kind of formalist approach is also related to analyses which attempt to explain art as exemplifying something called a *Zeitgeist*, or 'spirit of the age'. As Pointon notes (1994: 30), this emphasis on formal or stylistic aspects of art and design enables one to ascertain the general formal and stylistic characteristics of an artist, a school or a whole period of time. Analyses which invoke the spirit of the age are generally thought to be a product of Hegel's idealist philosophy and are strenuously opposed by materialist thinkers, following in the historical and materialist footsteps of Karl Marx. Those art and design historians who support the *Zeitgeist* theory of history argue that from the formal characteristics of works of art, their typical shapes, colours and styles, one may read off the spirit, the mood or atmosphere, of an entire historical age. The spirit or mood of a historical period somehow permeates the objects and images produced during that period. Wölfflin supports the idea of a *Zeitgeist*, noting that 'nothing is more natural to art history than to draw parallels between periods of culture and periods of style' (Wölfflin 1960: 9). 'Different times give birth to different art', he says, and proposes the transition from Renaissance to baroque as a 'classic example of how a new *Zeitgeist* enforces a new form' (ibid.). Something of this approach may also be seen in the chapter headings to Sir Ernst Gombrich's *The Story of Art*, first published in 1950. The chapter headings may be read as summarising the spirit of the age which is then found exemplified in the paintings and sculptures. For example, the eighteenth century is said to be 'The age of reason' while the nineteenth century is the age of 'Permanent revolution'. In his section on *Zeitgeist* and *Zeitstil* (the 'style of the age'), Walker proposes Penny Sparke's 1986 *Design Source Book* as an instance of this kind of approach in design history. Her chapter headings give the game away in the same way as Gombrich's did, including 'Arts and crafts 1850–1900' and 'The machine aesthetic 1900–1930' and so on (Walker 1989: 162).

A slightly different, although closely related, approach conceives of art and design as providing what is known in German as a *Weltanschauung*. The word *Weltanschauung* means world-view. Visual culture is studied in this approach as providing the world-view of an entire people. For example, at the beginning of the twentieth century, Wilhelm Worringer was attempting to explain the differences between what he unfortunately calls 'savage' peoples and 'primitive' epochs, on the one hand, and 'western' people and 'modern' times on the other (in Frascina and Harrison 1982: 160–1). He suggests that the abstraction favoured by the former and the naturalism favoured by the latter may be explained by the world-views of the different people. The 'psychic presuppositions for the urge to abstraction' are to be found in the 'people's feelings about the world, in their psychic attitude towards the cosmos', according to Worringer. The savages were unsettled by nature and its wide open spaces and consequently were anti-naturalist and pro-abstraction. But westerners found only happiness in the representation of nature and were consequently anti-abstraction and pro-naturalism. Thus, on a large scale, is the world-view of entire peoples alleged to explain their visual culture.

Unfortunately, attempts to explain visual culture in terms of either *Zeitgeist* or *Weltanschauung* are also circular. They are circular in that the only clues as to what either a *Zeitgeist* or a *Weltanschauung* might be are found in the works of visual culture that one is trying to explain. So, for example, if part of the explanation of the art and design of a particular time is that the *Zeitgeist* was one of unremitting gloom, the only place where the idea of unremitting gloom could have come from is the very art and design that is supposed to be explained. Similarly, if one attempts to explain the art of 'savages' by appealing to their view of the natural world as 'unsettling', it is the case that one of the sources for evidence of such a view is, precisely, the art that one is attempting to explain. Such attempts also run the risk of assuming that there is only one spirit or view present at any one time, when it could be claimed that the reality is more often that many spirits and views exist together, often actively and energetically opposing one another. They can tend to adopt a 'monolithic' account of *Zeitgeist* and *Weltanschauung*, in which alternatives are not possible and therefore cannot be accounted for.

Other object-based attempts to explain visual culture include those that use the concepts of biography and intention. Basically, this approach looks at the artist's or designer's life, their biography or life story, and attempts to explain their work in terms of that life. This might be called a 'popular' approach: it is somehow comforting or reassuring to link artists' and designers' works closely to the events of their lives. One of the earliest art histories to deal with individual artists was Vasari's *The Lives of the Artists*, published in 1568. A modern example of this kind of approach is to be found in John Elderfield's essay 'The drawings of Henri Matisse'. Elderfield's account begins in the year Matisse died, with Matisse remembering an episode in a post office in Picardy in which he 'drew without thinking' a picture of his mother's face (Elderfield 1984: 19). The whole of Matisse's life is explained on the basis of this one episode. This episode is explained in terms of rejecting the reasoning part of the mind and concentrating on the instinctive, the effect of 'the heart' (21); it is held to provide the key to understanding the whole of Matisse's drawn work and is referred to at many subsequent points in the essay. Elderfield also explains Matisse's drawings in terms of the intentions he perceives, in terms of Matisse's aims. One very clear example of this comes when Elderfield recounts how Matisse misquotes Courbet in trying to explain his aims and intentions. Matisse says, 'I have simply wished to assert the reasoned and independent feeling of my own individuality within a total knowledge of tradition' (Elderfield 1984: 25). This is, then, to try to explain how Matisse's work looks the way it does by recourse to his aims and intentions.

This approach may be applied to design. It is not easy and the results are not always encouraging. As design is often 'anonymous' in the sense that very often one simply does not know, and cannot find out, who the designer was and what their intentions and biographical details are, or were. If one cannot find out the intentions, one cannot explain the works. High street home furnishings, like carpets, furniture and wallpaper, for example, are often completely anonymous, in the sense that they are not the product of individual, named designers. When the individual designer is known, however, there is always the tendency to treat them as if they were an artist, producing works of art. It has already been established that art is different to design and that it is not always helpful to study design as if it were a one-off, unique piece of art. This thoughtless and unhelpful blurring of the categories is what happens to Giorgetto Giugiaro in Sudjic's book *Cult Objects*, discussed in more detail in the next chapter.

There is another problem inherent in such an approach. It is that it is not often made clear how an event, episode or period is relevant to the work. Elderfield's account of Matisse, for example, is full of tiny, and to all intents and purposes, irrelevant, detail. He writes that 'since 1899, Matisse had been working as a law clerk in Saint-Quentin' (1984: 20) and that his father had been keen for Matisse to follow a career in law. It is never made clear, however, why these details are recounted. They are never used to illuminate the work and the relation to the work is never made explicit. If a detail is relevant, then its relevance should be made clear; if it is not relevant, then it should be omitted.

Another object-based approach uses the idea of expression to explain visual culture. Ernst Gombrich's essay 'Expression and communication' is a good account of such 'expressionist' theories of art and of their 'misconceptions' (1982 and in Gombrich 1971). Essentially, this is the theory that the shapes, lines, colours and textures found in visual experience are naturally meaningful and naturally understood by spectators. There is, on the expressionist account, a 'natural code of equivalences' (Gombrich 1982: 179) between feelings or emotions and shapes, colours, textures and lines. On this account, 'forms or tones are analogues of feelings and will therefore convey a specific emotional experience' (178)). Dark colours, and blues especially, then, are said to be sad and even hostile while bright colours and reds especially are experienced as happy and friendly. Imagining a spectrum ranging from cold and unfriendly to warm and friendly, Gombrich suggests that angular and pointy shapes would 'go to the cold and tense end of the spectrum' on this account of expressionism, while 'round and undulating ones' would go to the 'friendly and warm pole' (180). As Gombrich says, if this account of the equivalence between shapes, colours, textures and lines and emotional states and feelings were true, it would be possible to explain paintings in terms of such an equivalence. A painter would select colours, shapes and textures that would naturally express his or her emotional state and make them into a painting. A spectator would experience the very same emotion as the painter, as the colours would naturally express the emotion (ibid.). The persuasiveness and popularity of this account led people to see 'spontaneous "natural" symptom[s] in abstract expressionism' according to Gombrich (ibid.).

Indeed, it would be possible to explain all forms of visual culture with such an account. The flowing lines, plump bodies, big eyes and rounded faces of the 'goodies' and the thin, bony, angular types with little eyes that make up the ranks of 'baddies' in animated Disney films, for example, could be explained as the natural expression of people's emotional responses to the characters. The 'goodies' would naturally elicit a positive, warm response while the 'baddies' would naturally be shunned as cold and unfriendly, all as a natural result of the shapes used in drawing them. In Hollywood films such as *Working Girl*, the dark-coloured, sharply tailored business suit, with its clean and uncluttered lines, favoured by the go-getting woman executive could be clearly distinguished from the fussy, flouncy blouse and patterned skirt of her secretary in these terms. The shapes and colours of the dark tailored suit would naturally be seen as colder and thus more efficient while the fussy blouse and patterns would be seen as warmer and more friendly. It is easy to see how such a 'theory' is so popular and plausible; it appears to make sense of everyday feelings and emotions in 'common-sense' ways that people seem to agree on.

However, that persuasiveness and popularity are mistaken, or misconceived, on Gombrich's account. According to Gombrich, concentrating on the ways in which shapes, lines, colours, textures and so on appear naturally to express emotions will 'never yield a theory of artistic expression unless it is coupled with a clear awareness of the structural conditions of communication' (1982: 182). These 'structural conditions of communication' are basically the sets of alternative choices that are available to the artist or designer at any time. It is the appreciation, or understanding, of the range of elements from which the eventual choice was made that creates the emotional charge. For example, if the executive woman above has a wardrobe containing only such dark, severe suits, the effect of sober efficiency is destroyed: she has no choice but to create such an effect. Gombrich uses the example of music to explain the point. He says that 'the *fortissimo* of a string quartet may have fewer decibels that the *pianissimo* of a large symphony orchestra' but he claims that 'our ability to interpret the emotional impact' of the quartet's *fortissimo* 'depends on our understanding that it is . . . the loudest end of the scale within which the composer operated' (ibid.). To paraphrase Gombrich, it is not the shape, line, colour or texture that elicits an emotional response but the choice of that shape, line, colour or texture from the range that is available to which we respond. The shapes, lines and so on are not naturally meaningful, then; the meanings they are given are not 'God-given' (ibid.), but chosen by the artist or designer to most closely match the emotion or feeling he or she wants to communicate.

This last point, however, introduces the main problem with Gombrich's account. If the meanings of the shapes, lines, colours and textures are not God-given, then where do they come from? Gombrich says that the artist 'will select from his palette the pigment from among those available that to his mind is most like the emotion he wishes to represent' (1982: 182–3). The problem is that the colour, shape, line or texture must also represent the emotion to everyone else, not only the artist. The understanding of the relation between a shape and an emotion must be shared between an entire community of sign users, otherwise the shape will not represent or communicate anything to that community. Communication is compromised, for example, if sharp, spiky shapes represent motherhood and nurture to an artist when they mean cruelty and viciousness to his or her audience. Gombrich's view does not account for the fact that there needs to be some form of social agreement, some form of social contract, as to which shapes, lines, colours and textures shall represent which emotions and feelings. This is the agreement or contract that ensures, for example, that a society agrees that black is mournful or red happy. In other societies, it is red that is mournful and used for funerals. This element of social agreement also introduces the mechanism whereby social and class conflicts can be explained in terms of the use of visual culture to create and differentiate different social and cultural groups. Different social groups, then, will use shapes, lines, colours and textures both to constitute themselves as social groups and to differentiate themselves from other groups, which use other different shapes, lines and so on.

Erwin Panofsky's method of explaining visual culture, iconology, occupies a somewhat ambivalent position in terms of Pointon's division of art history into object-based and structure-based approaches. It could be claimed to be part of an object-based approach in so far as it is concerned with the art object. But it could also be claimed to be part of a structure-based approach in so far as it relates the contents of art objects, like paintings, to things (narrative structures, conceptual schema) outside the painting. Panofsky's approach is not just to do with form and formal aspects of visual culture, then; it is also to do with subject matter or meaning (Panofsky 1955: 51). He introduces iconology by describing an event from everyday life, an acquaintance greeting him on the street by lifting his hat. As he says, from a purely formal point of view, what he sees is a series of changes in the colours, lines and volumes in the configuration which makes up his 'world of vision'. However, as he automatically identifies the configuration as a gentleman and the changes in colour, line and volume as hat-lifting, he has 'entered a first sphere of subject matter or meaning' (ibid.). This he calls the factual meaning. There is another sort of meaning, which he calls 'expressional'. Expressional meaning is what he understands when he ascertains, from the manner in which the hat is lifted, whether his acquaintance is feeling indifferent, friendly or hostile towards him. Both of these sorts of meaning are classified together as primary or natural meaning (52).

In addition to primary or natural meaning, there is secondary or conventional meaning. This level of meaning is understood when one understands why the acquaintance lifts his hat. The acquaintance lifts his hat as a sign of politeness. As Panofsky points out, this practice is a residue of medieval chivalry, when an armed man would remove his helmet as an indication of his own, and an acknowledgement of the other's, peaceful intentions. Now, Panofsky says that neither an Australian bushman nor an ancient Greek could be expected to understand this level of meaning, as they would not be familiar with the customs and cultural traditions specific to western Europe within which hat-lifting is made meaningful. Finally, there is a third level of meaning. Panofsky calls this level of meaning intrinsic meaning or content. It is what one understands when one understands the hat-lifting in the context of many other observations of the acquaintance and uses them to construct a picture of his personality. It is what one understands when one understands how those other observations construct a picture of the acquaintance's 'period, nationality, class, intellectual traditions and so forth' (52–3).

Now, these reflections may be applied to art, to paintings and sculptures. They may be taken as a method of understanding visual culture. And that is what Panofsky proceeds to do. In the fine arts, painting and sculpture, primary or natural meaning is apprehended by 'identifying pure forms' (53). One recognises arrangements of lines and colours, or shapes of bronze or stone, as representations of things in the world. These things may be 'human beings, animals . . . houses, tools and so forth'. This level of meaning is relatively easy to understand: after all, 'everyone can recognise the shape and behaviour of human beings, animals and plants and everyone can tell an angry face from a jovial one' (58). Secondary or conventional meaning is slightly more complex. It is understood, for example, by 'realising that a male figure with a knife represents St Bartholomew' (54). In understanding this level of meaning, 'we connect artistic motifs and combinations of motifs . . . with themes or concepts' (ibid.). This level is slightly more difficult to understand as one must know the concept, theme, story or allegory with which the motif is connected and not everyone will be equally familiar with all the concepts, themes and so on. In order to understand Leonardo da Vinci's painting *The Last Supper*, for example, one would have to know that part of the Bible which tells the story, the Gospel of St John 13: 21. Different people may or may not know this story as they will have had different educations, for example, as was noted in relation to Clark's account of civilisation in the previous chapter. Thus, for Panofsky, an 'Australian bushman would be unable to recognise the subject of a Last Supper', although curiously he would be able to see it as a 'dinner party' (61). It is worth pointing out that it is at this point that the explanation begins to refer to things, concepts, stories and so on, that are outside of the painting, sculpture or whatever being explained. The things that are 'outside' the item being explained may be referred to as structures. They are conceptual, literary, narrative and allegorical structures, for example.

Intrinsic meaning is more complex yet. It is understood when the 'underlying principles which reveal the basic attitude of a nation, a period, a class, a religious or philosophical persuasion' are understood (55). As Panofsky points out, there are no textbooks or literary sources to which one may turn for help in understanding this level of meaning (64). A 'synthetic intuition' is required. This synthetic intuition seems to be something like a delicate sensitivity to the cultural symbols or symptoms of a society, as Panofsky has it, a 'familiarity with the essential tendencies of the human mind' and the ways in which different historical circumstances manifest these tendencies (66). Panofsky cites the way in which, during the fourteenth and fifteenth centuries, paintings of the Nativity subtly changed. The traditional Nativity has the Virgin reclining in bed, whereas later Nativities show the Virgin kneeling before the baby Jesus in adoration. This, says, Panofsky, is evidence of 'a new emotional attitude peculiar to the later phases of the Middle Ages' (56). It is not a formal aspect, nor is it related to scripture. It is rather 'something else', some sign of an emotional shift, an indication of an underlying attitude.

Now, it is not immediately clear how this sort of approach might help in the understanding of works of design. Film and television seem to admit of such treatment, possessing formal aspects and relating to stories, concepts and so on. They may even be seen as giving away vital clues to the underlying attitudes of the times they are a part of and help construct. But things like cars, furniture, street signs, fashions and so on do not seem to be equally available to such analyses. Cars, furniture, street signs and fashion, for example, are not readily associated with stories, concepts and allegories in the same way as the characters in paintings and sculptures seem to be. These objects and items clearly possess formal aspects. They are shaped, coloured and textured. These shapes, colours and textures may aid the recognition of them as cars, fashions and so on. Maybe the way to proceed is to suggest that things like gender, age, class and so on are the concepts that the formal aspects are associated with on the second level of meaning. Those colours, shapes and textures may also be interpreted as masculine or feminine, as luxury or frugal objects or as appropriate to either the young or the old. These conventional meanings may then be seen as indicative of the third level of meaning, as indicative of underlying attitudes.

For example, a collection of shapes, lines and textures may be recognised as many things – a car, a shaver or a shirt. This would be the first level of meaning, natural meaning. One then recognises certain shapes, lines and textures as a certain kind of car, shaver or shirt. One recognises large-radius curves, pastel shades and smooth, shiny textures as a woman's shaver. One recognises flouncy sleeves, pale pink and slinky satiny textures as a woman's shirt. These would be conventional meanings; there is, after all, nothing natural about them. The objects are being related to concepts, to structures, that are outside of the object. In this case, the concepts are to do with gender, with masculinity and femininity, although they could also be to do with concepts of age, class and so on. Finally, one must look for the intrinsic meaning. This would be to reconstruct a society's underlying attitudes from its concepts of gender, age, class and so on. Thus, for example, one might conclude that a society was very strict about gender distinctions and needed carefully to indicate class divisions, perhaps, from the ways in which it signalled these things. The underlying attitude would be that such distinctions needed to be sharply made.

There are two main problems with an approach such as this. The first is that what Panofsky calls natural meaning can only be a form of conventional meaning. Panofsky admits as much in his discussion of how it is that the floating child in van der Weyden's *Three Magi* is recognised as a miraculous apparition but the floating city in the *Gospels of Otto III* is neither miraculous nor an apparition (1955: 59–60). The different pictorial conventions operating in different times and places account for the fact that one is miraculous and the other is not. Thus the 'natural' meanings of the motifs are not so natural; they are the product of different conventions that govern the depiction of objects and events and which change in time. (60–1). Panofsky avoids the criticism that this is to appeal to a vicious circle by arguing that it is a methodical circle, a circle that can provide a necessary corrective aid to the interpretation of visual culture (61n.). That is, by knowing the convention that determines that the city is in fact in front of an abstract background and not floating in empty space, one is prevented from misinterpreting the image as miraculous.

The second problem with Panofsky's approach concerns his use of words like 'revealing' (55–6), 'documenting' (56, 65) or 'bearing witness' (65) to describe the relation between works of art and the underlying political, philosophical and social tendencies. Words like 'reveal', 'document' and 'bear witness' are all neutral-sounding words: they all suggest that art and design are innocent. Panofsky also says, on numerous occasions, that works of art are 'symptoms' or 'symptomatic' of something else (56). He even writes at one point of a 'cultural symptom' (65). A symptom is also relatively innocent: a symptom is only the innocent signifier of 'something else' (56). That something else is the thing, the disease, the tendency, that is significant and to be worried about. It is also possible to argue that works of art and design are not innocent, that they are not neutral signifiers of something else that is more important. It may be argued that they are themselves something else, that they are the means by which social, philosophical, political and other tendencies are created and reproduced.

It was noted above, in the discussion of Gombrich's account of expressionist theories of art and design, that different social groups will use shapes, lines, colours and textures both to constitute themselves as social groups and to differentiate themselves from other groups, which use other different shapes, lines and so on. On a very simple level, this was the point of the survey of the different books in Chapter 1. In these books, different social groups used different kinds of objects as well as different colours, shapes and so on to differentiate themselves from other social groups. The aristocrats and upper classes in Clark's account of civilisation used fine art, paintings and sculptures to constitute themselves as distinct from other social groups, not to reflect or to bear witness to that difference. The paintings and sculptures are not symptoms of something else (social inequality), they are the means by which that inequality is established and reproduced. As was pointed out, if you do not have the education to understand the paintings and sculptures, you are not a member of the culture. Similarly, the reds, golds and greens of Rifat Ozbek's Spring/Summer 1991 collection do not reflect Rastafarian identity, they create it. The Rastafarian style was also a means of opposing dominant white social groups; these colours and styles are not simply a record or a document of opposition, they constitute opposition to other social groups. There is no sense in Panofsky's account of different social classes using art and design to construct their identities against other social classes in these ways and the analysis, explanation and critique of visual culture proposed here must take such insights seriously.

It was noted at the beginning of this chapter that, in addition to what might be called a traditional 'object-based' art history, there is in Pointon's account a more 'structure-based' art history, in which economic, social and political structures are used to analyse and explain cultural products, including art (1994: 30–1). Some of the more significant aspects of the object-based approaches, explaining the appearance of items of visual culture in terms of materials, style, expression, formal aspects, iconology/graphy, spirit of the age, intention and so on, have been examined above and some of their main weaknesses have been identified. The rest of this chapter will concentrate on some of the structure-based approaches. These are largely materialist accounts and they are largely historical accounts. Another way of saying this would be to say that they are largely Marxist accounts. Such accounts hold that social class is of major significance in explaining how and why examples of visual culture look the way they do and they hold that social class is largely defined in terms of economics. They also hold that visual culture has what is called an ideological function. That is to say that it is one of the ways in which the ideas of a social class are expressed and it is one of the ways in which the ideas of different social classes may come into conflict. This is in contrast to the accounts examined above which were characterised as being mainly idealist. They were idealist in the sense that they held that the explanation of visual culture could be found in ideas, divorced from material and historical 'reality'.

Michael Baldwin, Charles Harrison and Mel Ramsden identify the 'proper' concerns and themes of art history in terms of Wittgensteinian 'fuzzy families' of questions. These divide into the factual questions that most art history concerns itself with and more substantive questions. The factual questions include those concerning 'date, dimensions, location and so on'. And the more substantive questions include 'what is it? To whom is or was it addressed? What does it look like? What is it of? or What does it represent or signify? What does it express? or What is its meaning? and Is it any good?' (in Fernie 1995: 262). They explain that the answers to these questions are really the answer to the question of what caused the work of art to look the way it does. These questions 'demand that we enquire into the specific *causes* of its specific appearance' (263). Although Baldwin *et al.* are coming from a completely different tradition, with a different set of interests, this sounds like the question that visual culture has set itself, to enquire into why the thing looks the way it does, to ask after the social and cultural construction of visual experience.

They also point out that in 'normal' art history, the matter of the interpretation of a work has been thought to 'hinge' upon questions like 'what does it represent or signify?' and 'what does it express or mean?' and that these questions have traditionally been seen as separate from the question 'to whom is it or was it addressed?' The question of a thing's meaning has been seen as separate from the question of its audience or market and Baldwin *et al.* seek to correct this mistake. They also seek to establish the artist as a producer and artistic work as production (Fernie 1995: 265). This means paying attention to the conditions of production, something that not all traditional art history has been interested in. Baldwin *et al.* cite Michael Baxandall's example of Sassetta's painting of St Francis casting away his gown. This gown was painted using a kind of blue that was extremely expensive to buy at the time, metaphorically and effectively making the point to the contemporary spectator that St Francis was casting away something that was extremely valuable to him – his heritage. This aspect of the production of the painting is part of the meaning of the work for Baldwin *et al.* For 'Roger Fry and his epigones', for those who would explain works of visual culture solely in terms of lines, shape and colour, for example, or in terms of 'expression', this aspect of the meaning of the painting would remain forever unknown and unavailable (266). The material conditions of the production of visual culture would not be an aspect that was of any interest to such 'explanations'.

Baldwin, Harrison and Ramsden are also concerned that concepts such as class and ideology should play a part in their explanation of art. They propose the outline of an explanation of Modernism in terms of class and ideology. The characteristic ideas and attitudes of Modernism appeared towards the end of the nineteenth century. At this time, the 'upper bourgeoisie' was especially concerned to distinguish itself both from the aristocracy and from the 'petit bourgeoisie and the nouveau riche' (272). The upper bourgeoisie seized upon Modernist art, along with its characteristic ideas and attitudes, in order to thus distinguish itself. Although Baldwin *et al.* do not explain how, this class apparently used the ideas of 'change, renewal and novelty' to establish itself as the 'proper guardian of knowledge, civilisation and . . . the eternal verities' (273). Art is ideological, then, in that it serves the interests of a particular social class. Art was idealised by this class as the place where it could articulate its own meanings. Consequently, the notion of the 'artist' was developed into that of a 'creator', not a 'producer' or 'worker' as it developed elsewhere. And the creations of the artist were thought of, not in terms of the productions of other types of worker, but as 'bundles of properties' that the upper bourgeoisie were specifically interested in (ibid.).

Another account of art which stresses notions of production is that proposed by Janet Wolff in her book *The Social Production of Art*, first published in 1981. In this work, and in the important Afterword to the second edition, published in 1992, Wolff argues that art is a social product (1981: 1). She reconsiders conceptions of artistic creativity in terms of production, pointing out that the notion of the artist as single individual soul is itself a product of the romantic period. Following Marx's exhortations in the *Grundrisse*, to the effect that production and consumption must be conceptualised and understood as complementary, Wolff examines the reception of art.

Wolff's account of the ideological status of visual culture is slightly different to that of Baldwin *et al.* Where they emphasise the dominant aspects of the dominant ideology, saying that, after all, 'the function of a dominant ideology is to dominate' (in Fernie 1995: 272), Wolff stresses that 'the so-called "dominant ideology" of a society is never monolithic or totally pervasive' (Wolff 1992a: 53). She takes a point from Raymond Williams, who introduces the ideas of alternative ideologies, to argue that there are also 'residual', 'emergent', 'oppositional' or 'alternative' ideologies. Residual ideologies are those which, although formed in the past, are still active. Emergent ideologies are those of new groups, existing outside of the dominant groups. Oppositional ideologies actively mount a challenge to the dominant ideology, while alternative ideologies may happily coexist with it. Art, and artistic production, may represent any one of these kinds of ideology. In the Afterword to the second edition, Wolff again critiques the monolithic conception of ideology, citing the work of Gramsci as instructive and useful in explaining the oppositional nature of social and political life.

An example of visual culture producing and expressing a dominant ideology might be found in Sir Kenneth Clark's book, noted in the previous chapter. The works reproduced in this book share the values of the dominant social group; they are to do with classical antiquity, with the Established Church and with royalty, for example. As noted, the works demand a certain type of education and a certain type of interpretative work in order to understand them. In contrast, the fashions found in Polhemus's book might be thought of as both emergent and oppositional. They are indicative of emergent ideologies in that they are used to construct new social groups, and they are often oppositional in that they do not happily coexist with dominant ideologies. The fashions, products and 'architecture' of groups such as the Travellers and the Donga tribe are both emergent and oppositional, opposing, as they do, the environmental destruction inherent in dominant lifestyles.

Tim Clark also represents someone who adopts a historical and materialist approach to visual culture, an approach that is better known as the social history of art. He begins his work on Courbet by listing the subjects, themes and approaches that he is not interested in covering or following. He says,

> I am not interested in the notion of works of art 'reflecting' ideologies, social relations or history. Equally, I do not want to talk about history as 'background' to the work of art – as something which is essentially absent from the work of art and its production . . . Lastly, I do not want the social history of art to depend on intuitive analogies between form and ideological content – on saying, for example, that the lack of firm compositional focus in Courbet's *Burial at Ornans* is an expression of the painter's egalitarianism. (1982: 250)

This is a criticism of many approaches to the study of visual culture that he shares with Wolff. Wolff refers to the many books which purport to be about 'art and society' but which conceive of society only as a 'kind of painted backdrop, referred to only as a tableau of social groups and their practices, which are said to inform the works' (1992: 706). Works of art, examples of visual culture, then, do not simply 'reflect' ideologies; as Clark says, they 'work' those ideologies. Works of art, examples of visual culture, may give ideology a new form and may even subvert that ideology on Clark's account (1982: 253). Wolff supports this argument, proposing that 'far from reflecting the already-given social world, . . . cultural forms participate in the production of that world' (1992: 707). Similarly, for Clark, history does not exist as a simple background, or backdrop, to the production of visual culture; the artist is a part of history and may sometimes be historically effective (1982: 252).

Clark also begins to give some positive content to the project of the social history of art, much of which will be taken up in some form in the following chapters. As a set of 'starting points', Clark suggests 'the immediate conditions of artistic production and reception: patronage, sales, criticism [and] public opinion' (1982: 251). So, production and consumption, the institutions by means of which producers and consumers of visual culture have organised themselves, will be dealt with in the following chapters. This means looking at groupings of artists and designers, as well as the various economic formations into which audiences, markets or publics have organised themselves. As Clark says, however, this must be done in the context of some general theory of 'the structure of capitalist economy' (251). This book is predominantly concerned with what might loosely be called western modernity, as are Baldwin *et al.* above, and the dominant economic structure of modern western society is capitalism. Consequently, in the following chapters, these are some of the topics and themes that will be covered. The next section will consider the various disciplines in terms of which visual culture might be studied. It will be argued that, in order to cover all the topics and themes noted above, some form of interdisciplinary approach will be required.

Disciplines and subjects

Since visual culture is not simply the same thing as either art or design, it follows that the best way to study it is not going to be simply either art history or design history. Indeed, many would argue that most versions of art history are not even the best way to study art, suggesting that traditional art history should be complemented by other disciplines, such as sociology or film studies, for example. This section will consider the arguments of Marcia Pointon, Victor Margolin and Janet Wolff concerning the disciplinary bases best suited to the analysis and explanation of visual culture.

Marcia Pointon argues that 'art history is concerned with no single class of objects . . . every "man-made" structure and artefact, from furniture and ceramics to buildings and paintings, from photography and book illustration to textiles and teapots, comes within the province of the art historian' (1994: 28–9). Her version of art history encompasses all the things that the definition of visual culture includes. Her version of art history also includes studying the economic, political and social structures, or contexts, in which these artefacts are produced and consumed. She is interested in 'power . . . control and . . . economics' as they are manifested at art auctions, for example. The workings and transgressions of 'social and class boundaries' in the purchase of works of art are also of central importance to her version of art history (ibid.). Pointon's version of art history seems also to be interdisciplinary. She refers, for example, to the diverse approaches that may be taken to the 'documentation, analysis and evaluation of visual material' (29) and argues that 'there exists no single line of enquiry that we can label art history' (49). What Pointon calls art history may draw from many other disciplines: philosophy, sociology, psychology, history and anthropology are all cited as disciplines which may aid the documentation, analysis and evaluation of visual material (49–50).

In an essay published in 1995, Victor Margolin reaches some conclusions that are rather similar to those which Pointon reaches while starting from the realm of design history rather than art history. Reviewing the history of writing about design history, Margolin presents Nikolaus Pevsner and Reyner Banham as two central figures. Pevsner's work, in his *Pioneers of the Modern Movement* (later revised and published as *Pioneers of Modern Design: From William Morris to Walter Gropius)*, has established the concerns and approaches taken by much subsequent writing in the history of design. In these works, Pevsner told a story of the history of design as the development of design towards a high point, or culmination, that was reached in the Bauhaus, the German design school that flourished between the wars, and especially the work of Walter Gropius, its first director. This approach has elements in common with that of Clark, in *Civilisation*, where civilisation is seen as the development of mind through painting and sculpture to a high point. However, as Margolin points out, for Pevsner, 'the study of design was an act of discrimination by which ordinary objects were separated from those which embodied an extraordinary quality' (Margolin 1995: 7). All objects which were used on a daily basis by ordinary people, for example, were excluded from Pevsner's account of design. Clearly, this is not a good model for the kind of studies proposed here for visual culture.

Reyner Banham, however, writing in the 1950s and 1960s, was very interested in these ordinary objects, intended for everyday use.

Banham was a member of the Independent Group, an informal group of artists, critics, architects and intellectuals who would meet at the Institute for Contemporary Arts in London. Richard Hamilton, the so-called pop artist who incorporated vacuum cleaners, toasters, fridges, comic art and advertisements into his paintings, was also a member of the Independent Group and wrote a series of 'intelligent and perceptive' essays on mass media and design (Walker 1989: 66–7). Margolin goes so far as to suggest that Banham had an 'infatuation with popular culture' and that he showed tremendous enthusiasm for both mass-produced objects and the 'diverse products of contemporary popular culture' (Margolin 1995: 7). A design history that can deal with mass-produced goods of all kinds, and which does not conceive those goods as either unworthy of study or as leading to some culmination of good design, is clearly to be welcomed. Such an approach bears comparison with Sudjic's approach noted in the previous chapter, which also conceives of mass-produced objects as worthy of cultural study and these elements of it must be adopted by visual culture.

Margolin, however, is still not entirely happy with this as an approach for the history of design. Basically, Pevsner and Banham are arguing over which objects count as design or are fit to be studied by the history of design, whereas for Margolin design does not 'signify a class of objects that can be pinned down' (1995: 10). Designing, he says, is an activity that is constantly changing and he implies that it is impossible to establish a body of knowledge about 'something that has no fixed identity' (ibid.). (This rather begs the question as to whether any of the humanities or social sciences are productive of 'knowledge' but that must remain a question for another time and place.) It is at this point that his argument begins to resemble Pointon's. He notes the way in which art history has been deeply affected by theories from other subjects and disciplines being applied in the interpretation of works of art. He suggests that 'sociology, philosophy, anthropology, history, psychology, psychoanalysis, cultural studies and literary criticism' (1995: 11) have all made their contribution to discourses about art recently. This is a longer list than Pointon's but contains many of the same disciplines and essentially the same point concerning the nature of art history is being made by them both. Margolin wonders whether the term 'art history' still describes a discipline, if what is meant by a discipline is 'a common set of assumptions about what the subject matter is and what the methods for its study are' (ibid.). Pointon, likewise, wonders about the 're-evaluation of art history as a discipline' (Pointon 1994: 49). She asks what a 'legitimate line of enquiry' would be for art history, given that 'furniture and ceramics . . . buildings and paintings . . . photography and book illustration . . . textiles and teapots' (28–9) are appropriate objects of art historical investigation and given that philosophy, sociology, psychology, history and anthropology are all cited as disciplines which can help art history (49–50).

While Pointon retains the name 'art history' for the study of visual culture (1994: 1), Margolin suggests that 'we no longer have a discipline of art history but rather a field of art studies' (1995: 11). He takes this line of argument further, extending it into the area of design history. Given what he calls the 'crossing' and 'blurring' of disciplinary and intellectual boundaries that is taking place in other areas of study, he asks whether design history, 'as it has been constituted up to now is a viable enterprise' (12). He is proposing that the intellectual and disciplinary crossings and blurrings that are happening elsewhere render design history, conceived as possessing an identifiable and fixed set of objects and methods, impossible. The design history of Pevsner, Banham and the others must be left behind, to be replaced by a new 'discipline' known as 'design studies'. Rather than trying to define what is and what is not a design object, Margolin proposes redefining design as the 'conception and planning of the artificial' (13). By the artificial he means the 'broad domain of human made products . . . material objects, visual and verbal communications, organised activities and services and . . . systems and environments for living, working, playing and learning' (ibid.). Design studies will include history, but it will also include specialists from other disciplines, such as those mentioned above. It will study the ways in which everyday products have been made and used and it will deal with 'product conception and planning, production, form, distribution and use' (14). Margolin sees this kind of design studies approach as escaping the problems that surround the conception of design as the end product of a design process.

It is clear that, in order to cover the subjects, themes and topics proposed above, some form of interdisciplinary approach will be necessary. It is not the case, for example, that a traditional art history, as envisaged by Wölfflin, for example, will be able to explain the workings of class in capitalist society and how those workings affect patronage in the nineteenth century. As Pointon, Margolin and Wolff have all argued, insights from other disciplines such as sociology, cultural studies, economics, anthropology and history, for example, will be needed to explain the appearance of visual culture. As well as furnishing concepts and approaches that will enable the explanation and analysis of visual culture, these disciplines will also force greater or lesser changes in those disciplines themselves. They will not always necessarily sit together quietly: there must be debate between these disciplines. They will, then, effect changes in each other.

W. J. T. Mitchell's 1995 essay 'What is visual culture?' offers a chance to show how an interdisciplinary approach enables and forces changes in approach and theme, keeping the most useful and placing others in a more realistic perspective. As an interdisciplinary 'discipline', visual culture represents a series of 'complex and far-reaching' challenges to other subjects which concern themselves with explaining and analysing the visual. Art history, for example, will be challenged in various ways. It will no longer be able to 'rely on received notions of beauty or aesthetic significance to define its proper object of study' (1995b: 209). What he means by this, presumably, is that things which are not beautiful, and not produced with the primary intention of being beautiful, will have to be accounted for, analysed and explained by art history. As noted in Chapter 1, Mitchell also believes that art history will have to account for vernacular (the everyday and ordinary) and popular imagery, in addition to traditional fine art imagery as a result of the 'challenge' from visual culture. Notions of aesthetic significance, aesthetic hierarchy, masterpieces and the genius will also have to be rethought by art history. In particular, they will have to be rethought as 'historical constructions specific to various cultural place-times' (210).

Mitchell argues that, so far from being abandoned by the study of visual culture, notions like the genius, aesthetic hierarchy and the masterpiece will at last become objects of serious investigation. Their status, power and the pleasures that they give will be analysed and accounted for rather than being taken for granted and mindlessly repeated by each new generation of students. Similarly, where there are 'authentic artistic achievements', those achievements will 'not only survive juxtaposition with the productions of kitsch and mass culture, but become all the more convincing, powerful and intelligible' (1995b: 210). Where the art critic Clement Greenberg sees the self-criticism of modernity as leaving modern art in all the more secure possession of its proper area (Greenberg 1982: 5), Mitchell sees interdisciplinarity as providing a proper, respectable and intellectually powerful account of all items of visual culture. Visual culture, as an interdisciplinary and reflexive approach to art and design, will have some intellectual and aesthetic standards with which to judge the claims of other disciplines in the analysis and explanation of art and design. It will not uncritically and unthinkingly adopt a canon, standards or modes of explanation.

Wolff has a similar conception of the effects of interdisciplinarity. She suggests, for example, that the traditional, art-historical notion of the artistic producer is in need of 'rethinking' in the light of developments in cultural theory. There are various ways in which the individual artist has been 'displaced' or 'decentred' in recent theory. There is the notion of the collective production of visual culture, which occurs most clearly, perhaps, in film and television. The concentration on textual meaning has also caused attention to drift from the artistic producer. The role of the reader or spectator is another source of meanings which diverts attention from the artist. And the general decentring of the artist as a potential unifying source for meaning is also part of this tendency. In the light of these developments, Wolff suggests that the artistic producer be 'reconceptualised' or rethought. The producer, or producers, of visual culture need to be reconceptualised, on her account, as 'non-unitary, provisionally fixed, psychically and socially produced' (Wolff 1992a, 2nd edn: 153).

While it is true to say that Raymond Williams (1981) is not explicitly concerned with visual culture, it would also be fair to infer that both he and Janet Wolff are concerned that the themes and approaches of both sociology and cultural studies are employed in the study of visual culture. For neither, however, is it a received, or conventional, form of either sociology or cultural studies that is to be used. Williams points out that 'a sociology of a new kind' is required, one that sees culture as a signifying system and which understands culture as constitutive of a social order but which does not reduce culture to an 'informing spirit' or *Zeitgeist* (Williams 1981: 14). As noted in Chapter 1, this signifying system may be thought of as the institutions, objects, practices, values and beliefs by means of which a social order or structure is visually constituted, and either reproduced or contested.

Wolff is also concerned that the sociology of art and cultural studies learn from each other and adapt in the analysis and explanation of visual culture. She says that the problem with 'mainstream' sociology is that it is 'unable to acknowledge the constitutive role of culture and representation in social relations' (1992b: 710). Consequently, it identifies the social institutions in its area of specialisation and analyses their internal operations. In terms of visual culture, these institutions would include galleries, museums, fashion houses, advertising agencies, television companies and so on. The problem is that such sociology sees culture, and the products and institutions of culture, as simply reflecting a social order or structure, with all its inequalities of power and status, rather than as constitutive of that social order. Sociology, then, should learn to see visual culture as constitutive of a social order or structure, something which cultural studies has long understood. Cultural studies, however, while seeing visual culture and representation as constitutive of a social order, remains at the level of representation. As Wolff has it, while cultural studies 'insists on the recognition of paintings as social products, bearing the trace of their origins in relations of power and inequality . . . it remains at the level of textuality. The social is only there in the text' (708–9). In what she calls 'strong' versions of this argument, the social is alleged to exist only in representation or in the text; any independently available or 'real' existence of social reality is denied (712).

Conclusion

Clearly, the sociology of art and cultural studies must learn from each other in Wolff's account. What she proposes is a form of

> dialectical realism, in which the cultural constitution of social subjects, social groups and the social world is fully acknowledged, and at the same time the persistence, effects and power of particular subjects, processes and institutions is [sic] recognised. (1992b: 712)

The content of the following six chapters, then, may be seen as an attempt to apply the lessons learned concerning the strengths and weaknesses of the approaches and subjects investigated above. In particular, it may be seen as an attempt to learn from and apply the most appropriate and fecund elements of the approaches of such disciplines as the social history of art, sociology and cultural studies. The following chapters will look at things which are explicitly suggested by these disciplines and approaches. Chapter 3 will examine the different ways in which artists and designers have thought about and described the nature of their activities and the different ways they have organised themselves into groups or institutions. Chapter 4 will look at the many and various relationships which the producers of visual culture enter into with the consumers of visual culture. It is about how artists and designers relate to markets, publics and audiences, and Chapter 5 will be concerned with the ways in which cultures are made visible. There are many different ways in which a culture may make its values and beliefs visible, from bodily decoration to television programmes and Internet home pages. Chapter 6 will show how different cultural groups at different times and places have used different rules, or codes, to define what is and is not art and design and to distinguish one form of art or design from another. And Chapter 7 will explain how and why cultural products, such as works of art and design, or visual culture, are produced in different forms or types. It will explain the different types of art and design as the product of different social classes and fractions of classes existing and evolving in time and constituting themselves as class groups. Finally, Chapter 8 will attempt to explain the role of visual culture; it will argue that the role of visual culture is in maintaining and transforming society.

Chapter 3

Producers: Artists and Designers

Introduction

This chapter is about the different ways in which artists and designers have thought about and described the nature of their activities and the different ways they have organised themselves into groups or institutions. It is also about the relative status accorded artists and designers and the activities of art and design and how that status is related to the groups and institutions they are members of. In investigating these topics, this chapter begins what might be called the historical sociology of visual culture. It is claimed that the nature of the groups that artists and designers form is part of the analysis and explanation of their work; it is part of the explanation of visual experience and visual culture. This chapter and the following chapter will largely adopt the categories of groups and institutions proposed by Williams in his (1981) book *Culture* as they offer a clear and concise method of selecting and organising this complex and difficult material. This chapter will also, however, provide Williams's usually empty categories with historical and contemporary content. Some of this complexity and difficulty is a product of the fact that these groups in which artists and designers exist are closely bound up with the ways in which these artists and designers relate to their markets. The notion of the academy, for example, is closely related to the decline of a certain form of patronage; as the patronage of the church declines, so the academies grow in status and importance. So, while guilds, academies and so on all entail some form of relation to a market or public, markets and publics will not be discussed here but will rather be the subjects of the following chapter.

Portraits of the artist and the designer

These topics are important as they still colour, or inform, the understanding of the kinds of people who produce visual culture and of the sorts of relationships these people form. For example, a few years ago, in a newspaper careers advice column aimed at young people, a journalist related the popular view of one of the differences between artists and designers. According to this view, 'the artist is generally a loner; the designer is always a member of a team' (Cross 1988). This account may be unpacked or expanded. The artist exists as a lone individual, with few connections to other artists or the outside world, independently doing his or her own creative thing. Such a view of the artist and of artistic activity is known as the romantic view, as it was most popular during the romantic period of the nineteenth century. As Louisa Buck and Philip Dodd point out, this conception of the artist often involves the idea that the artist is 'special', possessed of greater imaginative powers and more sensitivity than ordinary people (1991: 44). In this conception of the artist, the artist is usually male, the phrases 'Old Master' and 'masterpiece' not fitting easily on female shoulders (see Pollock and Parker 1981). This lone, male hero conception of the artist is found in films such as Vincente Minnelli's 1956 *Lust for Life* which portrays Vincent Van Gogh as a 'tortured, struggling genius', who also suffers from 'artistic madness'.

There are various criticisms that may be made of such a view of the artist. Janet Wolff points out that such a conception is a product of a particular historical point in time (1992a: 11). She argues that the rise of notions of individualism, from around the fourteenth century, alongside the development of capitalism and the separation of the artist from any secure patronage or social classes, gave rise to this romantic notion of the artist. The fact that this conception arises only in particular social and historical circumstances means that it cannot be a natural or universal model of art and artistic production. As well as social and historical arguments, there is the argument, hinted at above, that the conception is gender-specific. Buck and Dodd argue that women simply do not fit into this conception of the lone, tortured artist: 'until recently Gwen John was simply Augustus John's neurotic sister'. . . just as Georgia O'Keefe was the eccentric wife of

Alfred Steiglitz' (1991: 51). Nor do they fit into the alienated, artistic madman mould: 'a woman was never an insane genius, she was just insane' (ibid.). And there is the postmodernist argument, that the simple individual of romantic theory is impossible, that the post-modern subject has been fragmented and decentred.

However, on the popular view recounted above, the designer is not such a lone, tortured individual; he or she exists as part of a team and subjugates the expression of his or her creative independence to the greater needs of the team. Artistic activity is creative and expressive on this view, then, and best achieved alone, independently. Design activity is not so expressive and is best done as part of a team. These are vast generalisations and, in the manner of vast generalisations, it will be possible to find evidence both for and against them. That the popular view of the artist is of a lone individual is probably correct; most people probably do think of artists as loners. One may wonder, however, whether a popular view of designers exists at all, and if it does, whether it does not rather follow the model of the artist as a lone, creative soul.

For example, designers like Neville Brody, Alexander McQueen, Giorgetto Giugiaro and Philippe Starck occasionally appear in pop-ular magazines or on television; Brody, McQueen, Giugiaro and Starck are known, then, but they are known as individuals. This point is effectively made by Brody's one-man exhibition at the Victoria and Albert Museum in 1988. People went to see an exhibition of one man's work, not a collection of anonymous design. Deyan Sudjic also makes the point in his *Cult Objects*: Giugiaro is probably known mainly for designing the Volkswagen Golf and Sudjic suggests that the Golf 'was one of the last single designer cars, produced . . . by an individual who left his individual stamp on it' (Sudjic 1985: 144–5). Sudjic leaves no room for doubt; the Golf was designed by a lone, single individual. This is in contrast to both the Ford Sierra, which was produced 'by an international team', and to the Mark Two Golf, which was the product of 'a studio full of technicians' (ibid.).

There are also problems involved in saying that the artist is 'a loner'; some artists are not loners. Andy Warhol (1928–87), for example, is usually thought of as an artist but he called the studio where he worked 'The Factory' and he employed numerous assistants to help produce large editions of silkscreen prints. His 'industrialisa-tion' of the artistic process involves something like a team, then, as did some of the work of Bridget Riley (b. 1931), who would leave her paintings to be completed by a team of assistants, according to her instructions. Part of the explanation of how these works look the way they do, then, is to be found in the way that artistic or creative activity is conceived by the 'artist'. Warhol has also been described as 'an androgynous dandy who played with the masculine myth of the genius' (Buck and Dodd 1991: 50), not simply reproducing a dominant masculine identity. However, his images of women are the traditional 'passive pin-ups' found throughout the history of art (ibid.). In the early twentieth century, the potter Bernard Leach seems to have fitted into the pattern of the lone artist. The popular image of Leach is that of him working alone, in the middle of nowhere, dedicatedly and self-denyingly struggling to produce his work. In all cases, the nature of the relationships which the artist or designer is a part of will form part of the explanation of their work.

Craft guilds

The first kind of organisation to be considered here is the craft guild. Craft guilds began to be formed as early capitalist economies were developing, around the beginning of the fourteenth century. It should be noted that these are craft guilds, and not art or design guilds: art and design are terms that are introduced later, as capitalism evolves a more complex social and economic system which demands that art be distinguished from design and craft. Craft guilds, then, were open to craftspeople; each craft would have its own guild. They were open to engravers, sculptors, printers, cabinet-makers, carpenters, tailors, builders and other artisans. They were also open to those who made paintings. Guilds controlled the education, training and professional practice of members of these trades. It was within the guild system that the master–apprentice relationship was instituted. The apprentice would be taken on by a master and educated or trained by him in the craft and after a specified time would be considered fit to practise that craft or trade. The guilds also determined and regulated production standards within the trades. The precise qualities and standards of workmanship, of materials and of specifications would be set by the guilds. And they controlled the prices of goods produced by guild members as well as the wages commanded by those members.

The guilds had, therefore, something of a conservative, or protect-ive, function. A system in which the transmission of skills and knowledges is restricted and rigidly controlled by the masters is necessarily going to be a fairly conservative institution. They were there to preserve the trade, to ensure that the old standards were upheld and passed on, whole and intact, to the next generation. Another way of saying this would be to suggest that they were there to institute a sense of professionalism in the members of a trade or craft. It would also be to say that craft guilds were there to defend the interests of the members of the guild, protecting them from other guilds and employers. In this respect, the guilds are the precursors of modern trade unions. The guilds worked to maintain the status quo. This is not to say that they were always successful in supporting the status quo. These guilds were unambiguously male-dominated, for example, run by and for men. However, Pat Kirkham points out that women were members of the medieval trade guilds, often opposing the male members who would claim that their work was too hard, too heavy or too dangerous for women (1989: 112). She notes that there were more women involved in upholstery than furniture-making because the latter was considered too dirty and heavy for women, but that there were no formal restrictions on entry to the furniture-making crafts or guilds (ibid.).

There have been periodic attempts throughout the history of art and design to revive some kind of guild system. In 1888, for example, Charles R. Ashbee founded the Guild of Handicraft. The Guild was joined by the School of Handicraft which, inspired by nineteenth-century socialism and the Arts and Crafts Movement, was an attempt to restore something like an apprentice system. This apprentice system would have been familiar from the Middle Ages. However, the division of labour demanded by new machine-based manufacturing processes had destroyed such a system. The School wanted to reestablish a unified experience of design teaching, theory and workshop experience. Consequently, it taught the development of practical craft skills, along with the works of Ruskin, and encouraged the study of how the principles of the arts and crafts could be applied to artistic materials. Again, the organisation of artists and designers into guilds is part of the explanation of why the products of these artists and designers look the way they do.

While the School could not compete with late nineteenth-century state-funded technical schools and while it failed to secure state funding, closing in 1898, the Guild went from strength to strength. The Guild developed as a cooperative, in which the workers owned and ran the Guild and shared whatever profits it made. The Guild was seemingly undaunted by the failure of the School and in 1902 moved to Chipping Campden to begin the extraordinary task of establishing an entire village as a commune, housing and employing Guild members and their families.

Academies

Although the term 'academy' derives from the grove near Athens where Plato taught philosophy around 400 BC, institutions with an emphasis on teaching the more intellectual aspects of painting and drawing began to develop in Europe around the end of the sixteenth century. The academies appear and grow as the significance of the Church as the main patron of art and design begins to decline. Academies were an early attempt at establishing and maintaining a series of differences between the activities that we now know as art and craft and design. Where, in the guild system, all manual activities were represented, in the academy, some are excluded. Thus, people who would now be called artists, painters and sculptors could be guild members alongside engravers, carpenters, tailors, builders and so on. The academies were an attempt to increase the social status and prestige of certain of these arts. Establishing new institutions, based on the universities, and differentiating certain arts from other arts was the way the academies attempted to increase the status and prestige of certain artists. The accounts presented here are indebted to Hutchison (1986) and Boschloo *et al.* (1989).

In the Middle Ages, activities had been divided into the liberal arts and the mechanical arts. The liberal arts included grammar, mathematics, rhetoric, music and astronomy while the mechanical arts included the production of what this volume calls visual culture. The mechanical arts included painting, drawing, sculpture, carpentry, tailoring and so on, both skilled craft and manual activities. The two kinds of activity were not equal in terms of prestige or status within medieval society. The liberal arts, and those practising them, enjoyed a higher status than the mechanical arts. In order to study the liberal arts, one needed time and money and only the wealthy could afford either. The liberal arts were taught at the universities: one would study for a Bachelor of Arts degree, or a Master of Arts degree. The mechanical arts were of much lower status. One did not go to university in order to learn the mechanical arts, one joined a guild. And, rather than be examined for a degree, one produced what was called a 'masterpiece'. The masterpiece was the piece of work produced in order to show that one was the master of one's craft and fit to be given full membership of the guild. The liberal arts involved more clearly intellectual activities while the mechanical arts were to do with more manual skills, and the social status of both the activities and those engaging with them was completely different. The liberal arts were of high status and the mechanical arts were of lower status.

After the Renaissance, however, the word 'design' entered the English language from the French *dessiner* and the Italian *disegno*. The word covered what would nowadays be called drawing and sketching as well as planning and designing. It meant the idea and the means by which the idea was communicated. There was, then, a new reference to something intellectual, the idea, that was involved in an activity that had hitherto been a mechanical art. Around this time, the word 'artist' was undergoing subtle changes. In the sixteenth century, it had meant something like an artisan, a skilled manual or craft worker (Williams 1976: 32–5). Towards the end of the sixteenth century, however, it began to be applied to painters, drawers, sculptors and engravers and it began to be applied only to these people, distinguishing them from other skilled craft and manual workers. The painters, including people like El Greco, were looking for a way of increasing the status of the things they did, and setting up academies for the express purpose of teaching artists and teaching them the more intellectual aspects of painting was one way of doing this. They wanted to raise the status of painting from that of a mechanical art to that of a liberal art. It is interesting to note, as Louisa Buck and Philip Dodd do, that the term 'masterpiece' survived the change in status of painters from artisan, producer of material artefacts, to artist, 'someone special, set apart from the rest of us' (1991: 30). The use of the term 'masterpiece' continued after its original context had changed.

Thus the academies were founded. Like the universities, they had lecturers and professors and they awarded prizes for their best work. Academies taught not just the practice of painting and drawing but the more theoretical or intellectual subjects like anatomy, geometry and history. The art that was produced, then, looked the way it did as a result of this kind of education; the academies were responsible for the appearance and experience of visual culture to this extent. Such curricula may be seen as attempting to be more like the high-status universities by teaching some of the same subjects as they did. The matter of status was pursued to quite extreme lengths by some of the academies. The Royal Academy, founded in 1768, excluded engravers; painting was evidently, or at least was evidently thought to be, of much higher status than engraving. An academy established in Holland in 1600 established distinctions of status between different kinds of painter (Wine 1996: 104). Artist painters were of higher status than either house painters or gilders. The founder of this academy went so far as to bemoan the fact that in most European cities the noble art of painting was being turned into a guild. Other academies would not teach painting at all, seeing it as too much like the lower-status manual skills of the gilder. These academies concentrated on teaching drawing. Generally, the academies were concerned to differentiate themselves from guilds, often demeaning the guilds as degenerate and as smothering the genuine intellectual creativity that the academies sought to nurture. All these measures were intended to distinguish the artist from the artisan and to increase the social status of the artist.

From around the end of the eighteenth century, however, it was the academies themselves that were beginning to be criticised in these terms. As the nineteenth century wore on, the academies were more and more seen in much the same ways as the guilds had been seen. They were accused of being out of touch, of stifling genuine creativity and artistic activity and of being sterile and mechanical. The growth of the art movements and groups, noted below, led to the ideals of the academies being questioned. These groups and movements, along with the ideas associated with romanticism, encouraged artists and designers to challenge the idea that creativity could be taught. These developments encouraged people to question the role of the academies, arguing against the mechanical copying of antique sculptures or of body parts and arguing against the schematic rendering of emotion and so on. Artistic and design activity was more and more seen as a free, individual activity, in which rules and lessons had little place, and the academy system began to decline in importance. At least partly in response to these developments, some academies allowed some changes. The curriculum in France, for example, altered to include landscape painting. Hitherto an extremely low-status activity, landscape painting was admitted into the academy, even if, at first, it was still largely judged according to the standards of history painting, where figures and character were all important.

Professional societies, cooperatives and unions

The academy in Holland mentioned above is unusual in that there were few academies in Holland (see de Klerk 1989: 284). What generally happened in Holland was that the craft guilds adapted. While artists continued to produce works for sale via dealers, the guilds continued to provide protection, training and a professional body for those who made books, furniture and other artefacts. The guilds continued to perform these functions until the Industrial Revolution, when they began to turn into professional societies and the organisations now known as trade unions. Other groupings into which artists and designers organised themselves can be included under the headings of 'cooperatives' and 'unions'.

Perhaps the best-known cooperative of modern times is the photographic agency, Magnum. Named after a bottle of champagne consumed by the founders in the Museum of Modern Art in New York (Blume 1985: 13), Magnum was formed in 1947 by Robert Capa, Henri Cartier-Bresson, David Seymour (known as Chim), Bill Vandivert and George Rodger. Many of these photographers had worked together during the Second World War and they had discussed the formation of such an agency at that time. In particular, according to Martin Caiger-Smith, Capa and Rodger had discussed their dream 'of an agency run by, and for, photographers' (1987: 8) during the war. Magnum established an office in Paris and set about the task of establishing a photographic agency that was owned and run by its members. Inge Morath, who became a member of the group, describes how the first such cooperative photographic agency had to fight with newspapers and magazines all over the world for the right to 'approve the captions published with our photographs and to own our negatives instead of having to surrender them to the morgue of some big magazine' (1981: 8). Caiger-Smith points out that Magnum also enjoyed a certain amount of 'independence from editorial control or censorship' (1987: 8). Magnum thus achieved the freedom to take whatever pictures they wanted and the power to ensure that the photographs only appeared with the captions that had been approved by the photographers. Morath and Caiger-Smith both point out that the collective also ensured that group projects, involving many of the members, were also a great success.

Magnum, then, was a curious and unique organisation. It was a cooperative which was commercially successful. It established and insisted on its own freedom, on the ability of its members to choose which projects they would photograph, and it promulgated a spirit of brotherhood and optimism, not only amongst its members but amongst all the peoples of the world. And it did all this while remaining commercially viable. It achieved these aims while proving that there was a market for such photographic projects.

Different kinds of union and association were found in post-revolutionary Russia. Between 1928 and 1932, many groups of artists and designers flourished in Russia, each proclaiming that it was the most revolutionary and the most socialist. There was the AKhRR (the Association of Artists of Revolutionary Russia), the RAPKh (the Russian Association of Proletarian Artists), and the October group, for example. These groups issued manifestos and were intended to provide revolutionary guidance for artists and designers in the turmoil that was post-revolutionary Russia. The October group, founded in 1928, included poster artists, photographers, architects, film-makers and book-designers, as well as artists and theorists. As John E. Bowlt points out, membership included Sergei Eisenstein, El Lissitzky, Alexander Rodchenko, Varvara Stepanova and, for one year, Diego Rivera (Bowlt 1988: 273). These various people were united by the Declaration of 1928, in which the role of the 'spatial arts (architecture, painting, sculpture, graphics, the industrial arts, photography, cinematography, etc.)' was to 'serve the concrete needs of the proletariat' (274–5). However, as Cullerne Bown and Taylor say, all the different groups were disbanded in 1932 by the Stalinist Central Committee, which led to the formation of artists' unions (1993: 11).

Indeed, in the years up to the breakdown of the Soviet Union into the Commonwealth of Independent States, artists' unions, under the umbrella of the USSR Artists' Union, were still the only ways in which artists could group together and they exercised considerable power. The institutional structure of groups in which artists and designers could exist survived, relatively unchanged, from 1932 to 1992. The USSR Artists' Union incorporated the artists' union of each Soviet republic, in addition to the large unions belonging to the cities of Moscow and Leningrad. Cullerne Bown notes that membership of these unions was crucial to an artist's existence. Membership entitled such an artist to studio space, as well as giving access to 'materials which otherwise may be impossible to obtain' (1989: 21). Membership of a union was also central to an artist's existence as, without it, a person was not really considered an artist at all and ran the risk of not being recognised as having a job at all. The Union itself was supported financially by the sale of its members' works: it took commission on each sale. Artists were not paid directly by the Union, but it did help support them by arranging for artists to provide works for 'schools, factories, public organisations and so on' (ibid.). In some ways, these unions are not unlike the guilds of medieval times. Membership of a union is gained by following a complicated and demanding path. Artists are expected to show work at 'exhibitions of a certain standard' and they are expected to submit both 'creative work and written references' (ibid.).

Art and design movements

This is probably the form of organisation that is best known to people today. There are many different forms which such organisations may take, and they are called many different names, from 'school', 'movement' and 'circle' to 'group' and 'association'. It is largely during the nineteenth century that these movements, schools and so on begin to expand and spread throughout western Europe. They are the ways in which artists and designers may attempt to declare and publicise the fact of their independence from the inflexibility of some academic training and from the control of the market. They are also the ways in which artists and designers may attempt to cope with the transition taking place in society from making things by hand to making things by machine. These groups, schools and movements, whatever they are called, offer artists and designers a way of protecting themselves from the changes in the market, which shifts from one-off, hand-made artefacts to mass-produced, machine-made artefacts. By associating themselves with certain classes in society, they protect their market and their social position.

As traditional forms of patronage, from the Church and Court, for example, begin to decline in the eighteenth and nineteenth centuries, the market develops and becomes more important. The way work is shown or displayed for sale also, therefore, becomes more important and artists begin to want more control over the exhibition of their work. These movements and groups offer the producers of visual culture such an opportunity. They also enable the idea to develop that the central values of art and design are not necessarily the same as those of modern society. It becomes possible for artists and designers actively to critique and oppose the dominant values of their society. Such movements and groups provide a way in which artists and designers may produce increasingly diverse and increasingly critical work. In doing this, the movements and groups of the nineteenth and twentieth centuries contribute to the changing status of artists and designers. Where they had been seen as skilled practitioners of crafts, artists and designers are increasingly seen as not being in complete agreement with the values of the society they live in and become associated with classes and parts of classes who are themselves not in agreement with the dominant groups of society.

These movements or groups are ways of identifying and making meaningful different examples of visual culture; these groups may be analysed and explained in terms of their internal organisation and in terms of their relation to other institutions and to the wider society. These forms of organisation and external relations also form part of the analysis and explanation of why the pieces of art and design look the way they do; they are part of the analysis and explanation of the appearance of visual culture. There are various forms of internal organisation. The movement or group may have a formal membership, where people apply to or are invited to join. Less formal modes of internal organisation include those based on manifestos, or exhibitions of work. And there are quite informal modes of internal organisation, with neither formal membership nor manifesto, where the movement or group is formed around something like a common mentality or consciousness, or even a place. There are also various ways in which movements or groups may relate to external factors like other art and design institutions or the society they are part of. Organisations may relate to these external factors in such a way that they actively oppose them, being critical or hostile to existing institutions and social conditions. Organisations may propose an alternative to those institutions and conditions, without necessarily being hostile to them or seeking to bring them down. And they may simply provide a way of distinguishing one specialist medium or form of visual culture from another. To reiterate, then: different types of internal and external relation are part of the analysis and explanation of visual culture in that they help explain why pieces of art and design look the way they do.

The following sections will consider various art and design movements in terms of their internal and external relations.

Memphis

Memphis is the name of a radical design group which was formed in the early 1980s in Italy by Ettore Sottsass. Sottsass gathered together a group of designers, including Michele de Lucchi, Nathalie du Pasquier, Marco Zanini, George Sowden, Martine Bedin, Andrea Branzi and Matteo Thun. These people were designers of furniture, glassware, textiles, ceramics, lighting and carpets and many of them had been involved with Sottsass in an earlier radical design group, Studio Alchymia. The 'postmodern' architects Michael Graves and Hans Hollein were also part of the group, designing furniture. Where Studio Alchymia had failed to find support from any manufacturers in its attempt to marry the styles of mass culture with those of elite culture, Memphis succeeded in getting support and put on its first show in Milan in 1981. It is the show, here, that first provides something like an identity for the group. The show is also very important in that it makes the group visible to the public; it constitutes the audience for the group and is the main way in which the visual identity of Memphis is manifested.

The Memphis group had no formal membership, unlike the Situationist International, discussed below, but it did issue a manifesto. The Manifesto, like the 1981 show, provides the group with an identity. It gives some forming energy to the group, enabling both the members and their public to understand their ideas. In terms of its external relations, Memphis had benevolent relations to some aspects of design and was hostile to other parts of the design world. The way the designs look, their visual appearances, may be analysed and explained in terms of these relations. As noted above, the group launched its first collection of furniture at the same time as the 1981 Milan Furniture Fair. This show was put on outside of the main, or dominant, furniture fair, however, as an alternative to that fair. It was an attempt to disrupt that dominant and mainstream fair and may be seen as an actively hostile exhibition. The designs, then, look the way they do because they are conceived as something of a challenge to mainstream, dominant designs and design institutions. Memphis may also be seen as a slightly more subtle critique of modernism in design. Where modernism in design proposes clear lines, uncluttered surfaces and the minimal use of colour and pattern, Memphis revels in colours, textures and patterns. De Lucchi's 'Lido' sofa, Pasquier's 'California' carpet, or Sottsass's own 'Carlton' room-divider (see Ill. 3.1), are multicoloured, striped, spotted and dotted. This relation is not actively hostile: cheerfully and exuberantly, it suggests that colours, textures and patterns can be acceptable and in good taste. Again, the relations to modernism are part of the explanation and analysis of the appearance of the designs.

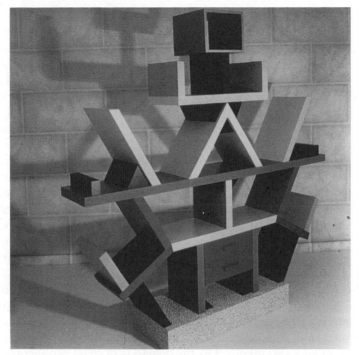

Ill. 3.1   Sottsass, 'Carlton' room-divider

In its relations to Italian and American popular culture, however, Memphis was more generous. The group borrowed from the coffee bars of both America and Italy, for example, taking motifs, textures and materials from the popular culture of the 1950s and 1960s. The name Memphis may refer to the capital of ancient Egypt, but it also refers to Bob Dylan's song 'Memphis Blues' and to American popular music in general. The laminates found in much Memphis furniture echo the easy-clean, fast-food outlets of modern America. In this way, they attempt to fuse, or marry, what is called mass culture, or low culture with high culture: these are high-culture objects, in that they are produced by individual, named designers, but they partake in the patterns and styles of low culture.

Der Ring 'neue Werbegestalter'

Der Ring 'neue Werbegestalter' is a German phrase which means 'The Circle of New Advertising Designers'. This group was formed in the late 1920s by a number of what might be called the international superstars of European graphic modernism. Paul Jobling and David Crowley describe this group as a 'professional alliance' formed in 1927 and including the German artist Kurt Schwitters, Dutch graphic designers Paul Schuitema and Piet Zwart, the Hungarian artist Lásló Moholy-Nagy and the Swiss typographer Jan Tschichold (1996: 139). Jobling and Crowley say that the group made decisions 'democratically', but that Schwitters was the 'guiding force' and that it was he who organised their 'sporadic meetings' (140). This represents another, slightly different form of internal organisation in that, while there does not appear to have been a manifesto, the group 'promoted their work and the forms of graphic modernism that they advocated through touring exhibitions which circulated through Germany, Switzerland, Scandinavia and Holland in the late 1920s and early 1930s' (ibid.). Membership also seems to have been relatively informal, with the likes of Herbert Bayer and John Heartfield being invited to join exhibitions of the group's work.

The group relates externally to other modernist groups and forces and to the institutions of modern capitalist society. Thus, the group was interested in developing typographies that were modern and functional and it was interested in the potential of photography. The group was also involved in the demands of mass production and advertising; they wanted to be involved in commerce, Schwitters going so far as to found his own advertising agency to this end. It is argued that these relations are partly responsible for the work of the group looking the way it does. As Jobling and Crowley point out, 'historic typefaces like black-letter *Fraktur* were rejected by Schwitters and his colleagues because they suggested origins in pre-industrial, calligraphic forms' (1996: 140). The modernist desire for clean, uncluttered lines is also expressed by Moholy-Nagy, who also complains that 'we do not even possess a type-face that is clearly legible and . . . that is based on a functional form of visual appearance without distortions and curlicues' (ibid.). For these reasons, the group preferred to use *Futura* (see Ill. 3.2), which was a 'geometric, sans serif type face' designed by Paul Renner (ibid.). The typefaces were a product of their relations to other modernist currents, which sought to escape the older, pre-modern, pre-capitalist hand-writing traditions. The interest in photography is represented by Tschichold, for example, who 'applauded the "supernatural clearness"' of contemporary advertising photography (141). The demands of advertising

FUTURA BOOK BOLD

ABCDEFGHIJKLMNOPQRSTUVWXYZ

abcdefghijklmnopqrstuvwxyz

1234567890

Ill. 3.2   *Futura* typeface

photography, then, prescribe the kind of aesthetic that is approved of by members of the group.

It would be wrong to suggest that the group was opposed to these other modernist influences or to the institutions of modern capitalist society. They are not a revolutionary movement, as it can be claimed the Situationist International, discussed below, was. They are not really alternative, in any very strong sense, either. Indeed, Jobling and Crowley point up the paradoxes of some of the members of the group in this regard (1996: 150). Schuitema, for example, combined working for left-wing publishers with producing advertisements for the Berkel scales company and Tschichold worked for trade unions as well as commercial companies. Tschichold is also aware of the ways in which his work and that of the others relates to and uses insights gained from earlier traditions. His book, *The New Typography*, charts the development of the group's modernist aesthetic from Marinetti's and Carra's Futurist experiments with typography in 1919 and from the abstract work of the Russian Constructivists in the early 1920s. The group, then, simply seems to be a way of distinguishing the membership from other modernist tendencies within early twentieth-century graphic design.

The Situationist International

The Situationist International (SI) was a group of artists and philosophers who were active in France between 1957 and 1972. In terms of its internal organisation, the SI actually had a formal membership. Indeed, membership was used as something of a weapon in the SI, being withdrawn and bestowed as the various members fell in and out with one another. It also held annual conferences and issued manifestos. In terms of its external relations, the SI was highly critical of the society it found itself a part of and of the artistic traditions it inherited. The Situationists saw themselves in combative and military terms; they saw themselves as an avant-garde. Indeed, John Roberts says that 'in many ways, the SI was the last of the great avant-gardes in which artistic proclamation and polemic fused with, and directed, political utopianism' (1992: 123). The work of the SI, then, looked the way it did partly as a result of the critical relations it established with other art movements and the society it was part of.

One of the ways in which artistic polemic and political utopianism fused was in the technique known as *détournement*, where changing context was used to change the meaning of words and images. Asger Jorn, for example, took kitsch imagery from everyday life, changing and modifying it so that its meaning was altered. In much the same way as John Heartfield used photomontage in 1930s Germany, the SI used popular, mass-produced images to make their political points, reproducing pornographic photographs with revolutionary slogans printed over them, for example. The SI was critical of previous avant-garde movements, including those that they seem to have learned most from. The SI criticised the Dadaists and the Surrealists in manifestos and disrupted their shows, claiming that SI work was more revolutionary. They also argued that contemporary abstract works, as well as socialist realism, still took the form of the commodity, a capitalist form, and could not, therefore, be truly revolutionary. This political critique developed after 1961, when Jorn left the SI and Guy Debord became more prominent. Debord initiated the critique of the 'society of the spectacle', mentioned in the Introduction to this book. This was essentially the idea that capitalism had reduced all human interaction to interaction with things or objects and that everything had been made into a spectacle. So, the kinds of work that the SI produced, as well as the way that work looked, are a direct result of the internal relations within the group and the external relations existing between the group and other groups in society. These relations are thus part of the explanation of the work's appearance.

Der Blaue Reiter

Der Blaue Reiter is German for 'The Blue Rider' and denotes a group of artists, including Wassily Kandinsky, Auguste Macke, Paul Klee and Franz Marc, working in Germany between 1911 and the end of the Second World War. The internal organisation of this group is informal, with no fixed membership and no clear methods of 'joining' or 'leaving'. Even the origin of the title is a matter of some confusion. Some hold that it derives from the illustration produced by Kandinsky of a horse and rider for the cover of the almanac. The group seems to be identifiable mainly through a common consciousness shared by a changing collection of artists. Having said this, the group did produce an almanac, *Der Blaue Reiter*, which included essays and graphic work, in which ideas could be circulated and used to form some kind of group identity. The almanac was the place where Kandinsky's central essay 'On the question of form' appeared and where the group's external relations to other traditions and other ideas could be discussed. The almanac is the place, then, where the identity of the group is formed and developed. It is also the place where the group's public, or audience, can see what the group is doing; it is the public face of the *Blaue Reiter* and thus essential to the constitution of the audience.

The external relations are perhaps clearer and more easily described. The group was formed largely as a result of Kandinsky's being rejected and criticised by the expressionist New Artists Association. Kandinsky was rejected by this group for his leaning too much towards abstraction. Other external relations include the relation to folk art, children's paintings and drawings and to the work of so-called 'primitive' cultures from New Caledonia, Easter Island, Malaysia, Brazil and Mexico. These cultures were featured in the almanac of 1912 and the influence of some of them can clearly be seen in much of Emil Nolde's work, for example. It should not be forgotten that, at around this time, 1906–7, Picasso was also being influenced by African cultures. It has been claimed, for example, that the appearance of some of the women in *Les Demoiselles d'Avignon* are the result of the influence of African masks on Picasso. The external relations of the group, to other cultures and to expressionist tendencies in contemporary German and European art are part of the explanation why the visual culture that is produced looks the way it does. It is as a result of these relations that the work is produced.

The Pre-Raphaelite Brotherhood

The Pre-Raphaelite Brotherhood was formed in 1848. The main names associated with it are William Holman Hunt, Dante Gabriel

Rossetti and John Everett Millais, who were in their twenties when the Brotherhood was formed. Again, the idea is that a group of painters are united by a common set of ideas, rather than by a formal membership or set of manifestos. It is, then, by means of their external relations that the Pre-Raphaelite Brotherhood and their works are largely to be explained. These painters were united in their disapproval of and antipathy towards contemporary forms and styles of painting. They said that they wanted to return to 'nature' and to the purity of certain medieval techniques and attitudes. They believed that contemporary painting was ugly, commercial and far too mannered and theatrical. Consequently, they tried to work in a more innocent and simple way. This paradoxical approach, for highly sophisticated and modern artists to adopt the attitudes and airs of some kind of medieval craftsman, eschewing current academic styles and subjects, was to characterise the works of the Pre-Raphaelite Brotherhood.

The Pre-Raphaelite Brotherhood appears rather insular; their relations are with other English traditions. It is the Royal Academy's style, subject matter and methods that they are opposed to. It is a certain version of Englishness that most often appears in their landscapes and interiors (see Ill. 3.3). More specifically, it is a certain version of bourgeois Victorian Englishness that appears in those landscapes and interiors. And it is a certain form of Christianity that is often to be found in their works. This is partly a result of their patrons being largely from that particular social group; parts of the Victorian bourgeoisie seem to have liked to think of themselves as dissidents and rebels in these matters. But it is also a result of the absence of relation to any wider European traditions. The Circle of New Advertising Designers, in contrast, was consciously internationalist and their work looks modern and European; it is partly where the idea of modernity and Europeanness comes from. The Pre-Raphaelite Brotherhood is not European in the ways that the Circle was in that they lack these external relations to those other traditions and styles. Their English, bourgeois and Christian values affect the ways that their paintings look.

Conclusion

This chapter has attempted to show how the various groups and movements which artists and designers form themselves into affect the appearance of visual culture. The groups, schools, movements and

Ill. 3.3   Holman Hunt, *The Awakening Conscience*, 1851–3

so on that artists and designers form and organise themselves into are part of the analysis and explanation of visual culture in that the visual appearance of art and design is partly the product of those social organisations. The nature of those organisations and the relations they enter into with other organisations affects the appearance of visual culture and is therefore part of the analysis and explanation of that visual culture. This chapter has tried to show, then, how the appearance of art and design may be explained and analysed both in terms of the internal organisation of these groups and in terms of their external relations to other groups and to other social forces.

It is not only the groups and movements that affect the look of visual culture. Visual culture is consumed, as well as produced, and if this chapter has concentrated on the producers of visual culture, the next chapter must begin to look at the consumers of visual culture. Chapter 4 will concentrate on the market, audiences and publics for art and design, showing how they play a part in the analysis and explanation of visual culture. So, visual culture looks the way it does, it has the visual appearance it does, as much as a result of the market, audience or public it is aimed at as of the people producing it. And Chapter 4 will look at those various forms and types of consumer.

Chapter 4

Consumers: Markets, Publics and Audiences

Introduction

This chapter is concerned with the types of relationships that exist between the producers and the consumers of visual culture. It is concerned, then, with the relations between the producers of visual culture and social institutions, the organisations, groups and more or less official bodies in society that consume visual culture. While obviously closely related to these matters, the nature and experience of the individual consumer of visual culture will be dealt with explicitly in Chapter 8. Conventional conceptions of the audience or public as the passive consumer or receiver of visual culture will be supplemented there by looking at the conception of the active consumer, who actively interprets and thereby transforms the products of visual culture. The active consumer is in this sense a producer of visual culture and the different experiences and pleasures undergone and enjoyed by the consumer will also be explored there.

The following events have either happened or may happen in the future. The Prince of Wales contracts an architect to design a church for the village of Poundbury in Dorset, Socialist Realism is adopted as the official art form in post-revolutionary Russia, Nokia appoint a salaried designer to style digital telephones, the Cadbury company sponsors *Coronation Street*, a fifteen-year-old buys a 'pirate' Oasis T-shirt from the dodgy character who designs and prints them and a bank manager purchases a watercolour from Harvey Nichols. All these events are very different. The nature and status of the people and institutions involved in them vary from individuals to corporations to governments, from secular to temporal and from royalty to commoner. The products are also very different, including a building, a television programme, a telephone, an item of clothing and a watercolour painting. The events also describe various different relations between people and institutions including contracts, sponsorships and purchases and it is these relationships that this chapter is interested in. To paraphrase Janet Wolff, social institutions affect who becomes an artist or a designer, how they become an artist or designer, how they are then able to practise their art or design and how they can ensure that their work is produced and made available to a public (Wolff 1992a: 40). One thing all the above events have in common, of course, is that they contain some kind of commercial relationship: as Greenberg says, 'no culture can develop without a social base, without a source of income' (1986: 10). This chapter is concerned with the many and various relationships which the producers of visual culture enter into with social institutions; it is about how artists and designers relate to markets, publics and audiences.

The relationships that artists and designers may enter into with their publics will be divided into three different kinds. The first kind of relationship will be explained as a form of patronage and the chapter will consider church, court, private, public and state patronage systems. The second will be described as the market, including all the ways in which art and design may be bought and sold with or without the aid of some form of intermediary. The third kind of relationship will be explained as sponsorship and the chapter will cover such manifestations of sponsorship as eighteenth-century subscriptions and twentieth-century corporate sponsorship, for example.

Patronage

The word 'patronage' denotes many different types of relationship that may exist between the producers and the consumers of visual culture. Some versions of patronage involved the patron protecting and supporting an artist or designer. Such a version may imply a close personal relation between patron and artist or designer. It may also imply that the patron is concerned for the well-being and domestic contentment of the artist or designer. And in such cases, it could be the case that the patron is less concerned with getting a specific, or specified, piece of work than in contributing to the development of the artist's or designer's work. However, it is not unlikely that this is an idealised version of the relationship that is patronage and that the patron is more often than not motivated by the desire to show off his or (less often) her power, social standing or religious beliefs. In this version of patronage, the patron would be less keen on the personal comfort, or otherwise, of the artist or designer and more interested in getting the work that they wanted.

And it should not be thought that patronage determines that the artist or designer is any less free to create according to his or her own desires or wishes. Patronage is not necessarily a constraint on the artist's or designer's creativity. Indeed, it may be that the public, or the patron, is a stimulus. Or it may be that the idea of the artist's or designer's free creativity is simply inappropriate, a product of a romantic and misguided conception of the production of visual culture. However, as Williams points out, one thing that all these patronal relationships have in common is the privileged situation of the patron (1981: 43). The patron is always the one who can, and can afford to, give or withhold their support.

The following categories should not be understood as discrete forms of patronage. It is often the case that any one example of visual culture is the result of more than one form of patronage and attention should be paid to the specificity of items of visual culture in the explanation of their appearance. Joshua Reynolds's work in the eighteenth century provides a suitably cautionary example. Reynolds, of course, was a member of the Royal Academy; he was in fact its first president. He was also in favour of history painting and thought that there should be a national school of history painting. In the eighteenth century, the art market was relatively undeveloped as far as paintings were concerned. There was, however, a wider and more established market for prints. John Boydell, an individual patron of the arts, was also interested in history painting and in 1786 he proposed that the most prominent artists of the time, Reynolds included, should paint a series of subjects from the plays of Shakespeare. Reynolds was commissioned by Boydell to paint the scene from *Macbeth* where Macbeth meets the three witches. Boydell was then to establish the Shakespeare gallery, in which prints, taken from the painted originals, would be sold. The paintings were to act, in effect, as advertisements for the prints.

The person who was to produce the engravings from which the prints would be made was a man named Thew; Thew's job was to translate the colours of the paintings into tones in a print. Consider the various roles and practices in this brief tale. Reynolds is a Royal Academician, patronised by royalty. He is commissioned by a wealthy private individual to produce a painting; he is to produce a painting to someone else's specification. That painting is to be used as an advertisement for a series of popular prints. Boydell has the idea for the theme of the paintings, he has identified the market and he knows what form the product will take. Thew, the engraver, is commissioned by Boydell to produce the engraving. There is some confusion as to Thew's place: some of the things he is to do are rather creative (turning Reynolds' colours into tones, interpreting the work), and others are more like those of a modern graphic designer (doing what he is told in exchange for money). Boydell is also the intermediary between the artist, whoever that turns out to be, and the public. And, finally, the whole sorry affair, which ended in bankruptcy for the promoters, is satirised in another print by Gilray, another engraver. The point of the tale is that the roles of artist, designer, patron, public and entrepreneur are not always straightforward or even readily identifiable in every case. Each case, then, should be treated in its specificity.

Church

Church patronage was probably the dominant form that patronage took in Europe between the tenth century, when the Cluniac monastic order was founded in France, and the fifteenth or sixteenth century, when the players in the economic game called capitalism began to take over as the main economic forces. The visual culture that survives from this time is largely the result of the Christian church's patronage of artists and designers. This visual culture takes the form of architecture, paintings, sculptures and stained-glass windows, for example, as well as the gold and silverware and the vestments worn by the clergy. Adrian Forty uses the work of the Cluniac and Cistercian orders (founded in *c.*910 and 1098 respectively) to introduce the work of twentieth-century corporate design consultants like Wolf Olins. Forty says that the Cluniac order's use of what became known as the Romanesque style of architecture and the Cistercian order's use of what became the Gothic style functioned in the same way as the corporate identity of modern companies. The visual appearance of their churches and monasteries could be used to differentiate the various orders, both from each other and from secular buildings; it also helped the members of the orders develop and recognise a sense of allegiance to the order (Forty 1986: 222–3). Where the Romanesque buildings at Cluny had massive walls, bare rounded arches and simple blunt mouldings, the Gothic church at St Denis, for example, had huge pointed windows, thin walls and ribbed vaults. Part of the explanation of why the architecture of this period looks as it does, then, is to be found in the patronage of the church; it looks the way it does because it has to create and communicate a sense of identity. It has to communicate the beliefs and values of the different strands of Christian belief.

Mentioning the abbey church of St Denis introduces perhaps the best-known example of medieval church patronage in Europe. Abbot Suger (1081–1151) is perhaps the best-known example because he wrote his own account of his patronage. The objects, architecture and imagery that Suger commissioned were recorded in some detail. The Christian church at the time was extremely wealthy and Suger brought designers, craftsmen and artists from all over France to decorate his abbey. He commissioned painters, goldsmiths, carpenters and stonemasons to build and decorate the abbey, believing that the images, paintings, sculptures, windows, furnishings and so on would aid the mortal soul to contemplate the eternal and heavenly truths of Christianity. The church is still relatively wealthy and continues to commission works of visual culture. In the twentieth century, Coventry cathedral commissioned work from Elizabeth Frink and Jacob Epstein and the Roman Catholic cathedral in Liverpool was built, for example.

Court

The Reformation and the Counter-Reformation of the sixteenth century had the effect of questioning not only the workings and devotional practices of the Roman Catholic church but also many of the preconceptions and traditions of European culture in general. At this time, mercantile capitalism was also expanding and becoming more powerful. New social classes were being formed, new towns and cities were appearing and growing. Secular, capitalist energies, united and fuelled by Protestant faith, according to Max Weber, were also questioning the validity and strength of many European assumptions and customs. Art and design, architecture, painting, sculpture and so on, could not escape the effects of these forces. While the countries which remained under the sway of the Roman Catholic church saw an increase in church patronage, those that became Protestant saw an increase in court and private patronage. Martin Warnke charts the origins of the court artist in more detail in his (1993) book, *The Court Artist*.

One of the earliest artists to benefit from such patronage was Hans Holbein (1497–1543). Holbein was introduced to Sir Thomas More, Henry VIII's Privy Councillor, by Erasmus and retained by the court of King Henry VIII, who broke with Rome in 1532. Being retained by the court meant that he received a place to live as part of the royal household. He was paid to produce portraits of the members of the royal household, as well as a number of other things. He was, in fact, expected to design the furniture for the king, and to take care of the interior design or decoration of the royal palaces. He was responsible for designing jewellery and costumes for pageants. And he designed weapons and the court cutlery and beakers. As well as being employed as an artist, then, Holbein was employed as a fashion designer and a furniture designer as well as an interior designer. It is worth speculating that it is only because he is famous as an artist that Holbein is even known of as a designer of furniture or jewellery. It is not the case that furniture designers from the sixteenth century are known in the same ways as the artists from the same period. This may be to do with the relative status of these designers: the lower-status designers were not studied, or deemed worthy of study, and their activities were not recorded and documented as were those of the higher-status artists. In the seventeenth and eighteenth centuries, however, names like Hepplewhite and Chippendale begin to become known as furniture-makers and upholsterers, as the prestige of such crafts and trades increases.

Founded under royal patronage and originally sponsored by George III, the Royal Academy of Arts is a slightly more modern example of the royal patronage of art. The Royal Academy was founded in 1768 at least partly in belated response to the opening in Paris of the Académie Royale de Peinture et de Sculpture (1648) and the Académie de France in Rome (1666). The idea was to provide training or teaching for the nation's artists as well as to generate a market for these artists. As well as providing a market for these artists, income from the exhibition was intended also to support the teaching of the students. Professors were appointed in geometry, perspective, painting, architecture, anatomy and design. And in the late twentieth century, the English royal family continues to support the production of visual culture. Numerous official photographic and painted portraits of the various members of the family are commissioned. The best-known of these include Cecil Beaton's 1952 Coronation photographs, Annigoni's 1955 and 1970 portraits of Queen Elizabeth II and Lord Snowdon's photographs of the then Princess Diana and her children. In addition to his involvement in Poundbury, Prince Charles is well-known for his views on modern architecture. Portraits of him, and of his mother, have also attracted much criticism. Judith Williamson explains the role of photography in the creation of the royal family's image in her essay 'Royalty and representation' (1985).

Private

Some of the complications of private patronage have been pointed out above, in relation to Reynolds and Boydell, where private patronage shaded into something more like sponsorship, discussed below and where roles generally became rather confused. Other examples are more straightforward. The private patron or collector of art in the more modern sense is generally thought to have emerged in around the early seventeenth century, although there have been, since the Renaissance, many private patrons of visual culture.

The Renaissance saw the emergence of individual patronage alongside that of the church. The Medici family of Florence is probably the best-known instance of such patronage, although Giovanni Ruccelai, a Florentine merchant, could also boast that he had in his house many sculptures and paintings, by artists such as Domenico Veneziano, Fra Filippo Lippi, Paolo Uccello, and Anrea del Verocchio (see Baxandall 1972: 2). Cosimo de Medici is generally credited with beginning a new tradition of patronage, competing with the trade guilds in the production and consumption of art and design. Although Cosimo is thought to be the very model of the free, independent patron, he is also known to have contributed to a common fund within the communal structure of republican Florence. However, he did put more money into this common fund than other patrons and he did 'suggest' which artists and architects might be used to complete the projects. While not wishing to draw too strong a line between the individual patron and the production of particular styles of painting, for example, it has been suggested (Haskell 1972: 124) that the

republican, bourgeois Florence of Cosimo de Medici was more likely
to encourage the classicising work of Masaccio and that the more
aristocratic, courtly character of his grandson Lorenzo was more
likely to encourage the more international and gothic work of someone like Botticelli.

Masaccio's painting *The Holy Trinity, the Virgin, St. John and
Donors* in Sta Maria Novella, Florence, shows the people who paid
for the work in the work. The donor, dressed in the scarlet robes of
the *gonfaloniere*, the highest civic office in Florence, and his wife
kneel in the foreground of this astonishing painting. Behind and
slightly above them are the Virgin and St John; the Virgin is gesturing
towards the crucified Jesus, who is in turn above and behind her and
St John, and to God the Father and the Holy Spirit. The use of
perspective in this painting is worked out so cleverly that the donors
are physically larger than the other figures, yet because of the way
that the perspective works one recognises that the other figures are
actually more important than the donors. The work looks the way it
does as a result of private patronage.

The control exercised by individuals over the production of items
of visual culture at this time could, of course, be extreme. Baxandall
actually reproduces the contract that was drawn up in 1485 between
the artist Domenico Ghirlandaio and the Prior of the Spedale degli
Innocenti in Florence for the *Adoration of the Magi*, completed in
1488. In this contract the prior specifies that he wants powdered gold
to be used 'on such ornaments as demand it', that the ultramarine
used 'is to be 'four florins the ounce' and that the final work will
follow the drawing, or plan, that all parties have agreed on (Baxandall
1972: 6). The prior insists in the contract that the colours generally are
to be of good quality, but he specifies the exact quality of ultramarine
that is to be used as the more expensive grades gave a better, stronger
and longer-lasting colour than the cheaper grades.

It was not only in southern Europe that individual wealthy patrons
supported the production of visual culture. In addition to working for
the court of King Henry VIII of England, Holbein also worked for
wealthy bourgeois families. He painted *The Virgin with the Family of
Burgomaster Meyer* in 1528, for example. This painting is not
dissimilar to Masaccio's *The Holy Trinity, The Virgin, St John and
Donors* painted around one hundred years earlier. In Holbein's
painting, the Virgin is central, holding the infant Jesus, while Herr
Meyer and his family are on either side of her, with their own infant,
praying or otherwise honouring the Virgin. Again, the appearance of

the painting, the way it looks, what it contains, is a direct consequence of the patron's desires.

The development in the seventeenth century of what became known as 'genre' pictures can be said to be the direct result of individual, private patronage. It could be claimed that such paintings would not exist at all were it not for the patronage of the Dutch middle classes. The Dutch middle classes at this time were mainly businessmen, merchants with little time for revelry or the disinterested philosophical enjoyment of classical tales or idealised landscapes. Consequently, they were not much interested in purchasing landscapes and history paintings. They were more interested in indoor scenes and everyday domestic life than in outdoor scenes, and the relatively small paintings of artists like Judith Leyster (1609–60) and Pieter de Hooch (1629–later than 1688) fitted perfectly into the homes of these people. The scenes depicted were also to these middle-class merchants' tastes, showing women peeling apples, sorting out the linen cupboard and sewing, for example. They often had an explicitly moral content, showing virtuous women resisting the amorous advances of men with beards, which the middle classes could enjoy. Jan Vermeer (1632–75) is also well-known for painting genre scenes, studies of young women playing the virginals, posing for artists, cooking and baking bread, for example. He is not a straightforward member of this group in that he painted very few such paintings; he was thus not in the same economic relation to his patrons as the others. Vermeer supplemented his income by running a pub and by dealing in art and consequently was not obliged to do exactly what his market demanded to the extent that the others mentioned were.

Even today, one or two of these forms of patronage have survived. It is not unknown, for example, for wealthy private individuals to commission portraits, either of themselves or of their families, from practising artists. It may be, however, that such portraiture more often takes what might be called a corporate form, where company chairmen and where appropriate chairwomen, founders of companies and so on commission portraits for the boardroom.

Public

This chapter will differentiate public patronage from state patronage by saying that public patronage is a more small-scale, local form of patronage; state patronage tends to be larger-scale and is more likely to be on a national scale. It is not an entirely satisfactory distinction, but a rough guide might be that public patronage is paid for by local authorities and bodies, while state patronage is paid for by national authorities and bodies. Public patronage of visual culture may take many forms. And it may be of larger or smaller scale. It could take the form of one-off, single contracts for projects such as designing civic regalia, the clothing and jewellery worn by civic dignitaries, street furniture or the layout of the local park. Or it could take the form of long-term projects, charting the appearance of the locality over a long period, or researching the pictorial history of the area. However, something that both public and state patronage, as they are defined here, have in common is that it is difficult or inappropriate to describe such bodies as doing exactly what the wider society wants. As Williams points out, the fact that public or state patronage involves bodies that are made up of more than one person, giving or withholding their support, makes the definition of public bodies as patrons either difficult or impossible (1981: 44). It is difficult or impossible to see public or state bodies as doing the 'general will of the society' (ibid.) and the definition of such bodies as patrons is therefore not completely straightforward.

Despite this, artists and designers may still be identified as producing visual culture that is supported by public patronage. Sixteenth-century Venice, for example, had managed to resist the political and economic domination of countries such as France and Spain and of the Roman Catholic church. It was a very affluent city, benefiting from trade with Asia, as well as the rest of Europe. It also retained a republican structure of government and public patronage was able to expand. Indeed, Venice at this time supported a post entitled 'Painter to the Republic'. Both Tintoretto and Veronese were patronised by the city to produce paintings at this time. Earlier, in 1334, Giotto had been appointed chief architect to his native city of Florence; he was expected to live in the city and to provide buildings which would enhance and beautify the city.

Cities, town councils and borough councils in Great Britain today still support the production of visual culture. In the English Midlands, for example, cities like Derby and Nottingham commission public sculptures and art works. Some towns have revived or created the idea and practice of town artists. While not on the same scale as sixteenth-century Venice, public money is put towards making the cities more attractive places to live and work in. Illustrating Williams's point about whether and to what extent such public bodies can truly represent the will of the general or wider society (1981: 44), both cities regularly upset their citizens with such public works. In Derby, for example, a sculpture of a ram, the symbol of the city, attracted much abuse, both verbal, written and graffiti-based. Another sculpture, in the central square, which involved a waterfall, was also not universally popular with the citizens. Nottingham had its own problems with water-related sculptures, as, like Derby's, it overflowed into the public's path. Both cases show that Williams's point is accurate; it is often impossible or inappropriate to say that such works are the result of public patronage because the public often does not like or does not understand the works commissioned in its name.

However, other forms of potentially public patronage might include community artists, or artists-in-residence in universities, towns and cities. In 1997, the land artist Andy Goldsworthy was commissioned to produce works in the Derbyshire Peak District. Basing his work on the characteristic dry-stone walls of the area, Goldsworthy caused consternation among the local sheep farmers as old sheep pens on remote and desolate hills were transformed into abstract art. On a more prosaic, although possibly also a more visible and genuinely public level, local councils and other authorities are obliged to furnish their streets. Streets must be lit, rubbish must be binned, shoppers and teenagers must have somewhere to sit and hang out. Maybe there must be somewhere for people to tie their dogs and bicycles while they enter shops. All of these things must be designed and built and artists and designers can benefit from public patronage by designing and building them. The artist Tess Jarray, for example, has been commissioned by the city of Birmingham to produce street furniture for Centenary Square. Parts of these regions and their towns, therefore, look the way they do as a result of these forms of patronage.

State

The various institutions that have made up the various national and civil governments throughout history have had many and various relationships with visual culture. Post-revolutionary Russia, for example, recognised that art and design could be used to further socialist revolution and prescribed socialist realism as the only appropriate revolutionary art. Louisa Buck and Philip Dodd describe the way in which the Spanish government has used art to raise the international cultural profile of Spain since the Second World War, persuading collectors to lend works and supporting a museum-building programme (1991: 112). Another way in which the state relates to or encourages the production of visual culture is in the area of education. Art and design education in Europe and America has always generated much debate: the content and direction of the artist's and designer's education have always been hotly contested. It is through education that the state most obviously determines who is trained as an artist or a designer – who becomes an artist or designer and how they become an artist or designer. As Pearson points out, the visual arts cannot be understood without a 'consideration of the role and function of the state' (1982: 1). The state's role in the selection and support of artists and designers must be studied and this chapter will outline some of the ways in which the state has fulfilled these functions throughout history.

Although granted the 'Royal' title by Queen Victoria in 1896, the Royal College of Art is more accurately described as an example of the state patronage of visual culture. The Royal College of Art was established in 1837, occupying Somerset House in London. Following the recommendations of the 1835 Select Committee, it was intended by the government of the day to improve the standards of British design and to train teachers of design. The content of British design education has always been debated; what is to go into the education of designers will, clearly, have an enormous effect on the kinds of things that they produce and on the ways that those things look. In 1950, the rector of the Royal College was Robin Darwin. He realised that the college had become moribund and old-fashioned and he reorganised the college into six schools. These schools were based on the different materials which could be used to manufacture goods, the development of new materials having been one of the causes of the college's becoming out of date. Concentrating on materials in this way repeats elements of the *Vorkurs*, or preliminary course, of the Bauhaus, taught by Josef Albers in the late 1920s. As Penny Sparke points out, these developments had the effect of encouraging industrial designers such as Robert Welch, Robert Heritage and David Mellor. She also argues that design education in Britain is too idealistic and fails to address social and economic changes taking place in society (Sparke 1986: 171–2). It might be added that there is much resistance from many design departments to the idea that design takes place in social and economic realities which must be analysed and explained. The design that is produced from within colleges and schools is clearly influenced by the different emphases found in those colleges and schools.

The Bauhaus of Weimar Germany, the Hochschule für Gestaltung at Ulm in post-Second World War Germany and to a lesser extent the Cranbrook Academy of Art in Michigan are all examples of the ways in which the state can encourage the production of visual culture. They also demonstrate how different states conceive of the nature and identity of visual culture, as well as the nature and identity of those best-suited to learn about it and produce it. The Bauhaus, for example, is well-known for its syllabus and its philosophy, and for the debates and changes that took place regarding that syllabus and philosophy. In addition to the early emphasis on mass production and geometric form, Gropius's famous pronouncement to the effect that we are all craftsmen, 'there is no essential difference between the artist and the craftsman', proposes very definitely the sort of people the producers of visual culture will eventually be (Gropius quoted in Naylor 1968: 50). The Bauhaus may also be seen as an example of art and design education resisting the energies of the state; much of the time it was concerned to oppose the policies of Nazi Germany, only giving up the struggle and moving to America before the Second World War. The Hochschule continued the concern with mass production, but saw the social, cultural and philosophical context of visual culture as extremely important. And the Cranbrook Academy, founded by the Finn Eliel Saarinen, took the view that design should be an artistic activity, enriching the rather commercial atmosphere of American design in the 1920s and 1930s. The kind of art and design produced in these different countries, as well as the way it looks, can be related back to, and partly explained in terms of, the input of the state in these cases.

Another way in which the state supports the production of visual culture is through organisations like the Arts Council of England, the Crafts Council, the Design Council and the Regional Arts Associations. The Arts Council of Great Britain was founded in 1946 with the aims of 'developing a greater knowledge, understanding and practice of the fine arts exclusively . . . increas[ing] the accessibility of the fine arts'. It was also intended to 'improve the standard of execution of the fine arts' and to advise and cooperate with the government on all the above matters (Arts Council Charter, quoted in Pearson 1982: 53). Quite whose standards were to be applied in order to measure any 'improvements' in the 'standards' of fine art is not made clear and the phrase was edited out of subsequent charters. The idea of state standards of fine art may appear ludicrous to many, with some justification. There were various problems involved in translating a national arts policy into many regional arts policies and in the late 1960s Regional Arts Associations (now called Regional Arts Boards) were formed to support local arts activities. The Crafts Council developed in 1971 out of the Crafts Advisory Committee. Initially, it supported the work of the individual 'artist–craftsperson', but was encouraged to adopt a wider definition of craft. Indeed, in 1982, the Council's exhibition 'The Maker's Eye' included motorcycles and letter boxes as examples of craft objects, considerably widening the accepted definition of craft. The Design Council, formed in 1944 as the Council of Industrial Design, had similar aims to the Arts Council. It was to encourage industry to make use of designers, to improve standards of British design and public taste, and to raise the profile of design in British industry.

In America in the 1930s private patrons were becoming scarce, as a result of the Great Depression. State patronage, in the form of the Public Works of Art Project, was an alternative. Set up in December 1933, as part of Roosevelt's New Deal, the Public Works of Art Project commissioned artists and designers to produce works of art for public buildings and institutions. The Federal Arts Project of the same period is another example of central government supporting the production of visual culture. In total, it is reckoned that nearly four thousand artists and designers produced 15 633 pieces of visual culture during this period. The Federal Arts Project was a nationwide system of art subsidy and it was administered by regional committees and art competitions. Originally conceived as a relief programme for the relief of the poor in the 1930s, the project eventually provided support and acknowledgment for avant-garde artists such as Willem De Kooning. While the Public Works of Art Project only lasted for six months, the Federal Arts Project ran until the time that the United States entered the Second World War. In one year, it employed over 5500 producers of visual culture: these were artists, photographers, designers, teachers and researchers, as well as craftsmen, and they earned $95 per month for 95 hours' work (see Harris 1995 for more on this subject). The project was unusual in that it supported easel paintings and graphics in addition to large-scale public sculpture and murals. The easel painters were expected to prove to the state authorities that they were actually working in their studios. In modern America, state authorities like the National Endowment for the Arts administer the state support of art, incurring the wrath of right-wing commentators when work that is considered obscene, blasphemous or otherwise contentious is given public money.

The market

Reference has already been made to the development of capitalism in Europe. Beginning around the fourteenth century and, as Marx says (1959: 332), growing at a tremendous rate in the mercantile revolutions of the sixteenth and seventeenth centuries, capitalism transformed the production and consumption of visual culture. It was not that patronage ended as capitalism began: patronage and the market may be seen coexisting today. There are, however, a number of differences which can be clearly distinguished. Within capitalist market economies, the work of art must be conceived as a commodity, as something that may be bought and sold, like any other commodity. The artist, consequently, must be seen as the producer of that commodity, like any other producer of commodities. This is different to many aspects of patronal systems, where the patron might take responsibility for the artist's well-being, taking him or her into their home, for example. Within patronal systems, the painting, sculpture, or whatever, is often not exchanged for money, it is not a commodity in this sense. Within the market, there are also a number of different ways in which the artist or designer may relate to their public, which is also known as a market. This section will look briefly at four such different relations: artisanal, post-artisanal, market professional and corporate professional.

The artisanal relation between producer and market is the simplest. Here the independent producer of visual culture offers his or her work for sale and is in total control of all aspects and all stages of the production and selling of that work. This is probably the most common form of relation in much of what is called 'craft work'. Self-employed woodworkers, ceramists, upholsterers and photographers, for example, would be included here. Indeed, Bernard Leach, the ceramist who was mentioned in the introduction to Chapter 3, represents an example of this kind of relation. He worked alone, in isolation, trying to produce work in this simple, self-sufficient way. Cheryl Buckley suggests that another ceramist, Susie Cooper, was this kind of producer in the 1930s. Cooper 'took the marketing and retailing of her products very seriously' she says, and the Susie Cooper

Pottery 'was a small- to medium-scale unit whose production was closely tied to the design skills of its owner' (Buckley 1989: 81). The relation of people like Leach and Cooper to their market is the most direct and they must either know that market well or be very adaptable in order to survive. The artisan's artistic freedom to produce whatever they like is also the artistic freedom to go hungry, after all. The relation between the producer and the consumer is direct in the sense that there is no intermediary between the two: the consumer goes directly to the producer. And the point about knowing the market or being adaptable is that, because the relation is so direct, the alternative to knowing exactly what the market wants is to be flexible and adapt to the specific and immediate demands of that market.

Only slightly more complex are post-artisanal relations between the artist or designer and their public. Here the independent artist or designer offers their work to an intermediary and, while they may more or less have control over the production of the work, they will have much less control over its subsequent marketing and consumption. The intermediary may be either distributive or productive and manufacturing. An example of a distributive intermediary would be an art dealer or an art gallery: an artist would receive a sum of money from the dealer or gallery in exchange for a painting or sculpture. In this case, the dealer or gallery intervenes between the artist or designer and the market. These dealers and galleries may, obviously, be large-scale, prestigious operations, such as those in Dover Street and Cork Street in London which sell works by well-known contemporary artists. Susie Cooper also provides an example of this kind of relation. She took space in Harry Wood's Crown Works factory in which she could display and sell her ceramic works (Buckley 1989: 81). These dealers and galleries may also be smaller, provincial affairs selling watercolour landscapes, for example. In these cases, it is the intermediary's relation with the market that is direct and that intermediary must know the market in order to make a profit. An example of a productive or manufacturing intermediary might be a film or television company: a set designer would receive a sum of money in exchange for a film or television set which the film or television company would then use in the production of a film. The freelance photographer who sells his or her investigative photographs of corrupt goalkeepers or titillating photographs of gullible royals to a newspaper would be an example of this kind of cultural producer. Another example would be a manufacturer of shavers, hair-dryers or some other consumer good: the designer would receive a sum of money in exchange for the design of such goods which the manufacturer would then produce. Again, it is the company or the manufacturer that relates directly to the market and which must know what the market wants in order to make any money.

The market professional is a more complex version of the post-artisanal worker. Like the post-artisanal worker, the market professional also sells his or her work to an intermediary but does not sell the work outright to them. Rather than sell direct, the artist or designer retains some form of title to the work in the form of copyright and rather than receive a one-off payment, the artist or designer receives royalties. A film or television company, for example, would use a script for a film or programme; the writer would receive acknowledgement of having written the script and may receive residual payments every time it is shown. Graphic designers might be examples of this kind of worker. A graphic designer might produce a design for a birthday card for the Hallmark company, or, until they ceased trading, a poster design for Athena; a contract between the designer and Hallmark or Athena would specify the form the publication would take and the period it was to be produced for and the designer would receive a royalty payment for each copy sold. This is not an especially new form of production. It was Hogarth, exasperated by unauthorised copies of his prints being made, who did much to secure a system of copyright in the eighteenth century. The 1735 Engraver's Act finally protected the designer against losing income from the pirating of his or her designs by outlawing the copying of engravings for fourteen years after they had first been produced.

In all the examples of the relations between the producer of visual culture and the market considered so far, it has been possible to see that the producer is what has been called the creative function. It has been the producer who comes up with the idea, the painting, the sculpture or the design, which the market is free to buy or not. In the case of the corporate professional, this is not the case. Large corporations are part of the latest phase of capitalism and much visual culture is now produced from within them. The corporate professional relation, then, exists between the artists and designers who work for these corporations and their market. In this case, the idea as to what is to be produced is generated from within the company, rather than by the artist or designer, as in the examples above. The artist or designer employed by the company is there to design what other elements within the company have decided should be produced. Here somebody else decides what should be produced, what the market wants, and the artist or designer is employed and salaried to carry those decisions out. The professional photographer, who is employed full-time by a newspaper or magazine, for example, will be sent to events and episodes which someone else has decided are newsworthy or interesting. Graphic designers, working for advertising agencies, will be told what products they will be promoting and what ideas the account managers and artistic directors have come up with. Dennis P. Doordan describes the origins and development of the CBS 'eye' in the early 1950s; this is another good example of corporate design and of how graphic design contributes to corporate culture (Doordan 1995b). Product designers, working for Sony, Kenwood or Braun, will be told that a new CD player, food mixer or hairdryer needs restyling. Furniture designers will be employed by Habitat, Ikea and Parker-Knoll to design sofas, dining tables and chairs according to the accountant's budget. Harry Bertoia designed the 'chicken wire' chair, for example, following a brief set for him by Hans and Florence Knoll in 1952. The buyers and colour specialists will dictate to textile and fashion designers at Wallis, Courtaulds and Brooks Brothers what colours, shapes and styles they will include in their spring collections. In all these cases, the artists and designers are told what to do as part of a larger corporation: the decisions are not theirs to make. A slightly different form of this kind of relationship is represented by the Shell company's support of many major artists and designers in the 1920s and 1930s. Artists and designers such as Edward McKnight Kauffer, Graham Sutherland, Vanessa Bell and Ben Nicholson all produced advertisements for the company and all appeared to have quite a lot of freedom to do whatever they liked, in their own style and with their own lettering, for example. Shell at this time employed a huge number of different styles and letterforms, dissipating what little corporate identity the company had.

All of the above artists and designers work to the perceived demands of the market, designing and making garish, overstuffed sofas for the working classes and lower-middle classes, designing party frocks for secretaries, prissy curtain materials for the lower-middle classes and so on. They are led by commerce: commercial and economic factors determine what gets made, in what shapes and colours. In this sense, the modern market is just as clear about what it wants as the Prior of Florence was in the fifteenth century. At least, another set of so-called 'experts' profess to be and give every appearance of being as clear about what 'the market' wants as the prior was.

So, while the market professional and the corporate professional are integrated into the capitalist market economy which dominates social relations within society, some cultural producers manage to resist incorporation into the market. First, in each of these areas there are a few designers who are allowed to exist somewhat outside the corporate, commercial realm and to produce more authentic and creative examples of visual culture. There are also a few occasions where such authenticity and creativity are allowed free rein. Someone like Vivienne Westwood, for example, is allowed to be creative and wacky; sometimes the dictates of the market are ignored. At these times, nobody says to her that because they do not see the customers of Bloomingdales wearing her frocks, she may not make them. The fashion shows of London, New York, Paris and Milan, for example, are occasions where designers are allowed to produce clothing that is often completely impractical, things that nobody could wear, ever, and things that will never appear in the high street shops. The motor shows of Birmingham and Geneva, for example, are similar sorts of occasions. What are called 'concept cars' without any apparent irony demonstrate absurd features which would enable convoys of cars to follow one another along motorways with only inches between them at seventy miles per hour, for example.

However, the idea is that these ridiculous frocks and these laughable cars draw attention to the manufacturer, or designer, as a form of advertising; the designers and manufacturers profit in the end when their everyday, comparatively reasonable, products are found in the high street shops and forecourts. What this means is that the relationship does not necessarily allow the designer the freedom it might appear. That freedom is eventually reined in and profited from by the company. Second, there is some freedom allowed in areas of visual culture that are not profitable in market terms. It is possible to see some of these less popular areas of visual culture as resisting the domination of the market, although it is also possible to make too much of this resistance. Some areas of visual culture, like theatre, opera and the arts and crafts, for example, that are not popular in the sense that they attract huge audiences are at least partly sustained by modern institutions of patronage. Foundations such as the Conran Foundation, trusts, organisations of subscribers and private patrons all help to promote examples of visual culture like opera, ballet and small theatre companies as well as painting and sculpture. This is sponsorship and the subject of the next section.

Sponsorship

Sponsorship may take many forms. It is the case, however, that they may be divided into two main types: private and corporate. Both can only exist where there is a market, a developed capitalist economy, as without this specific economic organisation neither the private wealthy sponsors nor the corporate sponsors exist.

The drinks company Allied Domecq were major sponsors of the RSC's September 1996 production of *A Midsummer Night's Dream*, for example. In 1997, BP sponsored the Portrait Award in conjunction with the National Portrait Gallery and the Booker company, along with British Airways, supported the same gallery's show on Ignatius Sancho, 'An African Man of Letters'. In the theatre, Barclays Bank sponsored the English Touring Theatre's version of *Henry IV*. The Montage Gallery in Derby, which puts on shows of what can only be called serious art photography, is sponsored by Boots the Chemist and the Canon Colour Copy Centre among others. Montage's sponsors are eminently appropriate, Boots being the place where everyone takes their holiday photographs and Canon being everyone's office photocopier, and one may speculate humorously on the association of Allied Domecq with the magical liquids used in *A Midsummer Night's Dream*, but these are large companies supporting what are some of the less popular and maybe more elite areas of visual culture. Sponsorship may, of course, become politically sensitive. In 1980, for example, the German artist Hans Haacke objected to Mobil's support for the 'Treasures of ancient Nigeria' exhibition in New York because of the way in which subsidiary companies of Mobil were supplying arms to the police and military forces in South Africa (Nairn 1990: 177ff.). Haacke also criticised United Technologies' part in sponsoring the Tate Gallery's 1986 Oskar Kokoschka show on the grounds that United Technologies produce parts for Cruise missiles (ibid.).

Another form of sponsorship mentioned above was the organisation of subscribers and private patrons. In the early 1990s, Opera North was supported by a foundation such as this. The 'Friends of Opera North' was formed to promote the activities of Opera North and in return for an annual subscription, members were able to attend social events organised by the company, as well as enjoy private bar and buffet facilities. It must be pointed out that many of these productions also received support from bodies like the Arts Council of England or the Crafts Council. As noted above, these bodies receive some or all of their money from public revenue but are not actually government departments. The English National Opera production and the English Touring Theatre production, noted above, for example, were also sponsored by the Arts Council of England. And the Opera North productions were often supported by the (then) Arts Council of Great Britain and Yorkshire Arts, one of the regional arts bodies largely funded by the Arts Council. And it must be pointed out that an organisation like the British Broadcasting Corporation, which produces television and film programmes, receives part of its income from the government, via the licence fee, but directs its own productions.

It is not immediately clear whether the example of Harvey Nichols's 'Art Supermarket', found in its Knightsbridge store, belongs in this category or not. At one level, they might be seen as sponsoring art in that they are providing, not disinterestedly, space for artists to sell their work. Other high street stores are using art, or allowing art be be shown in and alongside their window displays. Habitat on the King's Road and in Tottenham Court Road have let young artists like Gary Turk, Tracy Emin and Gary Hume show their work for a long time. Selfridges, in Oxford Street, shows art works in its window displays and the Original Levis Store shows artistic videos and has a gallery. Other developments in sponsorship include the way in which major companies appear to be starting to imagine themselves in the role of the Medicis, noted above. Sponsorship is becoming the responsibility of marketing executives and art is being put to work by these executives. As Richard Gott points out, 'these developments are not confined to the visual arts'; companies are also putting money into theatre and are commissioning plays and inventing prizes named after them (1997: 13). Gott quotes the development director of the Serpentine Gallery, who says that 'sponsorship has moved from being a simple act of philanthropic giving . . . Instead of giving money to arts organisations, people are beginning to think, "Why not do it ourselves?"' (ibid.). Whether sponsorship was ever a simple act of philanthropic giving may well be doubted, but the new form of sponsorship seems to be clear. The reason given for this new sponsorship is not dissimilar to the motivation that may be ascribed to earlier sponsors: it is to increase press coverage and give the sponsors 'hip status' (ibid.).

Companies like the Absolut vodka company sometimes appear to be playing the part played by the courts in earlier centuries, patronising a number or a series of artistic works. The main difference, of course, is that companies like Absolut are out to make money for themselves; the difference between art and advertising is becoming blurred by the efforts of some of these companies. Thus, while Beck's beer sponsors just about every show and gallery opening and, as Gott says, manages to be loved by everyone in the art world, Absolut vodka 'causes frissons of alarm' (ibid.). In the 1980s, Absolut had the idea of commissioning works of art which are subsequently used in its advertising. In this way, 'you might have an Absolut Warhol or an Absolut Keith Haring' and this is not approved of by everyone. Gott quotes a critic of what he calls 'post-sponsorship': 'they're the worst . . . they think they know about art' (ibid.). In yet another twist, Selfridges are to sponsor the Serpentine Gallery. Not only are they showing art works in the Miss Selfridge store, they are also giving money to a gallery. The relationships between sponsor, gallery, artist and audience get more and more complex.

Conclusion

These, then, are some of the major institutions that artists and designers come into contact with; they are the main ways in which artists and designers relate to their audiences or publics. One relation that has not been dealt with in any detail here is that of criticism. Art and design criticism are not really ways in which artists and designers relate to their audiences or publics, but they do affect those relationships. As Janet Wolff points out, the judgement and evaluation of visual culture are neither 'individual' nor 'purely aesthetic' phenomena, they are 'socially enabled and socially constructed events' (1992a: 40). They are 'socially enabled' in so far as only certain social groups, with certain kinds and levels of education, are in positions to produce art and design criticism; other groups, lacking such educations, are paid little or no attention. She cites John Ruskin's support of the Pre-Raphaelites and Turner in the nineteenth century and the ways in which that support was crucial in making the reputation of these artists. One might also look at Tim Clark's essay on the critical responses to Manet's *Olympia* in the late 1860s for a treatment of the socially enabled and located practice of art criticism (Clark 1980).

Having examined the social institutions which form the audiences or markets for visual culture, the various forms of patronage, sponsorship and the market, and having tried to show how these forms are part of the explanation of visual culture, the next chapter will study the various media that artist and designers use. All cultures must make themselves visible in some form or other and the next chapter will consider the different media used to do this. The media that are used to make visual culture visual will be analysed into different forms and explained in terms of access, control and ownership.

Chapter 5

Media, Access and Ownership

Introduction

This chapter concerns visual signs and media; it is about the ways in which cultures are made visible. The idea of a culture that does not manifest or represent itself physically in some way is meaningless. Every form of culture must use something to stand for or represent itself, first to itself and second to others. The way in which cultures represent themselves physically, in order that they may be perceived, is by means of visual and aural signs. Most cultures use both visual and aural signs or media to communicate their beliefs and values. What one hears, or does not hear, is just as meaningful as what one sees or does not see. In many cultures, for example, quiet, or even silence, is used to suggest solemnity or to indicate the presence of a God or gods; different kinds of music, singing and other vocalisations are prescribed for different occasions like weddings, football matches, parties and so on. The rules for the volumes at which one talks, for example, are strictly controlled in all cultures.

The many different ways in which a culture may make its values and beliefs visible can be divided into two basic sorts: human and material. The human resources are based on the body and the various ways in which it can be used to communicate visually. So, practices like cicatrisation (in which the scars left by intentionally wounding and scarring the skin are significant), tattooing (see Ill. 5.1) and piercing, for example, are considered as well as the gestures, expressions, actions and dance that are made by moving the body.

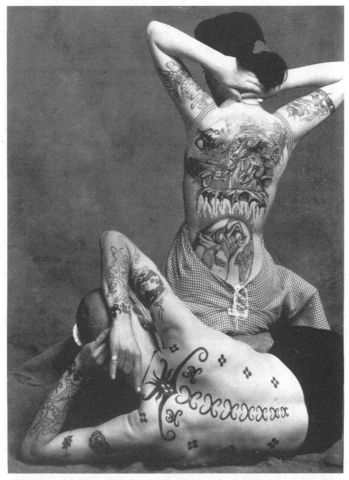

Ill. 5.1   Tattoo, photograph by Tim O'Sullivan, 1991

The material resources of visual culture include all those practices in which non-human objects and forces are used and transformed in order to communicate visually. Costume, clothing, writing, painting and drawing and so on are all ways in which material objects and materials are used to communicate visually. The material resources also include the many ways in which those objects and materials are reproduced or amplified and distributed.

Another way of categorising these media is according to whether the artefacts produced are predominantly hand-made, tool-made, machine-made or computer-generated. Handmade imagery is usually called drawing or painting, while handmade text is commonly known as writing. Both might be subsumed under the general term autography. Hand-made artefacts, similarly, might be called craft, or the ghastly but logical autotechnology. Many apparent examples of handmade texts and products in fact rely on the use of tools and it may be unwise to insist too firmly on this distinction. Machine-made images are often the result of photography and machine-made text should go by the name of typography. Machine-made artefacts are known as factory-produced or mass-produced and that is better than technotechnology. Digitally produced text has been word-processed, while digitally produced imagery and artefacts are often called virtual reality.

These different media, along with their different products, pose difficult questions concerning ownership, access and control, which this chapter must also address. As a medium of expression, the body might be thought of as exemplifying almost universal access and ownership. One is free to paint, pierce and pose one's body as one pleases and no special training is required to respond to such phenomena. Writing is slightly different, in that specialised training, or education, is required both to produce writing and to read and decipher it; it is a skill that until relatively recently was available only to a minority within western societies. Writing represents a completely different level of access from that of imagery; one may get some idea of what is going on in an image from a different culture where one may get no idea from writing from that culture (see Ill. 5.2). It was thus under the control of, even if it was not actually owned by, that minority. Media that are more obviously owned and controlled by a shrinking minority include the press and television. Three or four companies, including those recently headed by Ted Turner, Rupert Murdoch and Robert Maxwell, are increasingly in charge of more and more press and television production. Access to these media, therefore, is increasingly limited, as are the opportunities within them for alternative production and self-determination on the part of artists and designers.

Human resources

In one sense, the simplest and most basic media are the resources of the human body itself. Facial expressions, gestures and actions, as well as the surfaces and parts of the body itself, are the basic resources

Ill. 5.2   Hokusai (1760–1849), *Cuckoo and Azalea*, British Museum

of visual culture. With facial expression, gesture and action, mime, dance and the various forms of non-verbal communication may be produced. The surfaces and parts of the body, including the skin, hair, teeth and nails, for example, may be used to produce other forms of non-verbal communication. Clearly, different cultures will use different expressions to communicate different things, and different cultures will use the surfaces and parts of the body in different ways.

These differences are part of what constitute those cultures as cultures 'in the first place', as it were. Despite these differences, these resources are the most common, simple and basic forms of visual culture. Thus, while one may not know that according to Nigel Barley (1986: 58), in performing one of the commonest friendly gestures to be found in an English pub, one is summoning up one of the most potent curses to be found in central Africa, the moving of the body is common to all who have bodies and thus basic and popular. Similarly, in so far as one has teeth, hair and other body parts, and in so far as one can make gestures and facial expressions, these resources are also the most accessible. Gestures, expressions and hair are not only available to those with large disposable incomes or expensive educations. To this extent, then, the forms of visual culture which are based on these resources are the most popular, accessible and common.

Material resources

There are different sorts of material resource. This section will roughly follow Raymond Williams's classification of them (1981: 90). The first sort may be called combinations. Here the human resources discussed above are combined with non-human material, objects. This is a difficult way of describing the use of things like masks, costume and cosmetics, but the combination of human elements with non-human elements should be clear. The second refers to the production of independent and identifiable objects. Here, objects such as paintings and sculptures are produced using non-human materials such as pigments, oils, clay, wood and so on. Third, there are independent and identifiable systems of communication, such as writing, which use inks, made from pigments, and papers, made from cloth or wood, to produce signs. And, fourth, there are the various technical systems and methods by means of which all of the above material resources and products may be produced and reproduced.

There are also problems with the media concerning access and ownership. Indeed, it is in these areas that these questions are most sharply focused. The first two sorts of media (masks, costume and cosmetics, along with paintings and sculptures) are relatively accessible to everyone. In dance, drama and much visual art, even if they are very sophisticated or culturally alien forms of dance, drama or visual art, one can at least see what is going on and to that extent one has some access to them. The problem, famously raised by Marx, of how it is that one can respond meaningfully to art that is from distant places or from the distant past may have the beginning of its solution in the idea that there are perceptual resources, visual and aural, common to all humans. The fact that one can see patterns, shapes and textures (the fact that in so far as one can see these things one can respond to them) seems to ensure that one is guaranteed at least basic access to these forms of visual art. It may be, then, that being human is to be at least potentially able to respond to visual patterns, shapes, textures and rhythms.

The second two sorts of media (sign systems such as writing and the many ways of producing and reproducing those sign systems) are not so universally accessible. Writing, for example, is very different in terms of accessibility. Writing is a sign system which requires an enormously specialised training, for the people who are to read or interpret it as well as for those who will produce or write it. Even in the 1990s, literacy is far from universal. As Williams points out, 'while anyone in the world, with normal physical resources, can watch dance or look at sculpture . . . still some forty per cent of the world's present inhabitants can make no contact whatever with a piece of writing' (1981: 93). Writing still reproduces and strengthens social divisions in that it is still the possession of a minority of the world's population. Those who cannot read and write are hugely disadvantaged and have lower status as a result of not being able to read and write. The production and reproduction of texts also reproduces and strengthens social divisions. This is because those who can read are also those who can afford to own, and who are interested in owning, manuscripts and books.

While the only forms of books available were those copied out by scribes, up to around the fifteenth century, they were expensive and rare objects. They were therefore only available to the very wealthy and the powerful. They were only available, that is, to the dominant social classes. The development of more efficient methods of producing and reproducing books, movable type, steam presses and so on, represents a development of massive importance. If it is possible to produce visual material in large quantities and thus relatively cheaply by means of machines, then there is at least the potential for a larger audience for that visual material. Clearly, the political will to educate people into the skills and abilities of literacy has to be present, but the mass production of printed material has the potential to transform the divisions in any society.

In addition to being difficult to understand, Williams's schema is flawed. Any such schema will be flawed in that it is not possible to construct fixed categories that will unproblematically accommodate all the various forms of visual culture. However one casts one's categorical net, some cultural fishes will escape. For example, where might fashion go on Williams's account? From one point of view, clothing and fashions are three-dimensional objects, in the same way as paintings and sculptures are. From another, they relate to the body in much the same ways as masks or make-up and other cosmetics. And from a third, they might even be said to affect the gestures, poses and actions which it is possible to make and which were part of the human resources discussed above. It is not immediately clear from Williams's text where texts, images and three-dimensional objects that are not sculptures or paintings are to fit. In Chapter 1, visual culture was said to include street and house furniture, street signs, fashion, textiles, pottery and ceramics, hairdryers, shavers, cars, architecture, garden design, advertising, personal, public, corporate and popular images, film, television, computer environments and games, Internet home pages, newspaper and magazine design, typography, products and packaging of all kinds. If these things are to be included in the same category as the one in which Williams places paintings and sculptures, then that is fine. If not, then the following account will establish new categories. The following sections will deal with these examples of visual culture by looking at four categories. These four categories describe the ways in which objects may be made: hand-made, tool-made, machine-made and computer-generated. Questions concerning access and ownership will also be considered.

Hand-made

This category probably contains surprisingly little. Most things that are visual culture, even the things that might at first appear to be hand-made, often turn out to have been produced with the aid of a tool somewhere along the line. Thus, if basketware or ceramics are suggested as examples of handmade visual culture, it will always be possible to object that the willow had to be cut for the basketware and the clay had to be dug out of the ground for the ceramics. Another complication to this schema is represented by products such as Aston Martin cars. These cars are often referred to as being 'hand-built', but nobody is suggesting that no tools or engineering techniques are used to construct them. For this reason, it may be unwise to insist too strongly on a rigid distinction between handmade and tool-made artefacts. Handmade and tool-made may sometimes be almost the same thing but hand-built can often refer to heavily engineered artefacts. However, if such crafts as carpentry, basketware and pottery or ceramics are allowed as handmade, then it might also be allowed that they can in principle be produced and possessed by anyone.

Of course, the 'in principle' here hides many questions. To say that 'in principle' everyone could build their own Aston Martin car, or that everyone could produce their own ceramics, is to stretch the phrase almost to meaninglessness. Many people would feel, with complete justification, that they could no more make their own laundry baskets, dinner plates and flower vases than they could build their own V8 supercharged sports saloon. Ceramics, basketware, coach-building and engineering demand specialist skills and talents which are only 'in principle' open to everyone. It is not simply the case that hand-made or hand-built artefacts may be produced by anyone. Nor is it the case that such artefacts may be possessed by everyone. Many craft objects are extremely expensive to purchase, reflecting the enormous amounts of work and skill that go into their production. Some craft objects, like the ceramics of Bernard Leach or Lucy Rie, for example, are treated more like works of art than pieces of pottery. It remains true, however, that such artefacts are much more accessible to everyone in the sense that the work that went into them may be appreciated by almost everyone. To be told that the perfectly aligned, gleaming and polished wings of the Aston Martin were produced by a man hitting a piece of metal with a hammer will give rise to the same feelings of aesthetic astonishment as being told that the paper-thin, iridescent ceramic piece is produced by working a piece of clay and putting it in an oven.

Tool-made

Much more of what many people would agree is visual culture would be found in this category. Tool-made artefacts require special equipment and training to produce. Such artefacts may also be more likely to require special training and skills to understand or appreciate. They therefore are more likely to be exclusive and of high status.

Along with painting, sculpture, and possibly the practices noted above, writing is an example of such visual culture. Many of the considerations that had to be taken into account in the discussion of hand-made artefacts above have also to be taken into account when dealing with tool-made artefacts. Because they require specialised training to produce, they are not in fact available to everyone to produce as and when they wish. Because of this, they are often of great value. The illuminated manuscript books of the Middle Ages, for example, were nearly all produced in monastic *scriptoria*, where *scrittori*, well-educated monks who supervised the production of the manuscripts, would keep a watchful eye on the *copisti*, the monks whose task it was to copy out every letter and every word accurately. Such books were certainly not available for everyone to produce as they wished. These books were also extremely expensive to produce, with gold, silver, lapis lazuli and parchment or vellum all being used in their construction. The Lindisfarne Gospels (*c*. AD 698), the Book of Durrow (*c*. AD 680) and the Book of Kells (*c*. AD 800) are good examples of such illustrated manuscript books.

As well as being only available to the literate minority, these books were only available to the very wealthy. This is also true of other tool-made artefacts, like the Aston Martin car and the Bernard Leach ceramics. And it is true of more everyday items. Many upmarket kitchen, bathroom and bedroom furnishings and fittings are tool-made. These are typically the choice of the wealthier classes in society, who see mass-produced, machine-made goods as being of lower status than the hand-made artefacts.

Machine-made

It is with machine-made text, images and artefacts that the production and consumption of visual culture become for the first time large-scale, world-wide activities. Machine-made text, images and artefacts are mass-produced; they are made in enormous numbers, they are relatively cheap and they may be owned by many people. Thus, with the Industrial Revolution of the eighteenth and nineteenth centuries come mass-produced text, images and artefacts. For the first time, the masses, huge numbers of people, begin to have access to and, most importantly, choice in the possession of items of visual culture. It is the element of choice that gives rise to the possibility of different types of visual culture, and thus to the possibility of different social groups using those different types of visual culture to constitute and identify themselves as social groups. These will be the topics of Chapter 7. The effects of these developments cannot be underestimated. They have made the visual experience of modernity, as well as what many people call postmodernity, what it is. Were it not for these scientific, technological, artistic, commercial and domestic developments, the visual experience of everyday modern western people would be totally and unimaginably different. Consequently, the explanation of contemporary visual experience, and of visual culture, must take these developments into account. They form a large part of what makes the images, texts and artefacts of modern times, and many would say postmodern times as well, look the ways they do. The appearance of contemporary text, images and artefacts, then, is a result of the industrialisation of the techniques and aesthetics involved in the production and consumption of visual culture.

Mass production and reproduction of images, text and artefacts create the visual experience of modernity and of what many call postmodernity. The production and reproduction of text are transformed during the nineteenth century by the invention and refinement of Monotype machines, which cast individual characters, and Linotype machines, which cast whole lines of type. New typographic styles, involving either finer serifs or the complete absence of serifs, for example, are made possible by the use of metal type. Thinner strokes are made possible by finer paper and more accurate printing presses; the look, the visual experience of typography, is altered by the means of production. As early as 1791, for example, Bodoni was producing letterforms with very thin serifs; the thin strokes of his letters were also much thinner than had been seen before, creating a striking contrast with the thicker strokes (see Ill. 5.3).

The production and reproduction of both text and images undergo enormous changes as printing techniques are refined and take new forms. As Robin Kinross points out, in 1800 most European and

ABCDEFGHIJKLMNOPQRSTUVWXYZ
abcdefghijklmnopqrstuvwxyz
1234567890

Ill. 5.3 *Bodoni* typeface

American printers were using processes and equipment that 'had not changed for 300 years'. By the end of the century these printers would be using power-driven presses, machine-made paper, composing machines to set type and powered collating and binding machinery (1992: 25). Up until about 1870, for example, poster typography was produced by wooden type. It had been found that metal type was too heavy to be convenient for large posters and wooden type had been developed by people like the American Darius Wells. This technique prescribed a strong vertical and horizontal look to the posters as the type could only be placed in the press in horizontal rows. This technique also encouraged the proliferation of thousands of different typefaces, using a huge variety of shapes and textures.

Around 1870, however, lithography began to be developed and the use of wooden type declined. Lithography is a printing process which was discovered around the end of the eighteenth century by Aloys Senefelder. It was developed into chromolithography, which used many different colours, and although it was not much used in the production of text, it transformed the world of poster and print advertising. The visual experience of modern times, with its ubiquitous advertising, is partly the result of the development of colour printing. Lithography works on the principle that oil and water do not mix. Images and text may be drawn, or transferred photographically, in oil on to a flat stone. Water is then spread all over the stone, moistening all areas except the oil-based text or image. An oil-based ink is then rolled over the stone, sticking only to the oil-based images or text. Finally, a sheet of paper is placed on the stone and pressed, transferring the image on to the paper. This process is not limited to straight lines, to horizontals and verticals, as letterpress printing is, and words may form curves and even circles. Colour lithography proved an excellent medium for advertising posters and the work of Jules Cheret, Henri de Toulouse-Lautrec and the other Art Nouveau artists and designers proliferated as a result.

Lithography also changed the look of the packaging that the goods being advertised were sold in. Thomas Hine charts the development of packaging (1995). As mass advertising only really got under way at the end of the nineteenth century, with the development of powered presses and lithography, so packaging also only takes off at this time. Paper as a form of packaging was a luxury until machine-made paper made it economical for foodstuffs and other goods to be wrapped in it. As Hine says:

machine-made paper and widespread lithography spurred a dissemination of vibrant imagery on a scale the world had never known. It was part of a social transformation that, by the end of the nineteenth century, enabled even the working class to lead cluttered lives. (1995: 58)

The evolution of these methods of production and reproduction entailed a split between elite and mass culture. The mass-produced prints, books and so on that became available to the working classes were different from (and perceived as being of lower status than) the cultural objects and practices of the traditional middle and upper classes, with their paintings and so on. However, as well as enabling the working classes to 'clutter' their lives and adorn their walls with cheap prints of 'comely faces, pastoral vistas, or great moments from history, the Bible, or classical mythology' (ibid.), these processes enabled manufacturers to print, by means of offset litho, on to materials like metal. Manufacturers quickly recognised that the addition of even one colour to their packaging made it stand out on the shelf (59) and chromolithography flourished until around the mid-1890s, when photoengraving began to take over. The visual experience of consumption was revolutionised by these changes.

In addition, the production and reproduction of both text and images are speeded up as steam-powered and later electric-powered presses are developed. Artefacts, goods, packaging and so on, are also the subject of these developments. With steam- and electric-powered machinery, the production of all kinds of goods is made quicker and cheaper. The first steam-powered cylinder press was made in 1814 by Freidrich Koenig, a German printer working in London. This press could print four hundred sheets per hour, compared to the two hundred and fifty sheets which could be printed on the hand-press developed by Lord Stanhope in 1800. Koenig was later commissioned by *The Times* newspaper to build a press that could print over one thousand sheets per hour. The effect on the appearance of newspapers was considerable. There was an increase in the amount of advertising they contained, for example, as well as the visual and aesthetic changes which were taking place in typography and layout. In 1800, for example, the London *Times* contained an average of one hundred advertisements per day. Fifty-three years later, the number of ads per day was up to around one thousand five hundred (Presbrey 1929). The look of newspapers would have been quite transformed by these developments.

Combined with the reduction in the 1830s and the eventual withdrawal in the 1850s of stamp duty and advertisement taxes (Williams 1980: 173), these developments in print technology radically transfigured the look of towns and cities, as well as newspapers, posters and other printed matter. From the 1930s, the forms in which illustrated advertising appears increased; as well as posters, illustrated advertisements appeared on handbills, vehicles, balloons, sandwich-boards, buildings, railway carriages and stations and hoardings. Illustrated adverts appeared on the safety curtains in theatres, shocking theatregoers, and the Quaker Oats company incurred much ill-feeling by erecting a hoarding on the white cliffs of Dover. Again, these developments have a role to play in producing, or delivering, the mass markets that were to buy the products and services that were being offered to people in the new and growing conurbations.

The products themselves were also being produced by machines, in factories, and they were being produced faster and in ever-increasing numbers. Clearly, large numbers of things could only be produced economically by machines if they were all standard sizes and shapes, and made of standardised parts. Such forms of production also demanded the division of labour, where no one person saw the product right through the manufacturing process. Instead, each worker would be responsible for one stage of the production of the item. With these divisions of labour came distinctions of status. Designers would be of higher status than the mechanics who turned out the designs. In printing, lithographic or otherwise, clear distinctions are drawn between writers, designers and printers. Most importantly for this volume, modern industrial mass production, which entails 'the large-scale manufacture of standardised products, with interchangeable parts, using powered machine-tools in a sequence of simplified mechanical operations' (Heskett 1980: 50), has a distinct effect on the ways that manufactured goods look. Goods manufactured in these ways tend to all look the same. The way these things look, therefore, is as much a result of their being machine-made as it is of the function they are to fulfil. It is not the case, however, that people always want to buy artefacts that are too obviously identical, mass-produced items. Many objects, like the stacking chairs designed by Charles Eames (Heskett 1980: 137), are designed for communal dining and individuality is not required. But other equally mass-produced items need to be individualised in order that mass consumers may feel that they are purchasing something special. The relation between mass markets, production and con-

sumption is clearly a complex one and full of problems for manufacturers.

John Heskett (1980) describes a number of products whose visual
appearance is the result of the complex relations between the
demands of manufacturers and the desires of mass markets. He
reproduces a page from Doulton & Company's 1898 catalogue which
shows their range of water closets. In order to produce many water
closets, at low cost, Doultons had to standardise their production.
The problem is that a standardised water closet will not sell to many
people when all of them consider themselves completely individual.
As Heskett points out, the problem is solved by producing many
standardised water closets but then decorating them in a number of
different finishes (1980: 44–5). One basic mould produced thousands
of identical water closets, which were then decorated and sold in
various different finishes, with mouldings, transfer prints, different
coloured stoneware and so on. The way these water closets look,
then, is a function of their being mass-produced for a mass market
each member of which considers themselves an individual. Heskett
also cites the example of the Colt revolver. This revolver was mass-
produced as early as 1851, with standardised parts and with a very
simple form. Indeed, Samuel Colt is widely recognised for his
'thoroughgoing application of mass-production methods' (52). Despite this, the revolver of 1851 is covered in hand engraving. It is the
hand engraving which gives each gun its individuality and its appeal
to individual members of the mass market.

Something of the same desire for individuality in mass-produced
items may be seen in the BMW company's attempt in 1978 to
individualise its cars. John A. Walker (1983: 57) reproduces an
advertisement from *Time* magazine in which BMW show three cars.
Each of the cars has been painted, or decorated, by a different artist,
Frank Stella, Alexander Calder and Roy Lichtenstein, and BMW refer
to the 'discerning motorist, who wants to express his individualism'
and to the artists, who have been provided with a medium in which to
'express their individual point of view' (ibid.). There are various
paradoxes here, as Walker points out. First, the 'discerning motorist'
is expected to 'express his individualism' in a mass-produced car.
Second, the decorated cars are not for sale, having been turned into
'works of art'. And third, cars from the Model T onwards are
undecorated because they are 'manufactured according to the modernist principle that "form follows function" . . . the addition of
decoration is anachronistic because it attempts to endow the mass-

produced, engineered object with the qualities of a hand-crafted object' (ibid.). A slightly different approach to these matters is found in the 1996 Mercedes press advertisement which simply asks, 'Would you describe a Picasso as second-hand?' The reader is expected to understand that the Mercedes car is a work of art and, as one would not call a work of art second-hand, so one should not call the car second-hand.

Not everyone was impressed by these developments; the visual environment was becoming decorated and adorned to an extent that had never been seen before. Rudyard Kipling, for example, complained to *The Times* that railway platforms and trains had every piece of information and advertisement on them except the name of the station. Robin Kinross points out that the development of steam- and electric-powered presses led to many people arguing that the quality, the 'grace', of the typography declined around the end of the nineteenth century (1992: 27). The argument is that the development of these presses led to a decline in the quality of the typography, to typography that was not as good or as beautiful as that which had come before. Such feelings were the driving force behind the work of people such as William Morris, who founded the Kelmscott Press in 1890 with the intention of reviving the Venetian roman typefaces of Nicholas Jenson in the fifteenth century. In 1897, Charles R. Ashbee, mentioned in Chapter 3 in connection with the Guild of Handicraft, also founded the Essex House Press, using many of Morris's staff and equipment from the Kelmscott Press after Morris died. And in 1895, C. H. St John Hornby founded the Ashendene Press. All these presses were interested in reviving and printing much earlier and, they thought, much more beautiful typefaces. There can be no doubt that books produced by these presses are extremely beautiful books; the 1903 Doves Press Bible, Ashbee's Essex House Psalter of 1902 and Morris's own 1896 *Works of Geoffrey Chaucer*, are full of stunning typography and intelligent, clear layouts. But, as Kinross points out, that is not to say that the everyday, functional typography and layouts of the end of the nineteenth century do not contain much to commend them (1992: 27).

While not wishing to present lithography as the single source of the modern production and reproduction of images and text, it also has a part to play in the evolution of photography. Until photography was invented, the production and reproduction of text and imagery was inevitably done by hand in the sense that the text or image had to be drawn or engraved by hand at some point. Photography uses the action of light on certain sensitised papers to make images and text. Lithography had a part to play here in that Joseph Niepce (1765–1833), who in 1822 produced a print from an engraving using sunlight and light-sensitive asphalt, was a lithographer. Four years later Niepce produced a picture, a photograph, of his backyard by putting a pewter plate coated with the same light-sensitive asphalt in a camera obscura and pointing it out of his window. From these beginnings, a whole new medium was born. Photography was refined by people like Louis Jacques Daguerre, William Henry Fox Talbot and Sir John Herschel to the point where it could eventually be used to produce both image and text. The work of John Calvin Moss in New York and Firmin Gillot in France produced methods by which photographs could be mass-produced and printed in newspapers.

This mass medium also had private uses. George Eastman produced a camera for the Kodak company which could be used by anyone 'who could wind a watch' and popular photography became possible. This, of course, led to the appearance of whole new genres of photography, the family album, for example. The everyday lives of relatively ordinary people could be recorded and preserved in photographic form, transforming their visual experience in so far as, for the first time, they could make it themselves. The visual experiences of photography are distinct from many other media in that photography inevitably contains an iconic element. What this means is that there is with photography a guaranteed likeness between the photograph and what the photograph is of. This, of course, makes it particularly appropriate for press and documentary photographs, for example, where the ability of the photograph to show convincingly what happened is unsurpassed.

While they are undoubtedly part of the mass media, it is not the case that film and television are machine-made in the sense that some of the images, texts and artefacts dealt with above are machine-made. Film and television make use of artificial light and electric power, for instance, which is not necessarily the case with the processes above. The divisions of labour, first seen in the production processes above, are also found in film and television. One only needs to study the credits at the end of a film or television programme to realise quite how effectively the labour has been divided, with dozens of jobs rolling interminably past. Actors, singers and dancers are followed by directors, producers, executive producers, editors. Then there are the various trades, technical staff, caterers and hairstylists. The fact that so many people are involved in the production of film and television programme is one of the main differences between the way they are experienced and the ways in which media like painting, sculpture and some design are experienced.

In the latter, there is some place, the artist or designer, where meaning may be sought. In the former, there is no single clear locus from which meaning may unproblematically derive. Meaning, one's visual experience of a film, for example, may also be sought in the description of the film as 'a Hitchcock', or 'a Spielberg'. Here the experience is shaped by one's knowledge of the sorts of films characteristically produced by these directors. The visual experiences peculiar to film and television are also slightly different. Television tends to be experienced domestically, *en famille*, while film is more social or public. These are probably the most prevalent forms of visual culture for most people in modern western societies and much concern has been expressed about the audience passively receiving all kinds of politically conservative, or radical, messages through these media. Paradoxically, despite the attractions of the model of the active viewer of film and television, it is probably also the case that these mass media, led by the perceived desires of the mass market as they are, can be among the most anti-establishment of media.

Critiques of the mass media, of television in particular, have been made by means of television and video technology. This would be an example of using a medium to criticise the form, content and cultural connotations of that medium. The video artist Nam June Paik, for example, uses video in this way. He has made old televisions, from the 1950s and 1960s, into aquaria. He has removed their wiring and replaced it with candles. And he has constructed families out of these television sets, with members of the family constructed out of old sets. David Morley quotes Hanhardt, who says that the effect of Nam June Paik's treatment of television is remove it from 'its position in the home and strip it of its signifiers and traditional meanings as an object' (Morley 1995: 183). Such decontextualising serves also to draw attention to the constant bombardment of the senses that the mass media represent; if the usual content of the screen is removed or replaced with interference, that content and its omnipresence are effectively made more obvious. In that attention has been drawn to what is usually taken for granted, Nam June Paik may be said to have critiqued the form and content of this particular medium. Bill Viola is another video artist who is interested in using video to critique television as a form of the mass media. Where Nam June Paik's literal breaking-up of the television set suggests the metaphorical breaking-up of its authoritative place in people's lives, Viola is interested in the actual physical activity of sitting in one place, watching coloured lights and shapes on a screen (quoted in Morley 1995: 183). He is also interested in using video to critique the wider society. He cites the example of the way a home video was used to convict members of the Los Angeles Police Department of beating a black man in 1991. And he relates the story of how a group of 'kids' in the Bronx Video Collective challenged the New York City Police over the shooting of an old woman. He says, 'video is the medium of choice for both creating and narrating alternative history, and it's now in the hands of the people and *that's* exciting' (Viola 1992: 5).

Computer-generated

These are the most modern media, only coming into the public eye in the late 1980s. Computer-produced words and images were introduced into magazines, newspapers, films, videos and television. The means to produce such text and images were the new generation of relatively small, immensely powerful personal computers which could run the various word-processing and image-creation packages like Microsoft Word, WordPerfect, Quark XPress, Adobe Photoshop and the other graphic packages. Various artists took up these new media, pop groups like the Shamen entered into partnerships with university art departments and those departments themselves established a virtual identity for themselves.

Also included in the category of digital and virtual resources are various other computer-based media: electronic mail, CD-ROM disks and the Internet, for example. While electronic mail may not be the most visually compelling medium, it offers a way for written documents to be produced and circulated and Caxton's press, after all, is at one level just a way of producing and circulating documents. It could be claimed that e-mail speeds up the production and distribution of text, enabling one person to reach a potential audience of millions, via the Internet. Another form of computer-based visual culture is interactive television. At present confined to a tiny, experimental, minority of viewers, interactive television is being developed by major entertainments companies such as Time-Warner. The idea is that individuals subscribe to interactive television and can access, play, rewind and rerun programmes. These programmes may be sports, films or even computer games. People like Martin Lister have questioned whether these media are interactive in ways that are significantly different from other, supposedly non-interactive, media such as terrestrial television and cinema (Lister 1995: 20), but they do represent a different relationship between the viewer and the material. It may be trivial, but it is, after all, not possible for a member of the audience to stop or rewind a section of film at the cinema and this constitutes a different experience of visual culture. Such an experience is different from that provided by video, which also may be stopped and rewound, in that the programme is remotely accessed with interactive television, whereas the video cassette is concretely in one's machine.

These are interesting for a number of reasons, mostly to do with the questions they all raise concerning media control and access. David Cronenberg, the director of such films as *Videodrome* and *Crash*, both of which raised precisely a series of questions concerning media ownership, media manipulation and pornography, raised the matter of access and control in an interview. His film *Crash* having originally been refused permission to be shown in London's West End, Cronenberg pointed out that it would be possible to show the film on the Internet. He said that the Internet was 'instantly international': a book banned in France could be scanned in a cyber-café in Belgium and then made instantly accessible in France (Freand-Jones 1997). It would be possible for a viewer in France, Great Britain, or anywhere, to view a banned or censored film on his or her computer, via the Internet. As Cronenberg says, the book is not published in France, it is not in France; the film, similarly, is not shown in France, it is not in France. Questions are raised concerning its legality; questions concerning its legality are also impossible. There is a sense, Cronenberg implies, in which it is pointless to think of the legality of something when that thing cannot be stopped. This is quite different from the situation that obtains with interactive television. In the few examples of such media that exist, the major international conglomerates, like Time-Warner, own and control access to the programmes. They own the material and they decide when and where it is shown. They also control who has access to it and what they can do with that material.

There has, inevitably, been a lot of talk about how 'everyone' will have access to this technology. And, as with movable type, it is inevitable that this talk will prove to be nonsense. It will still be the case that only the wealthy, post-capitalist countries will ever have proper access to these media, just as it was the case that only wealthy, capitalist countries ever had full and proper access to the written and printed word. Having said that, the power of the people who currently own and control most of the world's print media to dominate most of the world's electronic media should not be underestimated. Their ability to penetrate new, hitherto suspicious markets should not be misjudged either. In 1997, for example, Rupert Murdoch launched an Internet service in China in partnership with the *Communist People's Daily*. Murdoch has secured for News Corporation almost unlimited and exclusive access to the Chinese people and while the service he provides will be censored by the Chinese authorities for politically and pornographically sensitive material, it will still offer them the major source of world information in Chinese.

Even the artists and graphic designers mentioned above do not represent the possibility of universal, unproblematic access to these media. Nor do they prove a challenge to the ownership of these media. There are two or three main players providing the hardware and software that are involved in digital and electronic media. Microsoft, owned by Bill Gates, Apple and IBM are probably the largest companies providing computer technology. Microsoft and NBC are collaborating in 1997 in the production of a supposedly interactive news service offered on the Internet. As with the interactive media noted above, it is unlikely that they will, or can, be interactive in any realistic ways. NBC and Microsoft writers and editors will still write and edit what is available on the web pages, after all. In order to produce anything in these media, these artists are obliged to use the technology produced by these large companies. Microsoft produces the majority of programmes used in word-processing and ultimately the disk-operating systems, Apple produces much of the image-manipulation and image-creation packages and IBM or IBM-licensed companies produce most of the hardware. It is as if Caxton had had the foresight to copyright and trademark every press and every piece of movable type, as well as the paper to be printed on.

Conclusion

Questions concerning the identity and nature of modernity and postmodernity and questions concerning whether certain media are more properly described as modern or postmodern have been hinted at but not dealt with in any depth here. These questions are also connected to questions concerning the nature and identity of production and consumption. Fredric Jameson, for example, draws a distinction between industrial and post-industrial capitalism (1971: 106); post-industrial capitalism begins to emerge at the end of the Second World War. According to Jameson, the distinguishing features of post-industrial capitalism include 'greater material abundance and consumption, freer access to culture . . . increased social, not to speak of automotive mobility . . . sophisticated forms of thought control [and the] increasing abasement of spiritual and intellectual life' (107–8). He also draws a distinction between two kinds of media, or two kinds of product. In the first kind, 'the human origins of the product . . . have not yet been fully concealed' (104). The second kind of media and product, the products of post-industrial capitalism, 'are utterly without depth' they lack any relation to human origins (105). Jameson's post-industrial capitalism is similar to what theorists such as Jean Baudrillard have called postmodernity and it is tempting to identify Jameson's implied industrial capitalism with modernity.

On this sort of account, then, the mass media are every bit as postmodern as computer-based media. Both the mass media and computer-based media lack the relation to human origins that Jameson says characterises post-industrial capitalism. The problem here, of course, is that it is precisely industrial capitalism that produces the mass media. The various print technologies of the mass media, lithography, offset lithography, Linotype and Monotype machines, for example, are all part of the industrial production of text and images. Similarly, the various machines which produced and still produce metal and plastic goods of all kinds are part of industrial capitalism. Neither of these forms of production could truly be said to have much to do with humanity; the texts, images and artefacts produced by these machines have little connection to the human origins mentioned by Jameson. The lesson appears to be that it is impossible to generalise: each product, each medium and each example of consumption must be dealt with individually in order to make sure that the confusing effects of difficult cases do not do too much damage.

This chapter has been concerned with the ways in which cultures are made visible. It was argued that the idea of a culture that does not manifest or represent itself physically in some way is nonsensical and that every culture must use something to represent itself. It must represent itself first to itself and second to other cultural groups.

Having considered the different media available to visual culture, the next chapter will try to look at the works of art and design themselves. Chapter 6 will develop many of the debates begun in Chapters 1 and 2, where it was noted that there are many problems surrounding the definition of art, design and visual culture. Chapter 6, then, will outline the main problems involved in trying to define art and design and begin to look at examples of art and design, visual culture, itself.

Chapter 6

Signs, Codes and Visual Culture

Introduction

This chapter will begin the attempt to examine works of art and design themselves. Previous chapters have examined the different ways in which artists and designers have conceived of their own activities, the various groups that they have formed themselves into and the assorted audiences or markets for visual culture. Many kinds of media have also been examined. One would be forgiven for thinking that maybe it is about time that this book actually began to look at some works of art and design. The chapter will begin the 'attempt' to look at works of art and design because, as Williams for example has pointed out (1981: 119ff.), and as has been seen above in Chapters 1 and 2, there are numerous problems involved in defining notions of 'art' and 'design' and of 'works of art and design themselves' and then finding examples of them. This chapter will inevitably, therefore, develop many of the debates begun in Chapters 1 and 2.

This chapter will outline the main problems involved in trying to define art and design. It will consider whether conscious performance qualifies something as art, or whether art has to be of high quality. And it will ask whether art is something that is beautiful or whether, as Baudrillard has argued (1981: 79), the beautiful is simply a product of difference. It will also consider whether these criteria are fit to define design. Is there any human artefact which is not in some sense a work of design? In 1988, for example, *The Sunday Times* reported on

124

'designer cars', 'designer water' (Philippe Starck designed the bottle for 'Glacier' water in America), 'designer jeans' and even 'designer gods' worshipped by Californian hippies (Burchfield 1988: G17). The idea of designer water and designer gods is likely to strike many as merely a characteristic of the 1980s but the notion of designer jeans and designer cars is genuinely interesting in that it seems to imply that the jeans and cars produced before the early 1980s did not have designers. This, of course, is absurd. Of course jeans and cars had designers before the early 1980s; what the prefix 'designer' does is to raise the status of the product concerned. It transforms the product almost into a piece of art.

It will be argued in this chapter that there are no neutral, objective and eternal definitions of art and design that could be used to analyse and explain them. 'Art', 'design' and even 'visual culture' are not innocent, neutral or objective terms. Different people, existing in different societies at different times and places, have defined these terms in many different ways. A simple postmodernist relativism will be avoided, however, by arguing that different cultures at different times and places have used different rules, or codes, to define what is and is not art and design and to distinguish one form of art or design from another. These are among the ways that cultural identity is formed. Following Williams (1981: 130ff.), these codes, which play a role in determining the interpretation of visual signs within a culture, will be explained as external and internal codes. External codes are used to indicate the places and occasions at which art and design may be encountered and internal codes govern the interpretation of signs within the work of art or design. For example, if one receives an invitation to a private show at an art gallery, one will expect a certain type of event to take place, with certain types of people present doing certain kinds of thing. Internal codes are used to convey a desired impression or meaning. These internal codes help us to understand, for example, that visible brushstrokes in a painting may signify an expressionist, rather than a realist, painting, or that 'Boom' written in large letters can signify an economic phenomenon in the *Wall Street Journal* or an explosion in a children's cartoon.

Art and design as conscious performance

The first definition of art and design to be considered is that art and design are conscious performance or exhibition, the product of some conscious planning process. This definition has the benefit of including all that would normally be called art: painting, sculpture and so on. It would also include all design products; there can be no design products, after all, that are not the product of a planning process. Film and television would also be included in such a definition, as would dance and various performance art forms.

Problems arise, however, if the idea of an unconscious or subconscious mind is admitted. It was Sigmund Freud, working in Vienna until 1938, when he moved to London to escape the Nazis, who is often credited with discovering the unconscious. The idea of the unconscious is needed in Freudian theory to explain aspects of people's behaviour that cannot be explained by recourse to our conscious minds. The notion of the unconscious implies that people are not as in control of their desires and actions, and of the pleasures they receive from those actions, as they would like to think. The unconscious, on this kind of account, is a reservoir of unacknowledged, and unacknowledgeable, desires, all of which actively fight independently to be satisfied in the things people do and say in everyday life. Some artists attempted to give expression to the contents and workings of their unconscious or subconscious minds. The Dadaists, for example, were very interested in their dreams, which for Freud were a special route to uncovering the contents of the unconscious. André Breton, Louis Aragon, Max Ernst and Robert Desnos were among the Dadaists who experimented with hypnosis and sleep in order to get at images from the unconscious which were normally repressed by consciousness. They also experimented with what they called automatic writing, writing which attempted to escape or bypass the conscious mind to reveal unconscious feelings and desires. The conscious mind was seen by the likes of André Breton as a sort of mental straitjacket, confining and restricting the imaginative impulses to be found in the unconscious.

The Surrealists, who many see as developing out of Dadaism, were also interested in the unconscious. Indeed, in the First Surrealist Manifesto of 1924, surrealism was defined in terms of a 'pure psychic automatism . . . thought dictated in the absence of all control exerted by reason'. The automatic writing of the Dadaists was supplemented by automatic drawing, introduced by André Masson in 1924, in which a line, or lines, formed supposedly unconscious images which could be embellished and developed by the conscious mind. Of course it is Salvador Dali who is most popularly associated with Surrealism and the unconscious. Although artists like Max Ernst, Giorgio de Chirico and even René Magritte have been understood as using dreams and other elements of the unconscious to produce paintings, it is Dali who claims most of the attention. Dali's work of the 1920s and 1930s is said to contain images from dreams and to use the mechanisms of dreams that were identified by Freud in his book *The Interpretation of Dreams*, first published in 1900.

Other artists, it is claimed, did their best work when in less than complete control of their minds. It has been suggested, for example, that Vincent Van Gogh, Edvard Munch, James Ensor, Ernst Ludwig Kirchner, Max Beckmann and George Grosz all endured mental health problems which were not unconnected to the impact and success of their work. Of these, it is probably Van Gogh whose work has most consistently been interpreted in terms of mental illness. The point here is that these painters were not always in control of their minds and that much of their work was produced during such episodes. It is difficult, therefore, to rule their work out, to say that it is not art because it was not always under conscious control. Munch's painting *The Scream* is usually explained as the pictorial representation of his psychological problems, as is much of Van Gogh's work, and the question of creative madness is raised above, in Chapter 3.

As far as design is concerned, the status of the unconscious is problematic. At one level, the notion of design appears to leave little room for the unconscious; at this level, every aspect of a product's design should be accountable to reason. This is not to argue, of course, that objects of design may not be said to be the result of the designer's unconscious desires. Nor is it to argue that consumers and users of designed objects may not be said to get unconscious pleasures from consuming and using those objects. It is, however, to use the popular notion of the design process as one that is totally rational, the result of reason, to question the notion of the unconscious having a large role to play in design. Nevertheless, it should not be forgotten that in the 1930s Dali, one of the most well-known of the Surrealist artists, designed hats and other accessories for Elsa Schiaparelli and in the 1940s he produced a sofa in the shape of Mae West's lips. In 1928, Dali also collaborated with Luis Buñuel, the film-maker, on the film *Un Chien Andalou* and two years later they made *L'Age d'or*. Fashion, furniture and film, then, may well be examples of some of the areas in which the unconscious plays a part: they are not necessarily always under the conscious control of their producers or consumers.

So, unless one is willing to argue that Dadaist and Surrealist painting, sculpture and performance are not art, then art cannot simply be a matter of conscious performance. In addition, art cannot simply be a matter of conscious exhibition, as there are images, cave paintings, for example, which many people want to call art but which do not appear to have been consciously exhibited. It is at least plausible to suggest, that is, that paintings and drawings found deep in inaccessible caves are not being consciously exhibited. Similarly, unless one is willing to deny that people may get unconscious pleasures from creating and consuming pieces of art and design, then art and design cannot be entirely conscious phenomena. This is because, in order to deny such a proposition, one must argue that creators and consumers are always in control of their desires, pleasures and reactions.

Art and design as high quality

This is the idea that for something to be considered 'real' art or design, it has to be something that is performed or produced to a very high standard. Ernst Gombrich proposes a version of this definition in his *The Story of Art*, where he says that 'we speak of art whenever anything is done so superlatively well that we all but forget to ask what the work is supposed to be, for sheer admiration of the way it is done' (Gombrich 1950: 456; see also Gombrich 1979: 152). There are various problems inherent in such an approach. First, there is the question as to how to define 'high standards'. Different people will have different ideas as to what is a high standard; producers will have different ideas of standards from the users and consumers of art and design. For example, some might hold that painting in oil is necessarily of a higher standard than painting in watercolours because it is more difficult or technically demanding. Others might believe that furniture from Ikea is of a lower standard than that from John Lewis or Habitat; such people would be committed to arguing that Ikea furniture is not proper design, as it is not of a sufficiently high standard. And there will be those people who see the camerawork or the acting in the *Dirty Harry* series of films as vastly inferior to that of Kieslowski's *Three Colours* series. However tempting or initially plausible, however, it is not easy to argue that watercolours are not art, that Ikea furniture is not design and that the camerawork and acting of *Dirty Harry* is neither art nor design. Is all watercolour painting not art? Is the whole Ikea range not design? And is there not a minute in the *Dirty Harry* series that does not become art? What, similarly, is to be made of art that uses poster paints, of furniture from Argos and of the acting in the *Police Academy* films? Is there some superlative form of non-art and non-design?

 The problem remains, also, as to what criteria are supposed to be applied to these items of art and design. Where are criteria of quality supposed to come from? Every single criterion will necessarily come from some socially located group from within a society. Each of these groups will have its own idea as to what constitutes quality in paintings, furniture and film. There are other problems. Even if it proved possible to arrive at criteria of quality that were acceptable to all the different social groups and classes of a society, there is still the problem that there are things which one might want to call art which have functions other than that of being art. For example, if it is agreed that items of 'real' art are those things that are produced to 'high standards', then items like the Swiss Army Knife, the Golden Gate Bridge and an Emanuel dress must be admitted as works of art. This may be no problem to many people. The problem is, however, that all of these items are functional items as well as being or not being works of art. They are all items that have uses, that are functional items, as well as being of high quality.

Art, design and aesthetic intention

This definition of art and design proposes that art and design is that which has some aesthetic intention or purpose. It was first broached in Chapter 1 above, which was trying to define visual culture and where Erwin Panofsky's account of art as that which was aesthetically affecting was introduced. On the broadest possible understanding of the aesthetic, art and design would be everything that could be seen, everything that affected one's visual senses. Clearly, this will not do. It was noted in Chapter 1 that natural objects, like landscapes, or the human body may affect one's senses but they are not works of art or design in any commonly accepted form. The idea could be refined, so that it was only objects that both affected one aesthetically and were 'beautiful' or 'harmonious' that were art or design. Again, this fails to rule out natural objects: both landscapes and the human body may be referred to as beautiful and harmonious and, as noted above, they are not the sorts of things that one would want to call art or design. There are also the problems that, first, the beautiful may vary between different class and social groups and, second, that the beautiful may only be a product of difference. The first argument is that, as different groups will have different ideas as to what is beautiful, they will have different ideas as to what is and is not art. The second argument, as put forward by Jean Baudrillard, for example (1981: 79), is that, as the beautiful is the product of historically shifting relations of difference, what counts as art is only the result of those differences. It is the argument that there is nothing substantial or significant in the things themselves that is beautiful, just that they are different from other things.

This kind of definition is useful in that it allows the serious consideration of items that fall beyond the traditional categories of art and design, but it is less helpful in that it does not rule much out. It also allows the discussion of the art and design of many different social groups, but it does not account for the fact that the aesthetically affecting may have other functions, which are not aesthetic. Thus, fashion and clothing, garden design, film and furniture design may all affect one aesthetically but, like the items considered above, they all have other properties and qualities as well as those of being aesthetically affecting. They may all be considered as items of visual culture. But they also have other functions. Thus, a garden is almost guaranteed to affect one aesthetically, but it may also be a garden in a primary school, that is there to teach the young about plants. It therefore has an educative function as well as an aesthetic function. The Armani raincoat is also likely to affect one aesthetically, but it also has the function of keeping anyone fortunate enough to wear one dry in a shower.

There are other problems involved in defining art and design in this way. The main problem is analogous to some of those noted above. It is that what counts as aesthetically affecting is also likely to vary between different social groups. Just as there are those who will remain forever ignorant of the tonal subtleties of Vermeer, there are those who will miss the energy and power of *Captain America* or *Batman* comics. There is, therefore, an element of truth in Clive Bell's pronouncement that Frith's painting of Paddington Station 'is not a work of art' (Bell 1982: 71). To someone of Bell's class and educational background, the thoughts and feelings evoked by Frith's work simply are not those that are recognised as aesthetic; the work, therefore, is not a work of art. It should be pointed out that many contemporaries of Frith would not have disagreed with Bell's later judgements. His 1889 painting, *The New Frock*, for example, was purchased by the Lever company and made into an advertisement for Sunlight soap, even suffering the indignity of being retitled *So Clean*. The argument is that the audience which saw the painting only in the form of an advertisement can be said to have responded to it aesthetically, but in such a way as to have bought the soap as part of their (aesthetic) response to the painting. To someone like Bell, however, such a response is not an aesthetic response and the work is not art.

Art and design as sign systems

The attempt to look at the works of art and design themselves, then, is not as straightforward as it might at first appear. As soon as a definition of either art or design is proposed, it seems that there are other social groups or other historical periods which would define them differently. Consequently, different objects, practices and so on count as art or design for different groups and periods. There are no objective, neutral and eternal definitions of art and design that may be used in the study and explanation of visual culture. Now, there are those people who will be cast into despair by thoughts such as these. It may well be argued that as there are no such objective and neutral definitions, there can be no definitions at all. Alternatively, it could also be argued that as there are no such neutral and objective definitions, there can be no useful work done in the study and explanation of visual culture. Both of these arguments may be presented as a form of relativism. If what is thought to be art, design, beauty and aesthetic feeling, for example, is relative to cultural time and place, then there can be no stable knowledge and analysis of those things. However, these arguments all presuppose that such thoughts are obstacles standing in the way of further thoughts.

It is possible to see such thoughts as starting points on the way to other thoughts. Rather than understanding the arguments above negatively, as signalling the impossibility of knowledge and analysis, it is possible to understand them positively, as being productive of knowledge and analysis. The attempt to provide answers to questions like 'what is art?' or 'what is aesthetic feeling?', for example, is itself also an essential part of the human process of cultural production. Just as people do not stop producing visual culture (despite having no objective and neutral definitions for it), so people should not stop trying to analyse and explain it (despite having no objective and stable definitions for it). Different groups within different societies define the artistic and the aesthetic differently as part of the process of their cultural life. It follows that debates concerning the artistic and the aesthetic may be seen as social processes, as part of social life (Williams 1981: 130). They may, therefore, be studied as cultural production. The analysis and explanation of visual culture itself do not need an objective and neutral account of culture, art and the aesthetic, for example, in order to study what different cultures understand by these terms. Nor does it need such an account in order to analyse and explain the ways in which they are used by those different cultures. Thus, that Clive Bell understands by the notion of the aesthetic something completely different from what Frith or the Lever company understood by it is not only evidence that these definitions are not objective terms or eternal truths. It is also evidence that the differences between Bell, Frith and Lever are part of ongoing cultural processes, part of a specific debate concerning the nature of the aesthetic, for example, in a particular society. They may be studied as such by visual culture.

So, distinctions between art and design, and distinctions between what is and what is not a valid aesthetic experience, for example, are made differently by different social groups. These social groups exist within different societies found in different times and places. As there are different societies, existing in different times and places, one may expect the distinctions and definitions that they make (between art and design, and between different forms of aesthetic experience, for example) to vary and to change. These distinctions and definitions are parts of and products of the cultural processes of those societies. As such, they may be studied, analysed and explained by visual culture. In this way, it is suggested that what some see as obstacles may in fact be seen as starting points. These sets of distinctions and definitions are themselves culturally significant; they indicate the values and beliefs of different cultural groups. Consequently, following Raymond Williams (1981: 130ff.), these sets will be thought of here as sign systems.

These sign systems may be found relating to all aspects of visual culture within a society. These sign systems may also be roughly divided into two types. They may, as above, be defining what is and what is not art and design within a society. This type of sign may be said to be 'external': it concerns the places and occasions in which what counts as art, or design, may or may not be found as well as the ways in which a society responds to that art and design. And they may also define what the conventions within individual art or design forms are taken to mean by that society. This type of sign may be said to be 'internal': it concerns the devices or conventions within particular forms of art and design. The way in which the floating baby in Roger van der Weyden's *Three Magi* is understood as miraculous while the floating city in the *Gospels of Otto III* is not miraculous, which was discussed in Chapter 2, would be an example of how such internal signs work. According to certain conventions, floating either is or is not interpreted as miraculous. The sign systems which determine how art and design or the conventions operating within art and design are to be interpreted are therefore part of and products of the social organisations in which they are found. They also contribute to the production and reproduction of those social organisations, although this will be taken up in more detail in Chapter 8.

External sign systems

The first types of signs to be explained here are external signs. These signs indicate, primarily, the presence or existence of art or design at some time and place. They indicate the nature of the experiences that one may expect to undergo at a certain time and place. And they indicate the nature of the relationships that will be found, and which one will be expected to enter into, at that time and place. External signs may be thought of as indicative of the sorts of experiences and relations that are to be expected; they are preparatory in the sense that they prepare one, make one ready for that set of experiences and relationships. Williams proposes the art gallery and the performance of a play as two cases in which the external signs for art and theatre may be clearly discerned (1981: 131–2). The art gallery, he says, 'is a place specialised and designated for looking at painting or sculpture as art' (131). The art gallery, then, is a sign that what is to be found inside it is 'art', as opposed to not-art. In the theatre, the sign system of 'advertised time of performance, arrangement of seating, raising of curtain and so on' indicate that one is in the presence of a 'play', or a piece of 'theatre', as opposed to 'real life', presumably (132).

In an art gallery, then, the external sign system consists in the advertisement of opening times, the displaying of paintings on walls and of sculptures set on plinths, the progression of rooms and corridors and the arrangement of ropes and other protective devices.

Such elements signify that one is in the presence of art, that one is to walk round in a prescribed order and not get too close to the works. In many ways, this is not so very different to the external sign system of many upmarket furniture shops, for example. There is a store on Third Avenue in New York called *Bon Marché*. Among other things, it sells chairs designed by the likes of Mies van der Rohe, Marcel Breuer and Le Corbusier. Various relatively minor cues will differentiate this store from many museums of modern design; the store advertises its willingness to accept payment by Visa and MasterCard and points out that its uptown branch is open at slightly different times from its downtown branch (see Ill. 6.1). The presence of credit facilities is one way in which the establishment externally signifies that it is a store and not a design museum. It alerts one to the fact that one may expect a slightly different set of experiences from what one would expect at the design museum. There is a commercial relation present at the Bon Marché store that is not present at the art gallery.

That is not to say that there is never a commercial relation present at an art gallery. Should one receive an invitation to the opening of a show, or a private show at a gallery, one would be surprised to find that there were no paintings or other art works present. More specifically, one would be surprised to find that there were no art works for sale. In this instance, there would be an art gallery, containing paintings and maybe sculptures, but there would also be price tags, as in the furniture store, and there may even be credit facilities available, as in the furniture store. The external signs are slightly different in each case, indicating a different set of experiences to be undergone and a different set of relations to be entered into. In the gallery, for example, there would be spectators, perhaps even connoisseurs and art lovers. In the store, there would be customers, salesmen and saleswomen, maybe even credit advisers. Alternatively, where the practice of holding swatches of fabrics or wall-paper against the items on display, to see if they 'go', would pass unnoticed in the furniture store, it would almost certainly attract whispers of disapproval in the gallery. The descriptions of people as either spectators or customers describe the different relations into which people enter in the different contexts and prescribe the different experiences and behaviours that are to be expected in those contexts.

The differences between books, pamphlets, newspapers, magazines and leaflets, for example, may also be explained in terms of external signs. The different aesthetic experiences associated with these

Ill. 6.1   Bon Marché store advertisement, New York, 1991

different types of printed matter are a product of their different external signs. As noted above, the external signs prepare people for various different experiences and ways of behaving. Thus, many people are more careful with a hardback book than they are with a paperback or a magazine; they simply take more care of it. The external signs of a hard cover, relatively expensive binding techniques and usually better-quality paper, indicate to people that a different form of behaviour is expected and a different level of response required. Many people behave towards some hardback books as if they were pieces of art, displaying them in full view, as if they were rare and precious things, on a coffee table. The pleasures of magazines and newspapers are generally much more ephemeral than those of books of any kind and this is suggested by the materials, the quality of paper and binding, for example, that make them up. In these ways, then, external signs prepare people for the kinds of experiences, behaviour and pleasures that are to be expected in and from a certain kind of product.

There are, of course, those artists who set out deliberately to confound the expectations set up by these external signs. This can be done in a number of ways. First, ordinary and everyday objects may be displayed in galleries. This is the tactic adopted by sculptors such as Carl Andre and Marcel Duchamp. Andre is famous for exhibiting one hundred and twenty firebricks at the Tate Gallery in 1976 and calling it a sculpture, *Equivalent VIII*. Duchamp achieved similar notoriety some sixty years earlier when he exhibited a men's urinal in New York with the title *Fountain*. Second, conventionally artistic objects and practices may be exhibited or performed in places which are not art galleries. The work of Richard Long, or Andy Goldsworthy, who creates often beautiful and moving sculptural objects from snow, ice, grass and other natural objects in natural settings like forests and fields, may be seen as an example of this strategy. The external signs which indicate 'art gallery' are absent but the objects nevertheless invite the description 'art'. And third, artists may challenge both the location and the object or performance conventionally labelled art by means of manipulating these external signs. The performance art of the Futurists and Constructivists in the early twentieth century may be seen as an example of such manipulation, as might the performance art of the 1960s and 1970s. Artists such as Stuart Brisley, performing arduous and strenuous pieces in their baths, for example, do not obviously exhibit conventional external signs for the performance or presence of art.

Internal sign systems

The second type of sign is internal signs. These signs may be thought
of as conventional signs and they indicate a relationship between form
and social structure. A simple example will make this difficult and
rather grand-sounding definition clearer. It is well-known that shavers
for men are often matt black and largely rectangular; they may also be
grey and set off with an orange or a red line, like the red line that
surrounds the Golf GTi radiator grille. Shavers for women are often
found in shiny pastel shades and in more circular and rounded shapes.
These shapes, colours and textures constitute internal signs. From
signs such as these one may understand that they are masculine or
feminine objects; the signs signify either masculine or feminine. That
the masculine object is matt, black and largely rectangular and that
the feminine object is shiny, pastel and largely rounded is the result of
conventions. It is entirely conventional that one set of shapes, colours
and textures is deemed to be masculine and another set feminine. The
difference in colour, shape and texture signifies a difference in gender
identity. These signs are interpreted according to these conventions,
thus indicating the relation between form (the shape, colour and
texture) and social structure (whether they are for men or women).

Different styles of art and design may be approached and explained
in terms of internal signs. There are, for example, styles of art and
design that draw attention to the methods and means of their own
production. And there are styles of art and design that attempt to hide
the methods and means of their production. In painting it is tempting
to arrange works on a sliding scale which has seventeenth-century
Dutch still life paintings at one end and twentieth-century abstract
expressionist works at the other. In the still life paintings, there is
every attempt made to efface the work of the artist's brush and in the
abstract expressionist paintings there seems to be every attempt to
draw attention to the work of the brush and the constructed nature of
the piece. Now, someone like Norman Bryson would explain this
scale as a common-sense and misguided attempt to explain realism, or
the lack of it, in painting (Bryson 1981: 1–28). On this misguided
explanation, realistic paintings would be the product of the brushstrokes being almost invisible and the lack of realism in abstract
expressionist paintings would be the result of the brushstrokes, or
knife-marks, or whatever, being highly visible. Whether the explanation is misguided or not, it is clear that there is something like a
convention operating here. The brushstrokes are constructed either to

be visible or to not be visible and meaning is ascribed to the paintings as a result. The former is understood by common sense to be realistic and the latter are said to be 'modern', 'postmodern' or even 'avant garde'.

Works of design may also be approached in terms of these internal signs. Some works of design seem to have appeared on the planet as if by magic, as if they were not made by human processes at all. Others look as if they are not yet finished, as if they should go back to the factory for completion, so apparent are the marks of their construction. The steel furniture of Ron Arad, for example, displays all too clearly the methods and means of its construction; sheet steel is difficult to present in a way that disguises the fact that it must be worked, bent, riveted and welded. The Lloyds building in London, designed by Richard Rogers, is a building that many have objected to because it displays the methods and means of its construction. It makes no attempt to hide the fact that it is constructed, and that it is constructed from certain, all too obvious, materials. Furniture that is available on the high street, however, never shows its screws or its staples; such features would be grounds for returning the product to the store. Similarly, most domestic buildings conceal their construction. Cement and plaster are always 'finished'; indeed, the latter is used to cover bricks and is itself most often papered over so that it will not be seen. Again, as with paintings, such buildings as do display the means and methods of their construction are variously described as 'modern', 'postmodern' or 'avant-garde'.

As Kurt Back has pointed out, fashion is also an area of design where the characteristic methods of construction have become of central interest recently. He argues that where modern painting displays the means and methods of its own construction to announce 'this is a painting', so modern fashion displays the means and methods of its construction to announce 'this is clothing' (Back 1985: 12). In the early 1990s, there was a group of fashion designers who routinely exposed the seams of their garments, who used fabrics that were more commonly used only in the construction and strengthening of garments, who left edges unfinished and who restricted their palettes to black, white and perhaps natural creams. These designers, who included the likes of Martin Margiela and Anne Demeulemeester, were known as deconstructionists and were thought of as postmodern designers. Again, the fashions and clothing found in high street stores are more likely to be rejected as faulty or 'imperfect' and returned to the manufacturer if they have exposed seams or edges left unfinished.

The different forms and styles of typography and layout used in books, in magazines and on television programmes are also good places to look for internal sign systems. In *Bugs!*, for example, a nature magazine for the very young, the typography used for the title is a form of handwritten script, mixing upper and lower case and appearing in a variety of lurid, often primary, colours. The close-up image of some hideous bug on the cover is surrounded by bright yellow lines which zig-zag at an angle across a blue background. Much of the headline type inside the magazine is placed at bizarre angles, getting larger or smaller as it progresses across the page. And some of it threads snake-like, or 'creepy-crawly'-like, as it promises to uncover 'the creepy-crawly world of minibeasts' (*Bugs!*, no. 6, 1994). The print appears on a variety of background colours, black, salmon-pink and a rather unsettling shade of green. The effect is extremely colourful, energetic and sometimes, frankly, exhausting to look at. The BBC's magazine *Wildlife*, however, has a rather different audience. It is read by senior members of the Forestry Commission, the British Bryological Association and Sustrans, if the letters page for the April 1994 edition is at all representative (bryology, of course, is the science of mosses and Sustrans is the name of a group that supports ecological transport policies). There are, admittedly, some rather racy diagonals on the front cover (an advertisement for Simon King's *Wildguide* video appears just off the vertical and the top right corner has a tiny promotion for a photography competition), but the tone is generally much more sedate. The typefaces are usually sans serif, they are always horizontal and they never get bigger or smaller as they progress across the page. These typefaces, layouts, colours and so on are internal signs. They are also conventional. It is, for example, a conventional idea of childhood that children like big, bold, exciting and colourful images. The more mature readers of the BBC magazine are conventionally held to be put off by such things. This is part of the explanation why the magazines look the ways they do.

It was argued above that the sign systems which determine how art and design or the conventions operating within art and design are to be interpreted are part of and products of the social organisations in which they are found. This is clear in the case of the shavers: the shapes, colours and textures are conventionally associated with different sex and gender groups. They also contribute to the production and reproduction of those social organisations. The continued and unthinking use of these shapes, colours and textures in these ways produces and reproduces sexual and gender identity. In the case of painting, furniture design and fashion design, the relation between form and social structure may be less clear. It is, nevertheless, still there. It is there, for example, in the reference to the avant-garde. The notion of an avant-garde only makes sense in terms of a social group that is apart from, and maybe opposed to, a larger social whole, the rest of the society. As such, it represents an elite form of visual culture, available only to those with the educational background, what Bourdieu calls the 'cultural capital', to respond to it, to understand it and thus appreciate it. The furniture of Ron Arad is not found in everyone's home, just as the fashions of Martin Margiela and Anne Demeulemeester are not found in everyone's wardrobe. They are found in the homes and wardrobes of a small educated and moneyed cultural group. The members of this small cultural group use such items to construct their identity as members of that group and to differentiate themselves from other cultural groups. Consequently, the internal signs here construct class identity, rather than sex or gender identity. This is the relation between form and social structure.

In the case of the typography, the relation between form and social structure is also fairly clear. The kinds of shapes, colours, typographies, layouts and so on used by the children's magazine are those conventionally linked with children. In the way that matt, black and rectilinear were deemed to be masculine, so bold, colourful, odd angles and different sizes are deemed to be appropriate to children. The use of these typefaces, colours and layouts, for example, both produces and reproduces the identity of childhood as a certain kind of thing: it produces and reproduces childhood as having a specific meaning. The more sober, horizontal and staid typography and layout of *Wildlife*, however, is understood to be more appropriate to older readers. It is a convention in certain cultures that maturer and possibly professional readers will not be attracted by the colourful and energetic approach of *Bugs!* but will require a more conservative approach.

Crossover

There is, of course, what might be called 'crossover' between internal and external signs. This is where external signs become internal and where internal signs become external. It seems to be more difficult and less common, however, for internal signs to become external than for external signs to become internal. Internal signs can become external signs when the design or style of a building raises questions as to the characteristic experiences to be had, and the appropriate forms of behaviour to be adopted, within it. The Pompidou Centre, designed by Richard Rogers and Renzo Piano in 1977, houses the gallery and library of the *Centre de création industrielle* in Paris. It is confusing enough for the word 'creation' to be used in conjunction with the word 'industrial', but when the gallery and library look like a factory, as some have suggested, people might be forgiven for not knowing what to expect or how to react to the objects within the building. What some people have suggested is that the Pompidou Centre does not look like a gallery should; it does not look like the Louvre, for example, or even the Guggenheim Museum. And it certainly does not look like the great municipal art galleries of Leeds, Liverpool and Manchester, for example. Consequently, the expectations as to what will be encountered within the building and how the contents are to be reacted to may well be unclear. The great municipal art galleries of the world engender an atmosphere of calm, of solidity and of civic prosperity and propriety in which the best of the world's art may be contemplated. Buildings like the Pompidou Centre adopt a different set of internal signs and disrupt the conventional understanding of those signs as they relate to what might be expected within such a building.

External signs may always be approached and analysed as internal signs, however. This is because those signs will always have to be done in some style or other. The style-free or neutral sign is impossible. Thus, for example, the invitation to the private show, or the fashion store shop-front, will always be done in some style or other. Consequently, it will always be available for analysis as an internal sign.

Conclusion

This chapter has shown that a neutral, objective and innocent definition of either art or design is impossible. It has, however, argued that, far from being a problem, this is a starting point for the understanding and analysis of visual culture in that different cultural groups, existing at different times and places, will define art and design, as well as what counts as aesthetic experience, differently, as part of the way they are constituted as a cultural group. These different definitions, then, may be used to analyse and explain those cultures' responses to visual culture. It was also argued that the notions of internal and external signs could profitably be used to investigate what cultures defined as art and design as well as the conventions in terms of which their art and design could be inter- preted. Thus, what different cultures defined as art and design, as well as the conventions they used to interpret those works, were linked to the social structures existing within those cultures. Indeed, it was claimed that they were the ways in which those social structures were produced and reproduced. These matters will be returned to in Chapter 8, on culture and reproduction.

The next chapter will consider the various different types of art and design. It will look at the ways in which paintings, no less than cars, trousers and typefaces, exist in many different forms. And it will consider potential explanations as to why these things exist in so many different forms. Specifically, it will consider the argument that these things look the way they do because different cultural and social groups use them to construct and reproduce their identities.

Chapter 7

Different Types of Art and Design

Introduction

This chapter begins to explain how and why cultural products, such as works of art and design or visual culture, are produced in so many different forms or types. It is difficult to think of an area of visual culture that does not offer products in different forms. This proliferation of forms exists in fashion, furniture design, photography and graphic design, in addition to painting, car design and film. There are different types or forms, then, and there are different types within these types. This chapter will begin to explain these different types of cultural products as developing in time and in relation to different social classes or fractions of classes. This chapter will explain the different types of art and design as the product of different social classes and fractions of classes existing and evolving in time. Different social and cultural groups, at specific times and places, use these different types of art and design to construct and communicate their identities. These artefacts exist in different forms in order to construct and communicate different social and cultural identities, then. Part of the explanation of why these things look the way they do, therefore, is that different social and cultural groups use them to differentiate themselves from each other. So, part of the explanation of the appearance of visual culture is found in the existence of different and opposing social and cultural groups.

Types of art and design

That the Model T Ford of 1908 was available in any colour you liked, as long as it was black, has become a commonplace of popular design mythology. It does not mean, however, that it is not difficult for late-twentieth-century people to imagine a culture where any product would be available in only one colour or form. There are different types of cars, as there are different types of painting and film, for example. Cars are an especially good illustration of this phenomenon, offering different engines, trim levels, paint options and body shapes in the same model. Indeed, it is partly the result of Ford's work in the 1960s on the Mustang and the Capri, the first production cars for which it was possible to specify a factory-fitted combination of engine, trim level, paint colour and so on, that there are so many different versions of each model of car. Ruppert reports (1997) that the Capri was said to have been available in over 900 derivative forms and that its central appeal was aspirational: as one moved from status group to status group, there was always a bigger-engined, more luxurious and better-equipped model to trade up to. Thus began the process which is found in a mature form in the different versions of the Citroen ZX, charted below. In 1997, advertisements for Fiat cars (see Ill. 7.1) stressed the fact that their cars are available in many different versions, appealing to many different groups of people. The Fiat Bravo and Brava are, or is, supposed to be the same car available in two different versions. As the young man who reads aloud the captions appearing on the computer screen in the television ad points out, one is a three-door hatchback and one is a five-door fastback. The implication is that the car exists in many different forms, as a number of different objects, to these people.

Paintings may also be used to illustrate the phenomenon. Of course, there is not just one kind of painting: there are landscapes, portraits, still lifes and there are abstract and representational paintings. There are even different types within these types. There are Mannerist, arcadian, productive and idyllic landscapes, for example. Film also exists in many forms. One does not go to the cinema and see only westerns: there are science fiction, comedy, film noir and horror films as well. The names of these genres prepare the audience for the kinds of stories, characters and events they may expect to see. Again, within any one type of film, there are variations and the intermingling of genres. So, for example, *Blazing Saddles* and *City Slickers* are comedy westerns, *Little Big Man* and *The Wild Bunch* have been

Ill. 7.1   Fiat Bravo/Brava advertisement, 1997

proposed as more thoughtful westerns and it has been suggested that the *Star Wars* series is a sort of science fiction western. The names of these genres and sub-genres prepare audiences for the kinds of experiences they are likely to have while watching the films. They also segment and identify the audience for each of these different types of film: the audience for *johns* will be slightly different from the audience for *Midnight Cowboy*, for example, and completely different from the *Con Air* audience. Films, as many other cultural products, are aimed at consumers who are ranked by what Stuart Hall has called their 'lifestyle, taste and culture rather than by the Registrar General's categories of social class' (1988: 24).

The relation between social classes, lifestyle groups and types of art and design is not a static or monolithic one, however. It is not the case that a social or cultural group will always and forever use a particular type of furniture design or film genre to communicate an identity. There is a more complex and dynamic relationship operating here in which social groups will seek to emulate superior social groups, for example, forcing those superior groups to find something else to distinguish themselves with. Aspects of this process have been described by Thorstein Veblen (1992), Georg Simmel (1971), and Adrian Forty (1986). All three have described the ways in which the upper classes are forced continually to discard their fashionable fabrics and styles once the lower orders gain access to them. Veblen (1992: 70) describes the ways in which the lower classes desire the 'scheme of life' of the class above them. Simmel describes fashion as a 'merry game' in which the upper classes distinguish themselves from their social inferiors, only to find that those inferiors begin to wear the styles of the upper classes and that the latter must find something new with which to distinguish themselves (Simmel 1971: 299). And Forty describes the way in which plain cottons had to be returned to by the upper classes of the late eighteenth century because the lower classes had become able to afford the printed cottons that were once the preserve of the upper classes (Forty 1986: 74–6; see also Barnard 1996: 123–5). Different types of visual culture will be explained as some of the many and changing ways in which social classes constitute and reconstitute themselves as social classes, with distinct identities and values, distinct from and often in conflict with other social classes and fractions.

The following sections will consider theatre, fashion, painting, automotive design and interior design as offering different types or forms of visual culture. It might be thought that interior design and fashion design are inappropriate topics to be discussed here as they both appear to be areas where individuals quite obviously express themselves freely. It seems at first glance that these are areas where the look, or appearance, of an example of visual culture must be explained in terms of the individual creativity and personality of the person wearing or designing the item, not in terms of the existence of different social groups. Where, after all, is one freer to express one's unique individuality than in what one wears and in what one chooses to surround oneself with at home, on one's own property? This apparent, although genuinely experienced, freedom is mistaken, however, and may merely be testimony to the power of the ideology of free, creative and purchasing individuality that is fostered by modern capitalism. As Forty points out, 'the extent to which individualism in the home is an illusion is brought out by the similarity of the interior to other fashionable interiors of its date' (1986: 118). In this sense, individualism in fashion and clothing is also an illusion. How could it not be when every frock and every pair of jeans are produced in their hundreds, if not millions? While not wishing to suggest that people are simply the unwitting dupes of the market, passively purchasing anything and everything that the economy supplies them with, this chapter will maintain that the appearance of items of visual culture is best explained in terms of the tastes and values of different social groups. It will look at some examples of how variation in visual culture may be explained in terms of the social groups using that visual culture.

Theatre designs

In the previous chapter it was noted how Raymond Williams (1981: 132) uses the example of theatre to illustrate the idea of an external sign; the advertised times of performances and so on are there to indicate that what happens within the theatre is 'art', or 'culture', as opposed to 'real life'. In this section, the actual buildings that are theatres will be considered; their different appearance will be explained in terms of their relation to different social groups. There are, then, different types of theatre; there is the Roman amphitheatre, there is the classical and the neoclassical theatre, there is the Baroque theatre and there is the Shakespearian theatre. All of these types of theatre have things in common, but they all look completely different. What they have in common, of course, is that they must provide somewhere for the audience to sit or stand and watch the action and they must provide somewhere for that action to take place. They must also, as noted above, indicate that the experiences to be expected in the building are of a certain kind. Thus buildings that are theatres have spaces where the action takes place and spaces where the audience can see the action and they distinguish the activities going on inside them from the activities going on outside them. The different ways in which they provide these spaces, the different ways in which they solve the problems posed by such demands, however, are the product of the relation to different social groups and they vary in time and space.

In what is known as ancient Greece and Rome, theatres offered what to modern eyes may appear an egalitarian approach to theatre. To be more precise, despite being founded on slavery, both of these societies offered an egalitarian approach to the audience. The auditorium was an amphitheatre, constructed as a circle, or semicircle, with rows of seats built in steps. Each of these rows of steps offered the same access to the action as the others, and in this sense may be said to provide a symbol and a model of an egalitarian approach: no spectator was privileged by being accorded a better view or a clearer hearing of the action. In total contrast, the Baroque theatre of the seventeenth and eighteenth centuries segregated tiny sections of the audience in small and exclusive boxes. The stage was very deep, in order to accommodate the scenery. It was also enclosed, and the entire theatre was elaborately decorated. And the Shakespearian theatre of the late sixteenth and early seventeenth centuries is different again. In so-called 'cock-pit' theatres, like the Globe and the Swan, social class was suggested by where one sat or stood. The lower classes, the 'groundlings', were accommodated on the ground, in the pit, while the upper classes were housed in boxes or galleries. As Bamber Gascoigne explains (1968: 116–17), a penny would gain one access to the pit. A further penny would admit one to the top gallery and a third penny would admit one to the boxes of the first and second galleries. Aristocrats could pay even more, probably twelve pennies, to sit in the 'gentlemen's room'.

These different social groups' ideas about the nature of their societies, and their ideas about how they fitted into their societies, partly determine how their theatres look. The visual culture that is their theatres looks the way it does partly as a result of these social groups' beliefs and values. While conveniently forgetting the presence of slavery, the Romans profess a belief in egality by means of their amphitheatres. All men are equal and all men shall have an equally good seat at the theatre would be the slightly bathetic formulation of this situation. The theatre-going classes of the Baroque era had different ideas about how society should be organised and of their place within that society. They clearly believed in a rigid social hierarchy and that their place in that hierarchy should be clearly demarcated. In Shakespearian times, social hierarchy seems to have been no less important. The different social classes were accommodated at the theatre, however, in such a way that they could at least see each other, unlike the Baroque theatre where the boxes did not always afford a view of one's companions. One could see the lower orders, the groundlings, from the vantage point of one's box, high above them. It may be worth speculating that the modern habit of performing theatre 'in the round' encourages a more egalitarian viewpoint. Like the amphitheatre, as many people as possible have as good a seat as the next person.

Fashions: the suit

Fashion and clothing are probably the most obvious areas in which to find the same items or objects existing in different forms. Any garment that one cares to think of is available in a multitude of different styles, colours, cuts, textures and fabrics. Fashion and clothing are also probably the most obvious areas in which to find these garments being used to construct and communicate a cultural and social identity. These different styles, colours, cuts, textures and fabrics are used to construct and communicate those social and cultural identities and the appearance of the garments, therefore, may be explained by the existence of those different social and cultural groups. It may be that fashion and clothing are the most obvious places to look for evidence of these phenomena because they are, potentially at least, cheap enough for almost everyone to afford. Fashion and clothing, that is, offer media which are available or accessible to almost everyone; with the exception of the very poor, most people have some choice as to what they wear and in so far as they have choice, they can use fashion and clothing in these ways. The gentleman's lounge suit, developed during the nineteenth century from the older frock coat, is a good example of how a garment has been used in different forms by different cultural groups. Zoot suiters in the 1940s, Modernists and Teds in the 1950s, Mods in the 1960s, Skinheads in the 1970s, Yuppies in the 1980s and businessmen and politicians since the 1890s have all worn a form of the basic lounge or business suit. Ted Polhemus's book *Streetstyle* contains images of these various forms of the suit and accounts of the various subcultural groups who wore them. The following is indebted to Polhemus's account.

The Zooties, who were predominantly young African-Americans and Mexican-Americans, adapted the basic lounge suit by elongating the coat until it reached the knees, tightening the waist of the coat and widening the knees of the trousers to around thirty inches (see Ill. 7.2). The shoulders of the coat were also exaggerated, as were the lapels, and the coat was fastened by a single, central, button. Zoot suits were part of the way in which disaffected black American youth could construct a separate and positive identity for itself. Indeed, this identity was so positive that it attracted hostility from whites and there were so-called 'Zoot-suit riots' in Los Angeles, Philadelphia and New York in 1943. This type of suit, this version of the basic lounge suit, exists and looks the way it does because these people wanted to create and communicate a specific identity. The suit had to be different enough from the original lounge suit to avoid being mistaken for such a suit, but it may be worth speculating that the lounge suit was chosen as a basic model because, as Polhemus points out, the Zooties were using it to mark a symbolic socioeconomic ascent. They wanted to say that they were upwardly mobile, to use a phrase from much later.

Modernists, who were also predominantly black and American, adopted the suit in the late 1940s and 1950s. Polhemus suggests that the suit as it was adopted and adapted by the Modernists was the 'apex of the pendulum's swing away from the Zoot suit' (1994: 39). The coat was now relatively short, the shoulders were not emphasised, lapels were narrow and sometimes absent entirely and the trousers were cut narrow all the way down. The style was single-breasted and 'slimmer and trimmer' than the Zooties'. Where the Zooties' ties were loud, colourful and, above all, wide, the Modernists' ties were more restrained, thin and sharp, cut straight at the bottom. Many Modernists were jazz musicians and they embodied the spirit of cool, minimalist style. At around the same time, white British youth, the Teds, were wearing their own version of the basic lounge suit. The Edwardian-style drape was produced after the Second World War by the tailors of Savile Row in London. These coats were single-breasted, longer than the Modernists' coats but nowhere near as long as the Zooties'. They were slim fitting and often had velvet on the coat cuffs and the collar. Trousers, often called 'drainpipes', were worn narrow, as in the Modernist style, and ties were even narrower than the Modernists', reducing to the bootlace tie favoured by Hollywood cowboys. Polhemus suggests that the working-class youth took over these styles from the dominant classes and

Ill. 7.2   Zoot suit, Savoy Ballroom, New York, *c.*1938

made them their own (1994: 33–4). The drapes and drainpipes became largely working-class styles, then, adapted and worn by the first generation of British teenagers.

Mods were another British subcultural group although, as Polhemus points out, they were perhaps more lower-middle-class than working-class. They also had a version of the lounge suit with which to distinguish themselves and express their beliefs and values. The Mod suit showed Italian influences. Polhemus quotes Colin MacInnes's *Absolute Beginners* on the visual style of the Mod:

> college-boy smooth cropped hair with burned-in parting, neat white Italian, rounded collar shirt, short Roman jacket very tailored (two little vents, three buttons), no turn-up narrow trousers with seventeen inch bottoms absolute maximum, pointed-toe shoes, and a white mac lying folded by his side. (1994: 51)

As with the American Modernists, the style is narrow, cropped and short. Some Skinheads also adopted aspects of Modernist and Mod style, the ones who wore two-tone or tonic suits. Polhemus shows a picture of 'Beano', a London Skinhead, wearing a very tight suit. It is single-breasted and has narrow lapels; the trousers are unpleated and also tight. He wears a white button-down collar shirt without a tie and braces. From this description it is difficult to differentiate 'Beano' from many sober city-suited types, except that 'Beano' has no hair on his head. Indeed, as Polhemus points out, those Skinheads who wore this style also often wore Crombie overcoats and bowler hats, making them even more like 'city gents' (70). This version of Skinhead is presented by Polhemus as an attempt to get back to the harder, sharper, stripped-down basics of the original Mod style; the tight, sharp, two-tone suit was the way they went about it.

Paintings: genres

It was noted above that there are many different types, or genres, of paintings. There are landscapes, portraits, still lifes, and history paintings, for example, as well as abstract and representational paintings. It was also noted, in Chapter 4, that these were and are produced in response to the demands of the market and of segments of the market. It should not be forgotten, however, that painting is itself a form or type of artistic production. The autonomous 'free-standing' painting that hangs on walls is a very important part of visual culture. It may even be what most people think of when they see the words art or visual culture. However, it is itself a distinct type of production, distinct from fresco paintings, murals, sculptures and so on, and it too is produced in response to the demands of certain specific social groups at certain specific times and places.

The appearance of paintings as a distinct type or form of artistic production is the result of a number of intersecting developments in artistic production and society. Until the great capitalist commercial revolutions of the sixteenth and seventeenth centuries, the main patrons of art in western Europe had been the church and the aristocracy. Between them, the church and the aristocracy commissioned most of the buildings and most of the art works that went into them. As well as frescos, in the churches, and tapestries, in the palaces of the aristocracy, there were free-standing altarpieces and movable panels being produced. These free-standing altarpieces had first appeared in churches in the Middle Ages. The aristocracies of Europe had noticed them and had smaller portable versions produced for their own private devotions in their own private chapels. Wooden panels, which could be moved from room to room and from palace to palace, as well as tapestries, which were equally portable, had been used to decorate princely courts for many years. The aristocracy had also been in the habit of using portraits in the process of arranging marriages. In addition to these artistic forms, there were prints, which were printed and sold once enough money had been pledged to finance the run. There was, therefore, a market already in existence that was to provide a model for a market in paintings.

The final force in these developments was the new class structure that evolved in the course of the progression of capitalism across Europe in the sixteenth and seventeenth centuries. In addition to the church and the aristocracy, there were now merchants, people who made a living buying and selling goods. There were the other class fractions, those administering and managing the buying and selling of goods. The bourgeoisie, as this class became known, wanted art works, either to emulate the princes or to set themselves apart from those princes. There was a distinct social class, with a set of demands, and there were the artistic forms that were developing in such a way as to satisfy those demands. The autonomous painting grew out of these specific historical and social circumstances as a separate and distinct form of visual culture. A market evolved for these paintings. There was the bourgeoisie and there was the aristocracy; both social groups wanted to purchase and own paintings, including what were to become known as portraits and landscapes. And there were craft painters, producing the works themselves, developing the topics of these paintings into what are known as portraits, landscapes, narrative paintings and so on. Painters of the early capitalist period, such as Pieter Brueghel and Hans Holbein, produced the first paintings that were to be hung on the walls in the rooms of merchants' houses and in the galleries of princes' palaces. The autonomous painting was not exactly born, but grew out of these various social and artistic formations.

As noted in Chapter 4, the market for these paintings grew and matured all through the seventeenth and eighteenth centuries and the independent painting itself grew and matured in this context. Within this process, the separate and discrete types or forms of painting were also becoming more apparent. These discrete types or forms are usually called genres and they include portraits, animals, landscapes, still lifes, history paintings and (most confusingly) the everyday scenes known as 'genre' paintings. These genres were not confined to paintings. Prints were produced that could be called history prints and genre prints. Someone like Bernini, working in sculpture, produced works that could be called history sculpture, portrait sculpture and animal sculpture. Of course, these genres were not produced in a vacuum, painted or sculpted randomly and offered for sale. There were markets for them. The aristocracy formed the market for what might be called gallery history, portrait and landscape paintings. The new bourgeoisie were interested in the portrait, in both corporate and private or domestic form, and in landscape paintings. And the bourgeoisie formed the market for personal works, to be displayed in the study; history paintings were especially popular.

A painter who produced works falling into many of these categories is Rembrandt. During the seventeenth century, he painted in Mannerist, realist, naturalist, Baroque and romantic styles. He also produced landscapes, group and individual portraits and history paintings, as well as the self-portraits. And he painted for a variety of different social groups. He produced work for the Prince of Orange, for the Dutch bourgeoisie and for the trade guilds of the time. It is suggested that the way to understand the appearance of these works is as a response to these social groups who are the market for the works. Rembrandt produced works for the aristocracy; he produced history paintings, portraits and landscapes, for example, to go in the galleries of princes, to be admired by other, visiting, aristocrats. He produced life-size public group portraits of the great and the good of the time to hang in the guild-halls of commercial guilds. He produced paintings that were to hang in the homes of the bourgeoisie; these were private domestic portraits of wealthy patrons. And he produced pictures for the private studies of merchants and other members of the bourgeoisie: these were often histories and became known as study histories.

Each of these different types of painting will take on a different appearance; the way the works look may be explained by looking at whom the works were produced for. This is because each of the social groups will represent a slightly different motivation for the picture. The princes will want their land to be admired and perhaps envied, the commercial guilds will want their members to be honoured and dignified and the private individual will want his family to be commemorated, for example. All these different demands and motivations, from these different classes and fractions of classes, will affect the way the finished painting looks. One of Rembrandt's most well-known paintings, *The Night Watch* (see Ill. 7.3), for example, was commissioned by a group of militiamen and completed in 1642. Each of these men paid a subscription towards the picture and each of them is portrayed in the picture. Those who paid more, like the captain, Frans Banning Cocq, were given a more prominent position in the picture than those who paid less. Thus, the picture looks the way it does because it has to accurately portray individual people and because it has to organise those people according to how much they had contributed towards the production of the picture.

Within even one of these genres, different types may be recognised. There are, for example, different types of landscape. In the sixteenth century, Pieter Brueghel and the other Mannerists produced what are known as 'world landscapes'. These contain a wealth of meticulously observed and presented detail and vast panoramas of space, and are crammed with all kinds of thing going on. Brueghel's *Hunters in the Snow* is an example of such a work (see Ill. 7.4). The entire scene, from foreground to horizon, is in sharp focus; a man fights a chimney fire, birds wheel in the empty, freezing air and human life is carried out in the bowl of the encircling hills. Landscapes such as these were produced for the walls of princes and the bourgeoisie. In the seventeenth century, Nicolas Poussin, Claude Lorrain and the other 'arcadians', like the eighteenth-century Englishman Richard Wilson, portrayed the landscape as a gentle, nostalgic and fruitful place. This was a place where man, usually in the form of a few Italianised peasants and shepherds, was in harmony with nature. These works

Ill. 7.3   Rembrandt, *The Night Watch*, 1642, Rijksmuseum, Amsterdam

were especially sought after by the English aristocracy, showing as
they did essentially humble and peaceful peasants. A change in the
perception of nature and the landscape had taken place in the
eighteenth century; with a more scientific and proprietorial attitude
to the land came a more 'businesslike' approach to landscape painting. The later landscapes of Thomas Gainsborough and many of the
animal paintings of George Stubbs show the land and the animals to
be productive, to be a capital resource that is to be tended and
profited from. These works were commissioned by the landowners
themselves: they wanted a record of their lands and of the excellence
of their animals.

   The relation between the market and the appearance of these
paintings is probably best shown in the two versions of Gainsborough's *The Harvest Wagon*. As John Barrell explains (1980: 59–70),
the first version, painted in 1767, shows a group of peasants, men and

Ill. 7.4   Brueghel, *Hunters in the Snow*, 1565, Kunsthistoriches Museum, Vienna

women, being taken to the feast that celebrates the end of the harvest. Here they will be plied with beer and encouraged to accept a contract of work for the next year. Two of the male workers are standing up in the wagon, fighting over a flagon of what could be cider while a third drags a woman roughly up into the wagon. The two other women are, as Barrell says, 'attractive, and attractively dressed' (60). The last worker is at the head of the lead horse, trying to bring it under control as it rears up and away from him. The second version was painted in 1784–5 and it also shows a group of peasants on their way to the feast to celebrate the harvest. This time, however, the two men fighting over the flagon are entirely absent. The two women in the wagon are now three women and two of them have babies with them. The woman being dragged up into the wagon is now being gently helped into the wagon. And the horses wait patiently until it is time to move on. These two paintings are significantly different and it is claimed that it is the market that has influenced the look of the second version. As Barrell notes, the first version remained unsold, Gainsborough eventually exchanging it for a horse (62), while the second version was snapped up by the Prince of Wales (70).

The point to be made is that the people who would have been in a position to have purchased the first version of Gainsborough's painting, landowners, farmers and so on, would not have been keen on the view of those working on the lands as drunken, wenching oiks who cannot keep the horses under control. Drunken, wenching oiks who cannot control the horses are not the sorts that landowners want working on their lands. Nor are drunkenness and wenching the sorts of activities that landowners want to see associated with the rural poor. Landowners are much more interested in seeing sober, responsible and family-centred characters, as found in the second version of *The Harvest Wagon*. These are the sorts of people they would like to have working on their lands and, to the landowning classes, sobriety and responsibility represent the values that should ideally be found among the rural poor. The content of the second painting, then, along with the ease with which it was sold, is directly explicable in terms of the interests of the potential market for the paintings. Not only is the type of art a product of the interests of different social groups but the portrayal of social groups in these paintings, the content of the works, is also directly connected to the interests of those social groups.

Cars: the Citroën ZX

It is possible, and increasingly plausible, to suspect that most people do not buy cars on the basis of what the car will 'say' about them. It is possible that many, if not most, people drive the car they do because their mother has given it to them, because their brother has sold it to them or because they could not afford to buy, run or insure anything else. There are those, then, for whom the inner circle of hell is a diesel-engined Peugeot 309 and there are those who could not tell a VR6 (a Volkswagen from the 1990s) from a TR6 (a Triumph from the 1970s). However, car manufacturers persist in producing different models, in different shapes, with different types and sizes of engine, with different levels of trim and accessories and in all different colours. Where there is choice and a complex social structure, there is meaning. This section will explain the appearance of different types of cars in terms of such a complex social structure. It will be argued that these cars look the ways they do as a result of there being different cultural or lifestyle groups.

In 1991, Citroën introduced the ZX to their range of cars. It was available in four forms, the 'Reflex', the 'Volcane', the 'Aura' and the 'Avantage'. The brochure produced to promote these cars illustrates rather clearly the different social types each car is aimed at. At least, it associates some different social types very strongly with each of the forms. The Reflex is advertised as 'tough, good looking and street-

Ill. 7.5   Citroën advertising, 1991

wise'; it is a car 'whose looks and panache turn heads in a crowd'. There is a picture of a single, very attractive woman with long dark hair alongside the pictures of the Reflex. A laughing young man with short hair wearing a bomber jacket and pleated trousers and using a mobile telephone is shown leaning nonchalantly on the Volcane. The Volcane is 'fiery, dynamic, assertive, stylish'; it offers 'high performance' and a 'red-blooded character'. 'Desirable property, luxury interior' are the words introducing the Aura; it offers 'pure, unspoiled elegance' and will 'spoil you with refinements'. This is the 'luxurious' and 'comfortable' model enjoyed by the expensively dressed young couple pouting moodily out at the reader. Finally, the Avantage cannot decide whether it is a 'first class cabin' or a 'luggage compartment', so 'spacious and versatile' is it. This 'flexibility . . . and economy' are no doubt much appreciated by the motherly woman with her two young daughters shown opening the hatchback.

A lot of work has gone into distinguishing these subgroups of the middle classes. What is more, the specifications and materials of the cars have been fine-tuned to pick up the slightest differences between these groups. And the cars therefore look slightly different according to which segment of the middle classes they are aimed at. These sorts of differences between social groups will be explained in more detail in terms of Max Weber's idea of 'status groups' (Weber 1978: 302–7) in the next chapter. However, it should be pointed out here that the idea of a status group enables the ways in which members of the same economic class make different choices in matters of consumption to be explained. It may be suggested that, in the brochure, members of the same economic class, the middle class, are shown divided into members of different status groups. Despite their being members of the same economic class, they are members of different status groups and members of these different status groups make slightly different choices as to what they consume. Citroën may therefore be thought of as producing different versions of the ZX, with different specifications and trim, in order to cater for these different status groups.

The Reflex, for example, has body-coloured bumpers while the Avantage does not, and the Aura has bumpers with chrome highlights. The Volcane has a three-spoke sports steering wheel and halogen fog lights set into the front spoiler, which none of the other models have. The Reflex has colour-coordinated piping on the dashboard and around the seats, which none of the other models have. These differences in appearance, which may often be minor differences, are partly to be explained as the product of the different status groups the models are aimed at.

These different status groups are interested in different things; they want different things from their cars, just as the Mods and the Zooties wanted different things from their suits. These different models are supposed to construct a different identity for each of these social groups. The Volcane is supposed to be the 'hot hatch' of the range. That is why it has the leather-trimmed, three-spoke sports steering wheel and why the young man with the mobile phone is pictured with it. The Avantage is the 'family runabout'. That is why the woman with her children is shown and why the car has a rear seat that moves forward to create more luggage space and back to create more leg-room for passengers. The Reflex is the car for the fun-loving younger set, represented by the young woman with beautiful hair. That is why it has the bright, if 'colour-coordinated', piping all over the seats. And the Aura is the more mature, sedate model. That is why it has the central armrest for rear passengers and the 'deep Omega velour' seats and why the sober but expensive couple are shown in front of it.

Interior designs: the parlour

In the late 1980s and early 1990s, the *Observer* newspaper ran a feature called 'Room of my own'. In this feature, prominent arts and media people were photographed in a room in their home that they were particularly fond of and interviewed about it. They would explain the furnishings, the pictures, the knick-knacks and memen-toes, the style and the contents of the room, for example. More often than not, the room the people featured chose was what has been called, at various times and places, the drawing-room, the parlour, the living-room, the sitting-room, the front room or the lounge. Almost nobody chose the bathroom, the kitchen or the bedroom. The first point to be made here is that, even before the type of room and its contents are considered, the name that is given to this room differs according to what class or status group the person doing the naming is a member of. Expectations as to what this room will contain and to the sorts of behaviour appropriate in it will thus also differ according to the social, or economic, class of the person doing the naming. The 'parlour', for example, dates from Victorian times and was a parti-cular middle-class phenomenon. The 'drawing-room' derives from the aristocratic 'withdrawing room', while the 'front room' refers to working-class two-up, two-down type housing, and the 'lounge' denotes a more modern, middle-class room, deriving from commercial and American contexts, where it meant a social room set aside for conversation and entertainment in a hotel or public house or on a train, for example.

The room chosen by the majority of the people interviewed for 'Room of my own' was the room that derives from the middle-class Victorian parlour. As Penny Sparke points out, the Victorian parlour was a room that existed primarily for the purposes of display (1995: 46). She quotes Gwendolyn Wright, who says that the parlour was where 'the housewife would show off the family's best possessions, strive to impress guests and teach her children about universal principles of beauty and refinement' (47). The furniture that was to be found in the Victorian parlour was itself often created with the express purpose of display. It was on display and it was used to display other manufactured items. Pieces of furniture like the chiffonier, the whatnot and the mantelpiece, and numerous cabinets and plant-stands were produced. These were often highly decorative themselves and they were intended to make the family's possessions look their best. The possessions that could be put on display multiplied. Various ornaments, jugs, jars, candlesticks, of glass, papier mâché, porcelain, metal and so on, were manufactured. The things that could legitimately go on walls also increased: clocks, cross-stitch samplers, wall-lamps and candles, mirrors, plates and pictures, including photographs, prints and paintings, were all hung on walls. The appearance of the room was a product of the Victorian middle class's desire for impressive and improving display.

And it cannot be denied for very long that the arts and media types appearing in 'Room of my own' were out to display. They were also out to impress and, where they had children, to impart their universal principles. Chosen almost at random is Peggy Prendeville, an interior designer and illustrator who appears in the edition for 5 April 1992. Despite what are described as 'minimalist preferences', exemplified in white walls and blond wood flooring, for example, and despite saying that she would 'prefer an interior with not a lot in it, with fewer objects rather than many', her room obeys many of these Victorian rules. There are still a lot of things on display: there are sculptures, paintings, a grand piano, a 'branch of contorted willow' and a collection of ceramics, for example. Moreover, unless the names of the people who made many of the items on display are included in the article for educational purposes, it is difficult to avoid the conclusion that they are meant to impress. And, unless little Isolde walks around with her eyes firmly shut, she will inevitably learn her mother's principles of good taste.

Having said that, it must also be admitted that Prendeville's room is indeed much more minimalist than many others in the series. In many of the rooms featured, there was hardly a surface that was not invisible because of the clutter on it. Some walls were similarly covered with pictures and so on. Jeremy James's room, for example, which appears in the 20 October 1991 edition, creates a much more 'cosy', 'cluttered' or 'claustrophobic' atmosphere, according to your tastes. Almost every flat surface has a pattern on it, the mantelpiece is covered with bric-à-brac and pictures adorn the walls. These differences might also be partly explained in terms of the difference between class groups and status groups, as noted above. These differences will be dealt with in more detail in the following chapter, but they may be introduced here as beginning to explain the differences and the similarities between these people's rooms. While they are all members of the same economic class, all members of the middle classes, these people are also members of different status groups. While both these rooms, indeed all the rooms that appeared in the series, were all obeying the basic Victorian rules for the 'parlour', 'living-room' or whatever it may be called, they are all slightly different in what they choose to display and the ways in which they choose to display it.

Forty shows how the parlour did not stand still, preserving forever the tastes and styles of the Victorian middle classes, but evolved, as different factions of that middle class evolved and developed their own views on interior decoration and design in distinction from other factions. The so-called 'art-furnishing' movement of the turn of the century clearly shows this process. It had been the custom, until the late nineteenth century, for domestic furnishing to be undertaken by a single firm of upholsterers; one firm would undertake to furnish an entire house. Forty reports that, at the end of the nineteenth century, a section of the middle classes objected to the fact that these firms did not produce furniture that 'met the moral and aesthetic standards of beauty they expected in their homes' (1986: 111). It was the middle-class intelligentsia that created the demand for what became known as 'art-furnishing'. This type of interior replaced heavy upholstered furniture with wooden-framed chairs and settees with loose cushions. Dark colours and gilding were abandoned in favour of lighter colours and woodwork was painted white. The moral standards were provided by eschewing furniture that disguised 'the way it was made'; as Forty has it, 'shams and deceits were forbidden' as dishonest (ibid.).

The two illustrations which Forty uses to illustrate art-furnishing are instructive here. An early version of this style from 1890 is, to the relatively untutored eye, virtually indistinguishable from the classic Victorian interior, full of dark wood, heavy fabrics and carpets. Apart from the white-painted wood, there is not much in this interior to distinguish it from the Victorian interior. A slightly later version from 1907, however, looks completely different from the characteristic Victorian style. There is less furniture and less patterning in the carpets and upholstery. Where there is patterning, as Forty says, it shares a white ground and creates an air of harmony (1986: 112–13). Again, the point to be made is that the rooms look the way they do because different social groups are using them to communicate different beliefs and values. This may also be seen in the differences between the two interiors chosen from the 'Room of my own' series. The two interiors look quite different and the differences may be explained by referring to the different status groups that the inhabitants belong to. Prendeville's room is full of pieces of art; it is, moreover, full of pieces of art created by people she knows and who are her friends. James's room is full of mass-produced things; it is full of things that are of local importance. The difference in status group may be used to explain the different appearances that these rooms take on. The rooms may also be explained in terms of their relation to the middle-class Victorian parlour.

Indeed, the room that goes by all these different names is developed from this social room. It is a type of room that is different from other rooms and it is in turn subdivided into different types, according to which social group is defining it. As free-standing paintings developed from other art forms, this form of room develops from earlier, preexisting rooms and as paintings developed into different types of paintings, this room then goes on to take various forms, differing in appearance according to which social or cultural group is using it. Thus the 'living-room' or 'parlour', or whatever, is distinct from other kinds of rooms in both public and private buildings. In terms of function, this room is distinct from reception rooms, halls and lobbies, for example, in both public and private buildings.

Conclusion

This chapter has argued that the existence and appearance of the different types of items of visual culture may be partly explained in terms of different classes and fractions of classes using those different types to create and communicate their specific cultural identities. The Zoot suit, for example, has thirty-inch wide knees because this is considered cool and smart by the people wearing them. The Citroën Volcane has a leather-trimmed steering wheel because leather is considered sporty. It is considered to be more sporty than plastic or rubber, or any of the other materials that could have been chosen, by the young men buying and driving it. And the middle-class living-room looks the way it does partly because the middle classes, like their Victorian forebears, want to display their possessions and impress their neighbours.

Now, reference was made above to Forty's claim concerning 'the extent to which individualism in the home is an illusion' (1986: 118). It was also suggested that, in this sense, individualism in fashion and clothing is also an illusion. The fact that every frock and every pair of jeans are produced in their hundreds, if not millions, was proposed as evidence of this. The problem arises as to how to avoid the suggestion that people are simply the suggestive dupes of the market, passively purchasing anything and everything that the economy supplies them with. Weber's idea of the status group was introduced to begin the explanation of how members of the same economic class make different choices in matters of consumption. However, the question as to whether these people are nevertheless the receptive pawns of the market, with no say in what is produced, has not been dealt with in any detail. The matter of how production, consumption, classes and status groups relate to the social structure has also only been hinted at in this chapter. The next chapter, then, must explicitly address these questions concerning production, as well as those concerning active and passive consumption and it must explain how production and consumption relate to the social structure. That is, do production and consumption merely reproduce the social structure, reproducing positions of inequality and exploitation, or can they criticise or resist that social structure, and provide an alternative? These are the topics of Chapter 8.

Chapter 8

Visual Culture and the Social Process

Introduction

This chapter will begin to unify, or draw together, the assorted and differing concerns of previous chapters by accounting for the place of visual culture within society, by looking at the contribution that it makes to society. It will consider the role of visual culture by looking at the relationship between visual culture and society. The relationship between visual culture and society may also be described as the function or purpose that visual culture fulfils within society as a whole. The chapter will argue that the role of visual culture is to produce and reproduce the social order. It will argue that visual culture is also a means of critiquing, or challenging, the social order.

In Chapter 2, it was noted that Janet Wolff refers to the many books that purport to be about 'art and society' but which conceive of society only as a 'kind of painted backdrop, referred to only as a tableau of social groups and their practices, which are said to inform the works' of art (Wolff 1992b: 706). These kinds of approaches are obliged to present art and design, visual culture, as ahistorical (as not existing and changing in history) and as universal (as everywhere the same kinds of activities). This chapter must investigate visual culture, not merely as a backdrop, then, but as being effective within society. It will argue that the role of visual culture is to produce, maintain and

166

transform the institutions, practices, media, objects and social classes analysed in previous chapters. This is effectively to argue that visual culture has a major role in the production, maintenance and transformation of society. That is quite a claim: society would not exist and continue to exist in the ways it does were it not for visual culture.

Visual culture's role in the production, maintenance and transformation of society will be investigated from two different perspectives. The first perspective is that of production and the second is that of consumption. It should be pointed out that the traditional sociological term for the processes in which society's continued existence is ensured is 'reproduction' and it is also common to refer to the production of society, as here. The production and reproduction of society, then, refer to the process known as hegemony (see Hall and Jefferson 1976: 39ff.), the way in which people's assent to the formation and legitimation of a social order is assured. These terms should not be confused with the term 'production' as it is used to denote one of the two perspectives from which the role of visual culture will be examined, that which is distinct from consumption. Of course, the social order or the structure of a society is not only produced and reproduced. The social order may also be challenged and attempts may be made to transform society. Many people have decided that the social order is unjust and unequal and they have tried to make it more just by contesting the positions of dominant and subordinate social groups.

The social order

Marxism

While there are many different versions or conceptions of Marxism, all agree that society as we are familiar with it is class-based. Marx and Engels propose that 'the history of all hitherto existing society is the history of class struggles' (Marx and Engels 1992: 3). They also agree that class is the product of economic conditions. Marx and Engels say that

> Insofar as millions of families live under economic conditions of existence that separate their mode of life, their interests and their culture from those of the other classes, and put them in hostile opposition to the latter, they form a class. (1968: 170–1)

This quotation may be taken as arguing that on*e*
product of one's economic conditions; it should *a*
'mode of life', 'interests' and 'culture' are als*o,*
explicitly considered to be a product of those eco*n*
What is meant here by 'economic conditions' is *w*
Marxism the 'means of production': social class is de*fi*
a relation to the means of production.

The means (or forces) of production are things like *th*
the knowledge and the machinery involved in the produc*t*
necessary for survival. In capitalist societies, then, *th*
production are the factories, machinery, tools, techno*l*
knowledge involved in the production of food, clothing a*n*
Consequently, if class position is defined in terms of a relati*c*
means of production, then one's class will differ according to *v*
one owns the means of production or whether one merely wor*k*
or in those means of production. The factory-owners, who *bu,*
own factories, plant, tools and technological expertise, will ther*e*
be of a different social class from those who work in factories, *u.*
plant, tools and so on. In this simplified Marxist schema, the ow*n*
of the means of production are capitalists, the bourgeoisie; and *th*
people who work in the factories are the workers, the proletaria*t.*

This ownership, this control, of the means of production has tw*o*
significant consequences. The first is that the class that owns an*d*
controls the means of production has more power than the class that
does not own it: economic control leads directly to political control.
So the class that owns the means of production may be thought of as
the dominant and superior class, while the class that does not own the
means of production may be thought of as the subordinate and
subservient class. There is a basic political and economic inequality
in the social order that results from the ownership of the means of
production.

The second consequence is that the class that controls the means of
economic production also controls what Marx and Engels call 'mental
production'. 'The ideas of the ruling class are in every epoch the
ruling ideas . . . The class which has the means of material production
at its disposal, has control at the same time over the means of mental
production' (Marx and Engels 1970: 64). The economically and
politically dominant class is also dominant in so far as its ideas are
dominant. The ideology of the dominant class, known by some
Marxists as the dominant ideology, is part of the way in which the
assent of the subordinate classes to the contradictions and inequalities

of the social order is assured. The dominant ideology says that it is right and proper that there is inequality in society and that it is right and proper that power and wealth are in the hands of one class (the bourgeoisie) rather than another class (the proletariat).

On such a view, culture is part of ideology and ideology, on this account, also reflects class positions. As there are different classes, each the result of a different relation to the means of production, so there will be different cultures and ideologies, and these will also be the result of a different relation to the means of production. The ideas, beliefs and values of the proletariat (its culture and ideology) will necessarily be different from and opposed to those of the bourgeoisie. This is because these different classes have different interests in the means of production. The owners of the means of production have an interest in the working classes continuing to work in the factories in that they make profit from the workers' labour. The workers, however, do not have an interest in the owners of factories making a profit from them; their interest is in profiting from their own labour. Where the interests conflict, leading to contradiction, so the ideologies conflict. The dominant ideology is the set of ideas and beliefs, belonging to the dominant group, which resolve those conflicting, or contradictory, interests. This is part of the meaning of Marx's suggestion that the history of society is the history of class conflict. On such a view, then, visual culture is a part of ideology and a part of the way in which class inequalities are either reproduced or contested.

Max Weber

Weber's account of class and capitalist society is slightly different to that found in Marxist accounts. It is not to be thought of as a replacement to those accounts, however: both Giddens and Bocock, for example, are agreed that Weber's accounts may be thought of as complementary to those of Marxism. Giddens (1980: 42) points out that he provides what is missing in Marx's account of class and Bocock (1993: 39) suggests that Weber provides a refinement of Marx's account. At its simplest, the refinement consists in two proposals. The first is that capitalist, class-based society cannot be understood only as the product of economic relations or conditions; a simple or 'vulgar' Marxist account of class needs to be supplemented by an account of status. The second is that the culture of capitalist societies cannot be understood only as a necessary reflection or product of economic conditions.

Weber's most well-known contribution to the theory of society is his distinction between 'class' and 'status group'. Indeed, class is a very complicated notion in Weber's work. Essentially, however, 'the factor which creates "class" is unambiguously economic interest' (Weber 1948: 183). In this sense, class for Weber has much in common with the Marxist formulation noted above; for both, class is a product of economic, or market, situation. Class is a product of a relation to the means of production. There are two definitions of class in Weber's work. He writes of the 'property classes' and the 'commercial classes'. The property classes consist of rentiers and entrepreneurs while the commercial classes consist of those who sell their services in the market. As Weber says, ' "class situation" is, in this sense, ultimately "market situation" ' (1948: 182).

In contrast to classes, however, 'status groups are normally communities' (1948: 186). The idea that status groups are communities introduces the idea that the members of such groups are normally aware of their common status. This cannot always be said of the members of class groups, who are usually unaware of their relation to the market, or to the means of production. What status groups have in common, what makes a status group, is a recognition of a shared level of 'social esteem' (Weber 1978: 305–6) or social 'honour' (Weber 1948: 187). Status groups also share what Weber calls a 'style of life' (1978: 305–6; 1948: 187). Now, where status may rest on economic class, it is not necessarily or solely determined by it (1948: 306). It may be that people have different economic class positions and yet share the same position in terms of status; 'the class position of an officer, a civil servant or a student may vary greatly according to their wealth and yet not lead to a different status since upbringing and education create a common style of life' (ibid.).

For both Marxism and Weber class is to do with the unequal distribution of economic power. For Weber, however, status is to do with the unequal distribution of social esteem or honour. For Weber, economic or market position is not sufficient to explain political power in capitalist society and the notion of status groups must supplement such an explanation. It is the differences in lifestyle, differences in consumption, for example, that are given different amounts or degrees of social honour, or held at different levels of social esteem by status groups.

Another difference, or refinement, concerns the distinction between production and consumption. Marxist accounts tend to stress the determining role of production in accounts of society. As Giddens points out, 'modes of consumption, according to Marx, are primarily determined by relations of production' (1980: 28). Weber enables a sharp distinction between production and consumption to be made. For Weber, 'the contrast between classes and status groups is . . . also one between production and consumption' (Giddens 1980: 43). For Marxism, the characteristic consumption of a class is determined and explained by the relation to the means of production. For Weber, however, consumption is related to and explained by the status group one is a member of.

On Weber's account, then, culture and ideology cannot simply be a reflection of economic conditions. The consumption of visual culture is related to status groups, not a simple reflection of economic class, on Weber's account. This enables a Weberian account to differentiate between members of the same class who pursue different cultural interests. Cultural consumption is not necessarily a product or a reflection of economic class but can be explained in terms of the membership of a status group. Status groups can divide class groups and can exist between or cut across different class groups. In the previous chapter, for example, members of the same economic class were seen to make different choices in the ways they displayed their ornaments in their 'living-rooms'. Members of the middle class were also seen to choose different models of the same car. These differences could be partly explained in terms of the different status groups these people were members of, despite them being members of the same economic class.

The next section will consider the production of visual culture as either challenging, reproducing or attempting to remain neutral with regard to the social order. It will look at the ways in which the production of visual culture has affected the identity and status of groups in society. The section after that will consider the consumption of visual culture as either reproducing or challenging the social order. It will look at some ways in which consumption has affected the identity and status of groups in society.

Cultural producers

Having explained the social order in terms of class and status groups, this section will look at the maintenance and transformation of the social order from the perspective of the producers of visual culture. It will examine cultural producers, artists and designers, who have

conceived of their work as contributing to the critique or transformation of the social order, as well as those who have conceived of their
work as being neutral with regard to the social order. And it will
consider the ways in which visual culture contributes, wittingly or
otherwise, to the reproduction of the social order. It should be
pointed out that producers are often not necessarily wholly either
reproducing or critiquing the social order. It may be the case that
parts of their work are critical while parts are simply reproductive
and uncritical. The Situationist International, for example, discussed
in Chapter 3, may be seen as exemplifying this fact. They were critical
of society in that they took the images and motifs of contemporary
society and showed them to be the products of capitalist and
bourgeois ideology. But, in that they lacked any theory or account
of the position of women, and thus had little understanding of the
effects of pornography, for example, they may be said to have simply
reproduced the gender relations prevalent in society. Groups and
movements, as well as individual producers, then, will have both
critical and reproductive elements. The ways in which fashion
designers and musicians produced the challenge to the social order
that was punk in the 1970s have been studied elsewhere (see Hebdige
1979 and Barnard 1996, for example), and will only be briefly
mentioned here.

Instead, William Hogarth and Barbara Kruger will be proposed as
instances of producers of visual culture that is intended to challenge
and contest existing class identities. Designers and design theorists
such as William Morris and Victor Papanek, for example, will be used
to explore the ways in which designers may challenge the existing
social order. The Bauhaus and Habitat will be proposed as examples
of visual culture that may be seen as attempts to be neutral regarding
the social order. They will be criticised, however, as providing
another outlet for the dominant groups' tastes and values and thus
being not at all neutral. And Thomas Gainsborough's painting *Mr
and Mrs Andrews* will be proposed as an instance of a piece of visual
culture that is explicitly reproducing the existing inequalities of the
social order. This painting may also usefully be compared with the
view of marriage proposed in Hogarth's work.

Challenging the social order

The first example of visual culture that is intended to challenge or
contest the existing social order is Hogarth's set of prints entitled

Marriage à la mode, produced in 1745. In these prints, the dominant ideology, the beliefs and practices of the English aristocracy, is being opposed by the ideology of the new, and increasingly powerful, bourgeoisie. In particular, the aristocracy's beliefs and practices concerning the institution of marriage are being challenged and contested. Around this time, aristocrats married for two main reasons. The first was to increase the amount of wealth possessed by the family; this would take the form of land, possessions or cash, for example. And the second was to increase the social status, or prestige, of the family; minor aristocratic families would, clearly, be keen to marry into more prestigious families. Aristocratic marriage at this time, then, was a specific institution, organised for specific purposes and defined by particular and class-specific beliefs and practices.

The bourgeoisie had a different set of beliefs and practices that defined marriage for them. They considered the aristocratic version of marriage to be both immoral and decadent. The basis of their ideological differences was their attitude to social status, wealth and money. The bourgeoisie, not surprisingly, believed that money and social status should be achieved through the efforts and hard work of individuals. It is not surprising because the bourgeoisie generally earned their living through the hard work of individuals; in capitalism, it is private enterprise that is rewarded and the bourgeoisie were the rising class of the developing capitalist economic systems of the eighteenth century. Consequently, they were opposed to the idea that social status, wealth and money should be gained simply by marriage. In *Marriage à la mode*, then, Hogarth is illustrating, and to that extent supporting, the opposition of the bourgeoisie to the aristocratic practice of marriage.

One of the images in the series shows the bargaining and dealing that took place before an aristocratic marriage contract could be signed. Hogarth wants to portray these people as greedy and stupid decadents, misguidedly and immorally defiling the institution of marriage. The picture shows the couple to be married and it shows the fathers of the couple. The couple to be married are hardly love's young dream, as Hogarth intends. Viscount Squanderfield is utterly indifferent to the endearing young charms of his bride-to-be, and prefers to study his own charms in a mirror. His prospective bride looks bored and miserable and one would be forgiven for thinking that it is not the happiest day of her life. The fathers are hardly any more attractive or sympathetic characters. His father, Lord Squander, is attempting to increase the stakes by holding up a picture of the family tree, as if his son was a horse at market. The idea is to stress what good and noble stock the boy is from and the father is apparently unaware that good and noble stock probably would not behave in such a way. Her father is also behaving badly, or at least vulgarly. He is being so coarse as to offer cash. Hogarth is suggesting that they are an unattractive bunch of people with an ideology to match.

The aristocratic ideology is being challenged from the position of the bourgeoisie; the series of prints is pointing out that this view of marriage is not natural or proper, it is a creation of a specific class at a specific time and place and may be contested by another class's view of marriage. In so far as this is happening, the social order is being contested; the dominance of the dominant group's ideology is being challenged by being shown as corrupt. The series of prints, then, contributes to the transformation of society, rather than to the reproduction of society. These prints encourage a way of thinking about marriage that is different from and opposed to the dominant ways proposed by the aristocracy and thus form a challenge to the existing social order.

The history of fine art and graphic design contains many examples of visual culture being used to challenge and contest the ideas and beliefs of dominant classes. Many works from the revolutionary periods of countries like France, the Soviet Union and America, for example, are obviously trying to change the social order. In post-revolutionary Russia, Alexander Rodchenko, El Lissitzsky and Kasimir Malevich all produced work, advertisements, political posters and typography, intended to help the forces of the Revolution. Vladimir Tatlin moved away from making sculpture and began designing clothes for the workers of the new Soviet Union; he also designed efficient stoves to keep the workers warm. Malevich was also active in the realm of fabric design. As Charlotte Douglas points out, weeks after the Bolshevik Revolution of 1917, along with Alexandra Exter, Olga Rosanova and Liubov Popova, he exhibited 'ornamented hand-bags, belts, collars, pillows and lengths of ornamented fabric' (Douglas 1995: 42). She says that 'under new slogans of revolution, internationalism and classlessness, Suprematist and Constructivist design continued until the late 1920s when geometric design . . . became politically suspect' (1995: 45). Emily Braun documents the way in which the Italian Futurists even produced manifestos for clothing and fashion. Giacomo Balla, for example, published the manifesto *The Anti-Neutral Suit* in 1914, which was essentially an attack on bourgeois 'good taste' and 'niceness', with its 'stripes, checks and diplomatic little dots' (Balla, quoted in Braun 1995: 39). As Braun says, 'the purpose of Futurist dress was to act upon the environment, to stun, to upset, to annoy and ultimately to liberate bourgeois society from its stuffy sartorial and social conventions' (1995: 35). Here, then graphic design, clothing design, textile design and industrial design are all used in a variety of attempts to change the social order.

The works of Barbara Kruger are also contesting dominant ideologies. They are contesting different ideologies in that, instead of those ideologies being class-based, they are based upon sex and gender. This immediately raises questions that cannot be dealt with in detail here. One question would be 'Are women an economic class?' Another would be 'Is capitalism sexist or does it affect everyone's life?' These are questions concerning the relation between sex, gender and class; they raise problems concerning the priority to be given class and sex and gender. For example, if inequalities of class are dealt with, will the inequalities of sex and gender also be dealt with or are there special and different difficulties involved with sex and gender? Whatever the answers to these questions, Kruger's work contests dominant ideologies; it proposes ways of thinking about sex and gender that are not the ways of the dominant ideologies of sex and gender. For what it is worth, Kruger considers her work to be about class. She believes that any challenge or critique of patriarchy (which is about the ways in which a gender dominates a social structure) is also going to be a challenge or critique of class (Roberts 1992: 113). In so far as her work does do this, it represents a challenge to those dominant ideologies and attempts to transform the social order. It attempts to change the ways in which the different sexes and genders relate to one another in a class-based society.

In the work entitled *Your fictions become history*, for example, Kruger is drawing attention to the ways in which, in a male-dominated society, males' ideas (fictions) concerning femininity become part of the dominant ideology and believed as if they were absolutely true (history). Because, generally, men are in positions of power in image-based industries like television, film, graphics and so on, because they are in positions of power concerning techniques of representation and the media, the ideas and beliefs about what women and femininity are are promulgated and believed as if they were fact. Kruger is drawing attention to this process and to that extent preventing it from working effectively. Similarly, in her work entitled *Your gaze hits the side of my face*, produced in 1981, the words of the title are placed down the left-hand side of a woman's profile. She is making a point about the gaze, in particular the male gaze, which has been characterised by such theorists as Laura Mulvey as an objectifying and powerful gaze (Mulvey 1989). The male gaze as a gaze that makes women into objects to be looked at, powerless and assaulted by that gaze, is being challenged by Kruger's work. In so far as the power relations that exist between men and women are being contested, the positions of dominance and subordinacy are being contested and the social order is being threatened.

The case of William Morris is more complicated than that of either of the producers of visual culture considered so far. It bears a resemblance to the examples of the Bauhaus and Habitat, which will be considered below. The problem is to decide whether Morris, the Bauhaus and Habitat are really challenging the existing social order or just reproducing the dominant ideas, beliefs and practices. It might also be claimed that they are really trying to be neutral regarding the social order, trying not to privilege or further the interests of any social group. Convincing cases can be made for all these positions. However, in the second half of the nineteenth century Morris, along with his partners in the English Arts and Crafts Movement and the firm Morris, Marshall, Faulkner & Co., was instrumental in providing a critique of the prevailing ideology. Morris referred to himself as a socialist and saw his work as helping to improve the lot of the working classes. Following people like John Ruskin, Morris thought that the Industrial Revolution had led to the spiritual and material impoverishment of society. In particular, he thought that the industrialisation of life had reduced the 'workman' to a 'skinny and pitiful existence' (quoted in Williams 1958: 155) and that it was the place of art to 'set the true ideal of a full and reasonable life before him' (ibid.).

It was through visual culture (furniture, graphic and wallpaper design) that Morris sought to set the ideal of a full and reasonable life before the working classes. The ordinary people, he thought, should not have to put up with the mass-produced, industrialised designs of the time. Traditional methods of producing furniture were to be preferred. Similarly, the garish synthetic dyes and pigments produced by using chemicals were also to be avoided and the natural colours of materials to be encouraged. Like Ruskin, Morris was concerned with the furtherance of social justice and saw to it that the workers at

Morris & Co. had decent wages and working conditions. All these aspects of Morris's production may be seen as attempts to challenge the existing social order.

They may also be seen as attempts to be neutral regarding the social order. It is not immediately clear, that is, whether wanting everyone to benefit from beautiful, authentic design is to be neutral regarding all social classes or whether it is to privilege one class above another. The idea does seem to be that class and status should not be reflected in the designs produced in so far as all designs should be equally available to all social classes. What is abundantly clear, however, is that Morris's project was not successful. His designs, in natural materials, handmade and using natural and time-consuming dyes, were expensive. They were too expensive for the working classes to be able to afford. Then, as now, they appealed to and were only available to the affluent middle classes; Morris himself said that he was 'ministering to the swinish luxury of the rich' (see McDermott 1992: 150). In that the designs were too expensive for all classes to afford, not all classes could possess them and economic class and social status is inevitably reflected in them. They have become one of the ways in which the wealthy middle class constructs itself as a class. Morris's designs therefore contributed and continue to contribute to the reproduction of the social order and not, as he hoped, to its transformation.

Another attempt to transform the social order by means of design and design theory is found in the work of the various alternative design groups of the late twentieth century, one hundred years after Morris. Designers and design theorists such as Richard Buckminster Fuller and Victor Papanek, for example, were worried about the way in which design had become the slave of consumer society, with no moral or ethical input. Buckminster Fuller raised questions concerning the economic, political and social contexts in which design was produced. Papanek's (1972) book *Design for the Real World* suggested that designers think about the needs of the underdeveloped countries of the third world and of the various disadvantaged groups within western societies, such as the disabled. Rather than devoting their energies and skills to restyling the fins on oversized and uneconomical American cars, or designing heated footstools for Americans, people like Buckminster Fuller and Papanek proposed that designers attend to the social and ecological aspects of design. Following Vance Packard's (1961) work on consumer society, *The Waste Makers*, Buckminster Fuller and Papanek brought questions concerning inbuilt obsolescence and the unnecessary waste of precious raw materials that it entailed to bear on designers. The elderly and the underprivileged, people with fewer material resources, were to be thought of when designing objects. The recycling and efficient use of materials were to be stressed. In these ways the members of the various alternative design groups sought to challenge and to change the world around them and the societies they were part of.

Buckminster Fuller was designing products in the 1930s and 1940s. This represents an early attempt at 'green' or 'alternative' design. In that many of the ideas of people like Buckminster Fuller and Papanek were taken up in the 1970s and 1980s, with ecologically-friendly design and products becoming ever more popular, they may be said to have been relatively successful. There are now groups like the Swedish Ergonomi Group, who design products for the disabled, for example. The point to be made is that the social order is challenged and transformed by such groups in that they are not constructing disability but rather ability. The social order is being transformed in that the group, 'the disabled', is no longer being reproduced even in the products they use. If a designer designs a plug that people with arthritis cannot use, then the social group 'the disabled' is simply reproduced. If a designer designs a plug that those with arthritis can use then that group and its status are no longer simply reproduced and the social order is transformed, in no matter how small a way. Similarly, if a designer designs a bush radio that uses electricity, then those in the bush without electricity are condemned to the margins; the social order is simply reproduced. If, however, a designer designs a bush radio that uses clockwork, then those without electricity are no longer marginalised and the status of these groups is transformed.

In contemporary western society, the most visible and conspicuous examples of visual culture which challenge the social order, refusing and contesting class, gender and ethnic identity and status, for example, are probably found in film and television. Television programmes may now be made by those who have not been educated and trained by either commercial film and television industries and shown on the so-called 'access' channels. Such shows have been seen on British television: New York's cable channel, as selected and edited by Laurie Pike, and Adam Buxton's *Takeover TV* have both provided evidence of the production of what can only be called 'non-standard' programmes, produced by people who are not professionals in the field. These programmes are a challenge to the dominant groups in that they do not use formally trained camera operators, sound crews and so on. They enable people to become producers of material which is of interest to them and are not always self-indulgent or adolescent. Contemporary attitudes to children, sex and pornography were ridiculed in Buxton's 1996–7 New Year's Eve show, *The Adam and Joe Show*, in which assorted teddy bears and other cuddly toys re-enacted the screenplay for the 1996 film *Kids*. *Kids*, produced by the photographer Larry Clark, who had already photographed the sexier side of teenage life in his work *The Perfect Childhood* (1993), attracted huge amounts of outrage by showing teenagers having unprotected sex. In film, although Hollywood continues to be the dominant reproductive force, it is still possible for the occasional critical comment to be made. Spike Lee, for example, provides constant contestations of white beliefs and attitudes, while showing a variety of black points of view. Such films and television pro-grammes challenge the social order in that they provide an alternative set of concerns, beliefs and attitudes and do not simply repeat the beliefs and attitudes of the dominant groups.

Of course, the very fact that these shows are seen on mainstream film and television screens will be evidence for some of the power of the dominant capitalist institutions to incorporate critical forces and render them relatively harmless. The process in which alternative and critical forces are taken over by the governing institutions and even used to those institutions' profit has been labelled 'hegemony' by Marxist analysts such as Antonio Gramsci and Dick Hebdige (1979). They argue that what is called 'counter-hegemony', the attempt to critique and challenge dominant groups, must always take new forms and must always take place in new locations as those groups recuperate and incorporate the challenges. Indeed, it might be sug-gested that much of the history of modern western art and design has been a demonstration of this process, as the avant-garde seeks ever new ways to be novel and shocking while the art and design establishments accommodate the supposedly novel and shocking pieces of visual culture. From John Constable in the early nineteenth century to Damien Hurst in the late twentieth century, strange and unusual art has eventually been exhibited and bought in the most mainstream and respectable galleries, by members of the dominant social groups. It might be worth speculating upon whether Harvey Nichols's attempt to sell contemporary art works in its 'Art Super-market' is another way in which the mainstream market takes over and profits from fine art. Richard Gott has described this process as the way in which 'the wild inventions and excesses of modern art (suitably tamed of course) are being brought in to form part of the modern shopping experience'; inventions and excesses are literally 'brought in' to the market and profited from (Gott 1997). Thus, in more than one sense of the word does visual culture become institutionalised as a result of hegemony.

Neutrality and the social order

The arguments surrounding producers of visual culture who claim to be neutral regarding the social order are complex. They are complex because the attempt to be neutral or innocent with regard to the social order may always itself be seen, by members of the dominant groups at least, as an alternative or challenge to the dominant groups; to adapt St Luke and St Matthew, anything that is not for them is against them. And they are complex because it may also always be argued that neutrality or innocence regarding the social order is impossible. Sometimes a whole industry, like graphic design, for example, claims that it is neutral or innocent with regard to the hierarchy of groups making up culture and society. It claims that it is just the messenger, innocently taking messages from one person or institution to another. It also claims to be the simple and neutral vehicle of other people's and institutions' messages. The argument is that graphic design as an industry and individual graphic designers themselves do not necessarily believe or agree with the meanings and messages conveyed by their work and that they have no interest in supporting the beliefs and values of the people employing them. Workers in other design industries, like fashion and textile design, for example, have also been known to claim innocence concerning the social order: if some people can afford the highest prices for haute couture and hand-made fabrics while others cannot, that is none of the designer's business, according to them.

The claim that certain designers, graphic, fashion and textile designers, for example, may be neutral or innocent concerning the social order is the claim that they do not support or further the beliefs and position of the dominant social group. It is the claim that they do not actively reproduce the dominant group's position. And it is the claim that they do not ensure the continued subordinate or alienated position of other non-dominant groups. As suggested above, there are two main arguments against this position which complicate the situation. The first is that such innocence is impossible because all design, as communication, makes some difference to the world it appears in. It might be questioned whether the communication that makes no difference to the world of the person sending or interpreting the message is even communication. What would be the point of producing an item of clothing or an illustration that did not affect the people who wore it or saw it? Indeed, it is quite likely that such an item would be impossible to produce (see Barnard 1995 for an application of these arguments to advertising). The second is that such innocence is impossible because the very attempt to be neutral is itself an attempt to affect the way power operates and is therefore a political act. If the social system that the designer is a part of consists in a hierarchy of social groups, then the attempt to 'flatten' that hierarchy, to accord each group equal status, is to change the power relations between those social groups and is therefore not innocent or neutral with regard to those groups.

These arguments are all rather abstract; applying them to concrete examples may make them more immediate and approachable. It is possible to present institutions of design education like the Bauhaus as well as commercial enterprises like Habitat and Ikea in terms of these arguments. The Bauhaus (meaning 'building house' in German) was set up in Weimar Germany in 1919 by Walter Gropius, who had been deeply impressed and influenced by the thought and work of Morris and the English Arts and Crafts Movement, discussed above. Indeed, it is tempting to describe the Bauhaus as a sort of Modernist and mechanised version of Morris. Whatever, one principle of the Bauhaus was to break down the division between the fine arts and the crafts and to take into account the increasing mechanisation of the production process. Thus, from Morris came the idea that designers should be true to their materials and to the functional demands of the objects they were producing and from the increasingly machine-oriented production process came the idea that the items should be cheap and made in large numbers. The chairs designed by Breuer, Mies van der Rohe and Le Corbusier (which featured in the advertisement discussed above in Chapter 6 – Ill. 6.1), for example, are good examples of work which used the materials appropriately, which could be mass-produced by machines and which related the function of the object in a pleasingly modernist way to its form.

In 1925, Gropius himself was involved in a project concerning modular, or serial, housing. The idea here was that industrial production methods, which were standardised and uniform, could be used to produce cheap and attractive housing for people at relatively low cost. The people would be served by being provided with housing and the community would be made more attractive in economically feasible projects. Thus, Gropius may be seen as combining economy with a social purpose. He may also be seen as joining aesthetics with industrial demands and methods. This is the sense behind saying that the Bauhaus was a modernist and mechanised version of Morris. Now, it is possible to see this project, and others like it that the Bauhaus carried out, as attempting to be neutral regarding the social order. The whole point of the serial or modular housing was that housing could be built from units that were standard, which were produced in standard sizes, colours, finishes and so on. Given such standardisation, it would be very difficult to signal social superiority or inferiority. The attempt to make it difficult to signal such status can plausibly be described as an attempt to be neutral with regard to the social order; it is an attempt to 'flatten' the hierarchy and treat everyone similarly.

Something of the same approach may also be claimed for the chairs discussed above. Given that they are mass-produced, or at least intended for mass production, they represent an attempt to 'flatten' the social hierarchy. It is difficult, again, to signal social superiority with something that everyone else also has in their house, after all. This is the basis of the case regarding commercial outlets like Habitat and Ikea. On the one hand it is possible to see such stores as providing well-made, good-looking and functional household items that are available to everyone. It is possible to understand their products as proposing a version of universal good taste, not supporting any one class identity over any other, and thus as trying to be neutral with regard to the social structure. On the other hand, however, it is arguable that they are presenting the tastes and styles of a particular class, the relatively affluent middle classes, and presenting them as if they were the only proper tastes and styles. This is the classic ideological move: presenting what is class-specific and the product of a particular time and place as if it were natural and applicable universally to all classes.

Reproducing the social order

It would be argued by many that examples of visual culture which reproduce the social order are easy to find. Many Marxist analysts of visual culture, for example, would claim that most, if not all, such work is supportive of the dominant classes and that it simply reproduces the social order. This may or may not be the case. However, the following paragraphs will consider Thomas Gainsborough's work *Mr and Mrs Andrews*, painted in 1748–9, as contributing to the reproduction of the social order (see Ill. 8.1). This painting combines a double portrait of Mr and Mrs Andrews with a landscape, showing the pair in front of a tree and surrounded by their extensive property. Drawing on the analyses of the work to be found in John Berger's book, *Ways of Seeing*, and Anne Bermingham's *Landscape and Ideology*, the first thing to point out is that the work is an oil-painting. The medium itself is a prestigious medium; it is not cheap, especially when produced by such a famous and fashionable artist as Gainsborough, and it is not therefore something that everyone has access to. On a very simple level, then, choosing to commission Gainsborough to produce a portrait in oil-painting reproduces the system of institutions and practices (the signifying system) in which Gainsborough can first appear as well as the form, (the portrait), and the medium (oil-painting), with which Gainsborough works. On a slightly more complex level, such a choice is explicitly intended to secure and reproduce Mr and Mrs Andrews's position in the social order. It is right and proper that Mr and Mrs Andrews continue to own and enjoy these lands because they are the sorts of people who

Ill. 8.1   Thomas Gainsborough, *Mr and Mrs Andrews*, 1748, National Gallery, London

commission oil-paintings of themselves and they commission oil-paintings because they own all these lands. The ideology supports itself in a circular fashion.

The rightness and legitimacy of the social order are confirmed, or reproduced, not only by the form and the medium employed by this painting but also by various elements of what might be called its content. Much of what is going on in this painting is there to suggest the fashionable enjoyment of moneyed leisure. The couple have portrayed themselves as being as fashionable and up-to-date a couple as was possible in eighteenth-century Suffolk. Frances is wearing a closed robe of blue silk over the wide oblong hoop popular in the 1740s. Her 'round ear' cap is worn under the fashionable *bergère* hat whose brim has been rolled after the manner of a milkmaid's. The 'milkmaid' look came into style in the 1730s, as part of a general taste for the informal and rustic look of the lower agricultural classes. Robert lounges casually wearing a sporty satin shooting jacket and knee breeches. His large tricorne hat, the 'kevenhuller cock', was all the rage among the beaus of London in 1746. These fashionable clothes emphasise how wealthy the couple are and how much leisure time they have: Frances's spotless shoes, for example, do not suggest that she has just stopped work for a rest. The shooting jacket, dog and flintlock are not there by accident either: at this time, the game laws permitted only those with an income of over £100 from their land to hunt game on that land. Even the stacked and harvested corn shows how progressive and trendy they are: the corn has been planted in straight lines, something that an early mechanical seed drill could achieve but which could not be done by hand. They are thus at the forefront of land management in the agrarian revolution of the eighteenth century.

The painting is also intended to commemorate the marriage between these two. As such, it is portrayed as secure and fecund. There is no intended criticism of the institution, as there was in the Hogarth discussed above: the marriage pictured here will be as productive as the fields it is set in and it is confident of its position. As the marriage is the legitimation of their relationship, so the painting is a legitimation of their ownership of the lands. Of course, Berger famously points out that the proprietorial, self-possessed attitude of these people can even be seen in their faces and their expressions. Their coarse, pinched and mean little faces do indeed speak eloquently of their ownership and their determination to enjoy their private wealth. Every aspect of the work seems to confirm the existing social order; they are upper-class and, while they may ape the look of the lower classes in their fashions, the difference in status and power is visible and confirmed in the painting. The couple are securely posed in the middle of their own lands, exercising their rights to shoot small birds and to profit from the crops and animals raised on those lands. The claim is, then, that the portrayal of the couple in this way, wearing expensive clothes, enjoying the 'rights' that ownership brings, posed casually looking out at the spectator, and in oils, reproduces the institutions and the social order that make the portrayal possible in the first place.

Consumption

This section will examine the production, maintenance and transformation of the social order from the perspective of the consumption of visual culture. Reference was made in Chapter 7 to Forty's claim concerning 'the extent to which individualism in the home is an illusion' (1986: 118). It was also suggested that, in this sense, individualism in fashion and clothing is also an illusion. The fact that every frock and every pair of jeans are produced in their hundreds, if not millions, was proposed as evidence of this. Indeed, the argument may be generalised so far as to suggest that individualism in many aspects of modern visual culture, be it the fashion one wears, the furniture, pictures and objects one surrounds oneself with, the film and television one watches or the car one drives, is under threat. Mass-produced objects, mass-produced visual culture, appears to pose the threat of reducing everyone to making the same 'choices', which are, in fact, not choices at all. The problem arises as to how to avoid the conclusion that people are simply the unconscious prey of the market, passively purchasing and consuming anything and everything that the mass market supplies them with. This section will address these problems. It will explain the debates surrounding active and passive consumption and it will explain how this consumption relates to the social structure. That is, does consumption merely reproduce the social structure, reproducing positions of inequality and exploitation, or can it criticise or resist that social structure, providing an alternative?

Passive consumption

The idea that people are reduced to making the same 'choices' from the mass-produced products of modern capitalist societies, and the related idea that their consumption is thus controlled and manipulated, are perhaps most closely associated with the Marxist analyses of Max Horkheimer, Theodor Adorno and the rest of the Frankfurt School. Instead of 'mass culture', Horkheimer and Adorno use the phrase 'the culture industry' to analyse and explain the relation between consumption, culture and mass production (Horkheimer and Adorno 1972; and see Adorno, 'Culture industry reconsidered', in Adorno 1991). They prefer 'the culture industry' to 'mass culture' because it prevents one from making the mistake of thinking that mass culture is in any way something that arises spontaneously from the masses themselves (Adorno 1991: 85). To the contrary, the culture industry, which for Adorno includes music and literature, as well as the visual arts and design, provides the masses with an ever expanding range of goods and products. In the culture industry, 'products which are tailored for consumption by the masses . . . are manufactured more or less according to plan' (ibid.); the culture industry controls and manipulates the masses, providing products for them to consume. On this sort of account, the culture industry does for consumption within people's culture and leisure activities what industry does for the production of things. The culture industry makes the products of both high and low culture into commodities, to be advertised and sold to everyone.

Horkheimer and Adorno's account of the culture industry depends upon this notion of the manipulated, passive consumer. The customer, as Adorno has it, is not king (1991: 85). She is not queen, either. The consumer is rather deceived and 'fettered' by the culture industry, which tells the consumer that they want this and that commodity, rather than letting them decide for themselves. As Adorno says, the culture industry 'impedes the development of autonomous, independent individuals who judge and decide consciously for themselves' (92). This has several harmful effects. First, autonomous and independent individuals being needed for the production of a democratic society, the culture industry thus stands in the way of democracy (ibid.). Totalitarianism is encouraged in so far as a passive audience that is accustomed to being told what it wants is an audience that will be particularly responsive to dictators. Second, the individuals making up society are also harmed, or damaged, by the culture industry. The culture produced by the culture industry generates false gratifications, false desires and pleasures, desires and pleasures which are aimed at the lowest common denominator. These desires and pleasures, which are not genuinely of the people, but which are forced on to the people, may even be emotionally harmful.

It is perhaps the fact that these passive and manipulated consumers are standing in the way of democracy that the Frankfurt School and Adorno in particular are most opposed to. To put the matter in the terms of this chapter, the Frankfurt School argue that the culture industry encourages the reproduction of the social order, rather than its transformation. In his essay 'How to look at television' (in Adorno 1991), for example, Adorno shows how the consumption of something as apparently trivial as an 'extremely light comedy' encourages the acceptance or tolerance of social inequality. The acceptance and toleration of social inequality, of course, are necessary parts of the reproduction of that inequality. Adorno's example concerns the charming and witty American sit-com teacher who is underpaid and constantly fined by her bullying school principal to the extent that she is in fact starving. The 'jokes' apparently revolve around her trying, and failing, to cadge meals from friends and colleagues. However, she is so intellectually superior and high-spirited that the audience is invited to identify with her 'and compensation is offered for the inferiority of her position and that of her ilk in the social set up' (1991: 143). The final implication of the script is that 'if you are as humorous, good-natured, quick-witted and charming as she is, do not worry about being paid a starvation wage' (ibid.). The script encourages the passive audience to accept their position on the social order; as Adorno has it, 'the script is a shrewd method of promoting adjustment to humiliating conditions by presenting them as objectively comical' and by showing the person suffering such social inequality as 'free of any resentment' (143–4).

This account of the consumer and of consumption, therefore, involves the consumer participating in the reproduction of the social order. Giving an account of consumption in which the consumer is passive, manipulated by the culture industry, leads to theorising consumption as simply reproducing the social order. It also leads directly to the problems noted above, in which consumers and audiences can only be thought of as the witless dupes of modern capitalism. If the consumer is passive and manipulated like this, it is difficult to explain individualism, or even the experience of individualism, in fashion, the home or anywhere else.

Active consumption: reproduction

There is, however, another way of theorising consumption. And, as Mike Featherstone has pointed out, it also begins with the work of Adorno (Featherstone 1991: 14). This way of theorising consumption centres on the notions of use-value and exchange-value. The use-value of a commodity is the meaning of the thing, a corset, handsaw, or chair, for example, expressed as the function of that thing. The exchange-value of a commodity is the meaning of the thing expressed as the price of the thing. According to Featherstone, Adorno describes the way in which, once the original use-value of a commodity has become less important than the exchange-value of that commodity, the commodity becomes 'free to take on a wide range of cultural associations and allusions' (1991: 14). This is the situation that is familiar to consumers in the 1990s, in which it is possible for everyday, mundane items like car tyres, washing machines, cigarettes, cosmetics and so on to be associated with 'images of romance, exotica, desire, beauty, fulfilment, communality, scientific progress and the good life'. These associations are, of course, made by the advertising industry: washing machines and toilet cleaners are regularly sold on the basis of their being the product of 'science', cigarettes always used to be linked with desire and fulfilment and the good life is now unthinkable without cars. The last step in this process is to think of these commodities as signs and to conceive of consumption as the active manipulation of these signs (15).

This process is not an easy one to grasp but it may been seen in a concrete form in the history of advertising as described by Leiss, Kline and Jhally (1990). They show how advertising changes between the end of the nineteenth century and the end of the twentieth century. In what they call stage one, which lasted roughly between 1890 and 1925, advertising concentrates on the qualities of the product itself; the reasons advanced for using it are those qualities. This might be described as concentrating on the use-value of the product as it is the function of the product which is used to sell the product (1990: 153). In stage two, which lasted from about 1925 to 1945, advertisements put less emphasis on the product and its uses and begin to sell the product as a symbol. The product becomes a symbol of qualities that are desired by consumers, qualities like status, glamour and the happy family (155). Between 1945 and 1965, advertisers begin to use the idea of a 'prototypical' mass consumer in their strategies. In stage three, that is, psychological techniques are employed in order to find out what this ideal mass consumer wants (158). And in stage four, which lasts from 1965 to 1985, advertisers concentrate not on the personality of the consumer but on the activities of different subgroups of consumers. The 'lifestyle attitudes', the 'consumption preferences' of increasingly small subgroups are sought out and appealed to in adverts of this period (ibid.).

Advertisements from the nineteenth century, then, stress the use-value of the product: they say what the function of the product is and how well it fulfils that function. After about 1925, however, a major change takes place and products begin to take on a symbolic role: the commodity is freed to take on associations and allusions. The commodity is on the way to becoming a sign, signifying romance, exotica, desire, beauty and so on. And once it has become a sign, it is available to the various different subgroups to use it to create and communicate themselves as subgroups. As Featherstone says, this is also the basis of Jean Baudrillard's account of the commodity (Featherstone 1991: 15). Baudrillard's (1981 and 1993) work also stresses the way in which the commodity is liberated or freed from its determination as use-value (1981: 66ff., 146) to become a sign.

On this view of consumption, the consumer is active, rather than passive. The consumer uses the commodities to construct and communicate an identity. This contrasts enormously with the version of consumption found above in the Frankfurt School's account. While Judith Williamson says that 'the conscious chosen meaning in most people's lives comes much more from what they consume than what they produce' (1986: 230), Adorno's more passive consumer is deceived by and unconscious of the meaning of commodities. The consumer also uses commodities to demarcate social relationships; the commodities take on a political function in that they may be used to show how different social groups relate to one another. Now, this is where the relation to the social order may be seen. The consumer is using the goods to create and communicate a social identity, membership of one or more social groups. Thus, products may be used to signify maleness as well as middle-classness. The consumer is also using the goods to signify a place relative to other social groups. Products may be used to signify that one is of a higher social class than someone else who does not, or cannot, consume those products. It can be seen that consumption here relates directly to the social order. Where passive consumption was seen only to reproduce a social order and even impede the progress of democracy, active consumption can either reproduce the social order or it can challenge and transform the social order.

One of the best-known examples of the analysis of consumption and status is found in Pierre Bourdieu's (1984) work *Distinction*. Consumption here is a way of creating or establishing differences between social groups. It is not as if one is working-class and then says that paintings are 'nice but difficult' (1984: 266); saying such things constitutes one as a member of a specific class. Nor is it that one is working-class and then seeks 'value for money' rather than aesthetic pleasures from one's clothes. Looking for 'value for money' and stressing function and substance in one's clothes are part of what constitute one's identity as working-class (200–1). Echoing Weber's account of status groups above, Bocock says,

> consumption . . . can be seen as a set of social and cultural practices which serve as a way of establishing differences between social groups, not merely as a way of expressing differences which are already in place as a result of an autonomous set of economic factors. (1993: 64)

Reading Bourdieu, the differences between the working class and the lower-middle class are found in the ways in which they watch television, furnish and decorate their houses, and in which cars they drive, as well as in the ways in which they relate to art and clothing. Visual culture is used here to constitute these different social groups. More accurately, the consumption of visual culture is one of the ways in which social identity is created and communicated. The lower-middle classes consume these things in order to be 'respectable' and look to the higher-middle-class groups for clues as to what to consume. The working classes are more interested in instant pleasures to be had from such commodities and in having a good time. And, as Bocock says, this is not simply a matter of income: 'it is cultural, symbolic, factors which affect their consumption patterns not income alone' (1993: 64).

Bourdieu says that 'nothing more rigorously distinguishes the different classes' than the various different types of aesthetic capacity. The working classes are much less likely to 'constitute aesthetically', for example, an object or image that is 'ordinary' or 'common' (Bourdieu 1984: 40). Bourdieu uses the example of a photograph of some pebbles to make his point; most of the working-class spectators thought it a 'waste of film' and dismissed it is 'bourgeois photography' (41). The working classes are also much less likely to apply what Bourdieu calls a 'pure' aesthetic to everyday visual culture such as dress or home decoration. This aesthetic is a sort of reverse of Kant's theory of the beautiful. Kant distinguishes 'that which pleases' from 'that which gratifies'. He also separates 'disinterestedness', which is the guarantee of a specifically aesthetic quality, from 'the interest of the senses', which is to do with sensual gratification. 'That which pleases', available to disinterested contemplation, is more characteristic of middle-class sensibilities while 'that which gratifies', which is apprehended through the senses, is more characteristic of working-class sensibilities. Bourdieu suggests that 'working class people, who expect every image to fulfil a function, refer . . . to norms of morality or agreeableness in all their judgements' (1984: 41). The different responses of these classes to photographs of dead soldiers (ibid.), or of arthritic hands (45), or to the work of Severini and Mondrian (51) is used to map out the different class identities.

Now, clearly, consumption conceived in this way is productive of society in that it is productive of the identities of the different social and cultural groups that constitute society. It is also part of the process that produces and maintains the institutions, practices, media and objects that those social and cultural groups are part of and which they use to constitute themselves as social and cultural groups. Bourdieu's secondary or higher-education teachers, who visit the avant-garde theatre and the art gallery (Bourdieu 1984: 580–1), help to ensure the continued existence of those institutions, as well as the practices and objects that are customarily found there. The lower-middle and working classes do not have the purchasing power of the higher classes, and they also lack what Bourdieu calls the 'cultural capital' to enjoy the objects and practices enjoyed by the higher classes; they do not have the education and the interpretative skills, for example, to analyse and understand much contemporary and avant-garde art and design. Consequently, there are not so many examples of visual culture open to them as are open to the higher classes. Herbert Gans suggests that 'most Hollywood films were once made for the low culture public, until it gravitated to television' (1974: 92). And it might be suggested that certain genres of film, especially as they are available on video, for home entertainment, are used by these classes. Thus, action thrillers, like the *Die Hard*, *Rambo* and *Terminator* series, for example, produce and reproduce working-class identity. The viewing, in the form of rental, purchase or attendance at the cinema, helps to ensure the reproduction of these forms of entertainment, as well as the institutions and practices involved in their production and distribution.

Active consumption: resistance

Consumption conceived in this way may also be a challenge to the social order; it may not simply produce and reproduce society in the ways the examples above do. Rather consumption may be a weapon in a class's or a cultural group's struggle to redefine its identity or its status in the social order. Culture is political in the sense that not only does it contribute to the production and maintenance of society, it may also contribute to transforming society. It has a role to play in changing the ways in which the different groups in a society relate to one another. It is probably in fashion and clothing that this phenomenon is most clearly seen. Ted Polhemus's (1994) book *Streetstyle*, Angela Partington's (1992) essay 'Popular fashion and working class affluence' and Dick Hebdige's (1979) book *Subculture* all chart some of the ways in which fashion has been used to challenge and contest the social order. As seen above, in Polhemus's account of the Zooties, fashion here is used by young black men to proclaim a status that is not that of the poor, humble black. They were trying to change the perception of black men by taking over and adapting the very sign of white respectability. Partington's essay charts the way in which working class women adopted and adapted one of the most famous and well-known signs of the fashion world, the New Look, in an attempt to forge a new identity and status for themselves. And Hebdige shows how punk challenged dominant ideals of dress and feminine beauty by using materials and patterns which those dominant ideals considered ugly and repellent.

These are well-documented examples of the consumption of visual culture being used to challenge and contest a social order and they will not be dealt with in any more detail here. Less well-documented attempts to challenge the social order by means of visual culture might include the ways in which different classes disagree over the interpretation of items of visual culture. Avant-garde sculpture and what is called either pornography or erotica might be usefully examined as examples here. There is in Bourdieu's (1984) *Distinction* a reference to an episode that happened at the Beaubourg in Paris soon after it had opened. Bourdieu is discussing the way in which evidence of working-class people's responses to art is hard to obtain. At the Beaubourg, however, high art and avant-garde works are available to everyone; it is as if the Beaubourg provides a kind of laboratory in which 'experimental situations' arise. Bourdieu says that some exhibits induce in working-class people 'confusion . . . a sort of

panic mingled with revolt' (1984: 33). Bourdieu mentions an exhibition of sculpture by Ben, which consisted of a heap of coal. Many
working-class people who saw this work apparently interpreted it as
'a sort of aggression, an affront to common sense and common
people' (ibid.).

Something similar appears to have happened a few years earlier in
London, when the Tate Gallery exhibited Carl Andre's sculpture
Equivalent VIII. The Tate had bought Andre's work in 1974 and
exhibited it in 1976. *The Daily Mirror*, a popular tabloid newspaper
hitherto unknown for its arts coverage, got hold of the story and ran
the banner headline 'What a load of rubbish' alongside three photographs of the work. Rather than adopt an aesthetic approach to the
work, rather than speculating on the rhythm of Andre's work, or
emphasising the sense of space and interval it established, or even
commenting on the tradition of using found or prefabricated items in
art, the *Mirror* chose to concentrate on the monetary value of the
work, saying that the Tate had wasted £4000. Even the Arts Minister
at the time, Hugh Jenkins, was less than convincing in his defence of
avant-garde aesthetics, wondering feebly whether the Tate had in fact
made a 'mistake'. The point to be made regarding both examples is
that different classes are disagreeing over the interpretation of works
of art. In particular, working-class people, or their representatives, in
the case of the *Daily Mirror*, are contesting and challenging the
interpretation made of visual culture by the dominant social groups.
In doing this, they are trying to change the social order; if their voice
is heard and their arguments are successful, then their subordinate
position in the social order will have been successfully challenged.

The second example of visual culture being used to contest and
challenge a social order is pornography. Visual culture has generally
been explained in this book as one of the places where these battles
take place, but the idea of pornography challenging dominant ideas of
class or gender is not uncontroversial. However, Laura Kipnis argues
that the consumption of certain pornographic magazines may provide
a challenge to the ideas and beliefs of the dominant classes and the
claims are worth examining. In particular, she says that *Hustler* is
'counter-hegemonic in its refusal of bourgeois proprieties' (Kipnis
1992: 388). Hegemony was explained above as the ways in which a
dominant class (or classes, or fractions of different classes) ensures
that the dominated classes consent to the values and beliefs of the
dominant classes. Something that is 'counter-hegemonic', then, will
be something that prevents the dominated classes from agreeing to or

accepting the beliefs and values, the ideology, of the dominant class. Kipnis is claiming, then, that *Hustler* disrupts and challenges the proprieties, the sense of what is right and proper, of the dominant classes.

That the consumers of 'mainstream' pornography are middle-class men is confirmed by Roger Cranshaw, who traces this group back to *Life* magazine in the 1880s, with its 'Gibson girls' and covers by Coles Phillips (Cranshaw 1983: 27). He quotes the Kinsey Report of 1948 to provide the link between social class and masturbation; according to Kinsey, it was the college-educated professionals that 'masturbated most frequently' (28). Kinsey says that what he calls 'upper level males' are the ones who are most likely to find erotic stimulation in pictures and other objects. What he calls 'lower level males' generally do not do this and, indeed, may find the 'use of pictures or literature to augment masturbatory fantasies' the 'strangest sort of perversion' (ibid.). In a paragraph that really would not look out of place in Bourdieu's Kantian account of taste and class, Kinsey speculates that this use of pornographic pictures may be more common among these 'upper level males' because they have a greater capacity to visualise situations which 'are not immediately to hand (*sic*)' (ibid.). Cranshaw concludes that the use of such magazines as *Playboy* and *Penthouse* in male masturbation has been accorded the status of an 'entirely proper and "natural" mode of sexual behaviour for the "upper level", "professional and managerial" corporate man' (ibid.).

It is precisely this group, along with their notions of what is proper and natural, that the consumption of *Hustler* challenges, according to Kipnis. She says that 'the discourse of *"Hustler"* is quite specifically constructed against – not only the classical body, a bourgeois hold-over of the aristocracy, but against all the paraphernalia of petit-bourgeoisehood as well' (Kipnis 1992: 378). The kinds of pictures found in *Hustler*, the cartoons, and the treatment and poses of the body are distinctly different in *Hustler* from the pictures, cartoons and bodies in *Penthouse* and *Playboy*. The pictures, for example, have consistently been much more explicit than in *Penthouse* and *Playboy*, (375), and the political cartoons are more 'gross' and contain more toilet humour than in *Penthouse* and *Playboy* (ibid.). It is on the matter of the body, however, in its treatment, that the two kinds of magazine are most different. The body of *Penthouse* and *Playboy* is a 'sleek, overlaminated' body, it is airbrushed and vaseline-lensed into silent perfection (374). The *Hustler* body, however, is a 'gaseous, fluid-emitting, embarrassing body, one continually defying the strictures of bourgeois manners and mores' (375). This use of imagery and this version of the body is presented as a class-based critique of the dominant values and beliefs. Those dominant values and beliefs are, of course, those of the white middle classes.

On this reading of Kipnis's essay, one would be forgiven for thinking that *Hustler* is 'porno for pinkos' and she does say that 'much of "*Hustler*'s" humour is, in fact, manifestly political and much of it would even get a warm welcome in left-leaning circles' (383). However, she also says that 'if "*Hustler*" is counter-hegemonic in its refusal of bourgeois proprieties, its transgressiveness has real limits' (388). Much of the transgressiveness can be incoherent and banal, for example, and it often appears to set out simply to offend anyone and everyone. Thus, *Hustler* is often full of the most appalling racism, it is anti-liberal, anti-communist and anti-feminist and it is anything but a model of left-wing progressiveness. However, in that it provides a critique of the beliefs and values of the dominant classes, it is transgressive and may be seen as attempting to change the way in which groups in society relate to one another. In this sense, then, it is an attempt to transform the social order.

Conclusion

This chapter has tried to show the role of visual culture. It has tried to show that society, in which different groups exist, is not a simple backdrop or context for art and design. Society is not something that goes on in the background of visual culture. Rather this chapter has tried to show that visual culture has the role of producing, maintaining and transforming society. Visual culture is one of the ways in which society is produced; it is one of the ways in which the different social groups constitute themselves. Visual culture is also one of the ways in which society is either reproduced or transformed; it is the means by which social groups can either reproduce their position concerning other social groups or attempt to transform it. Visual culture is thus the means by which social groups, institutions, practices, beliefs and objects are produced and reproduced. It is one of the means by which a social order, the hierarchy of those different groups, practices, beliefs and so on, is challenged and contested.

Chapter 8 has attempted to demonstrate, then, how the production and consumption of visual culture contribute to the production, reproduction and transformation of society. The production of visual culture has been shown to have a role in the production, reproduction, and transformation of society. And consumption has also been explained as playing a part in the production and reproduction of society. Passive consumption of visual culture was shown to contribute to the production and reproduction of class and status groups. Active consumption was shown to contribute to the production, reproduction and transformation of class and status groups. In these ways, then, visual culture has been shown to be more than the context in which society is produced; visual culture is one of the ways in which society is produced.

Chapter 9

Conclusion

This book is intended as a contribution to the definition, analysis and explanation of visual culture. It has tried to define what visual culture is and it has tried to explain how visual culture might best be studied. It has attempted to show what the analysis and explanation of visual culture might consist in and it has attempted to explain the role of visual culture in society. Above all, perhaps, it has taken seriously the idea of visual culture as a discipline, distinguishing it from other disciplines such as art history, design history and cultural studies-type approaches. Beginning from W. J. T. Mitchell's point that visual culture may seem like an idea whose time has come, but that it is not entirely clear how the study of visual culture might best proceed, the book has tried to show how that study might best proceed.

Chapter 1 began the attempt to define visual culture by looking at how visual experience, what is seen and the sense that is made of what is seen, may be defined and conceptualised. Visual culture was introduced in this chapter as the study of the social and cultural construction of visual experience: how one sees what one sees and why what one sees appears as it does. Raymond Williams's idea of the 'signifying system' (the institutions, objects, practices, values and beliefs) by means of which society is visually produced, reproduced and contested, was used to explore this aspect of visual culture.

Chapter 2 developed the definition of visual culture by considering how it may best be studied. Existing disciplines, such as art history and design history, as well as cultural studies, were critically examined and their characteristic approaches, along with their strengths

197

and weaknesses, were investigated and assessed. This chapter also investigated the different topics or subjects in terms of which visual culture may be studied. Approaches which concentrate on formal elements, on expression, or on visual culture as a reflection of the *Zeitgeist*, for example, were assessed. The chapter argued that lessons may be learned from such approaches as the social history of art, sociology and cultural studies.

The contents of Chapters 3, 4, 5, 6 and 7 were presented as exemplifying some of the ways in which visual culture may be usefully studied. Chapter 3 began to look at concrete and positive matters, the substance of visual culture, as it were; it considered the ways in which artists and designers have thought about and described the nature of their activities and the different ways they have organised themselves into social groups and institutions. It also described the relative status accorded artists and designers and the activities of art and design and showed how that status is related to the social groups and institutions they are members of.

Chapter 4 was concerned with the many and various relationships which the producers of visual culture enter into with the consumers of visual culture: it explained how artists and designers relate to markets, publics and audiences. These issues were introduced by looking at traditional forms of audiences and markets and at some modern versions of those forms. Chapter 5 was to do with visual signs and media: it concerned the ways in which cultures are made visible. It was argued that all cultures must make themselves visible in some way and this chapter was an attempt to analyse and explain those different ways, looking at the different media, from the body to electronics, that may be used to produce visual culture. The debates surrounding the definition of art, design and visual culture which were introduced in Chapter 1 were revisited in Chapter 6. Chapter 6 argued that there are various codes ('internal' and 'external' codes) which govern what different cultures, existing in different times and places, call 'art', 'design' or 'visual culture'. This chapter explained the working of these codes and provided examples of the ways in which visual culture is coded and understood.

In Chapter 7, the explanation was begun of how and why cultural products, such as works of art and design, or visual culture, are produced in different forms or types. The proliferation of forms exists in fashion, furniture design, photography and graphic design, in addition to painting, car design and film. This chapter began to explain these different types of cultural product as developing in time and in relation to different social classes or fractions of classes, looking at theatre design, landscape painting, men's suits and automotive design, for example. Chapter 8 tried to draw together and contextualise the objects, practices, institutions and ideas covered in previous chapters by explaining the role of visual culture. It was argued that the role, or function, of visual culture is the production, reproduction and transformation of society, that visual culture maintains and transforms the institutions, practices, media, objects and social classes analysed in previous chapters.

Visual culture, as an interdisciplinary approach, has been distinguished from art history, or the various versions of art history, in that visual culture does not use one aspect or topic to analyse and explain art and design. It does not insist that form, style, biography or expression, for example, is the true basis of analysis and explanation. These things are themselves to be explained and analysed; they are to be shown to have strengths and weaknesses as explanations of visual culture. Visual culture, as a discipline, has been distinguished from some versions of design history in that it is not overly concerned with universal, eternal definitions of design. The definition of design (and art) is itself a cultural matter: different social and cultural groups define design (and art) differently as part of the way in which they constitute and identify themselves as cultural groups. And visual culture, as a discipline, has been distinguished from the various cultural studies-type approaches in that while culture is seen as constitutive of social identity, it is not reduced to an ideal and intangible *Zeitgeist*. What Wolff calls the 'real' existence of social reality (1992b: 712), the fact that power relations are established and reproduced through the products and institutions of visual culture, has been proposed as a major part of the analysis, explanation and critical evaluation of visual culture.

In this way, the book has tried to identify and adopt the most useful aspects of these various disciplines, it has tried to learn from their strengths and to avoid their weaknesses, and it has tried to give some concrete sense to what the, or a, practice of visual culture might look like. It has tried not to take from disciplines in a random or haphazard fashion. Nor has it argued that, in the absence of eternal standards and truths, all approaches are equally valid, as some postmodernist approaches have been accused of doing. Rather, Mitchell's point, that in the light of visual culture, the idols of the art-historical and design-historical tribes will be tested and a more interesting and informed idea of their worth arrived at (1995b:

209–10), has been used as a starting point from which to escape what might be called postmodern relativism and modern absolutism. The idea of the genius, the idea of artistic expression and the idea of a specifically aesthetic hierarchy, for example, will have to be subjected to the kind of critical analysis as is proposed above. But it is claimed that, having undergone such a critical analysis, they will be seen in a more interesting and informed light.

For example, it is clear that different social and cultural groups call different artists and designers a genius and it is not suggested that just anyone is or may be called a genius. Nor is it being suggested that all works are of equal aesthetic value: different social groups equally clearly give different objects and images different aesthetic values. As Janet Wolff has insisted (1992b: 712), the effect of inequality, of power, in these judgements means that the groups with power, and with what Bourdieu calls 'cultural capital', set and regulate these standards. To this extent, they are in no way relative. It has been claimed, then, that these approaches are more worthwhile than either simply and uncritically adopting the dominant ideas and approaches of art and design histories or simply and uncritically asserting that there are no standards. The methods, ideas and processes adopted by this book are proposed as being better than others but they are not proposed as the only methods, ideas and processes to be adopted. They are proposals, to be developed, criticised, adopted or abandoned in the light of how well they help in the further analysis and exploration of visual culture.

Bibliography

Adorno, T. W. (1991) *The Culture Industry: Selected Essays on Mass Culture*, London, Routledge.

Albrecht, M. C., Barnett, J. H. and Griff, M. (eds) (1982) *The Sociology of Art and Literature: A Reader*, 2nd edn, London, Duckworth.

Appignanesi, L. (ed.) (1989) *Postmodernism*, London, Free Association Books.

Ash, J. and Wilson, E. (eds) (1992) *Chic Thrills: A Fashion Reader*, London, Pandora.

Attfield, J. and Kirkham, P. (eds) (1989) *A View from the Interior: Feminism, Women and Design*, London, The Women's Press.

Back, K. (1985) 'Modernism and fashion: a social psychological interpretation', in Solomon, M. R. (ed.) (1985).

Banham, R. (1960) *Theory and Design in the First Machine Age*, London, Architectural Press.

Barley, N. (1986) *A Plague of Caterpillars*, Harmondsworth, Penguin.

Barnard, M. (1995) 'The rhetorical imperative', in Jenks, C. (ed.) (1995).

—— (1996) *Fashion as Communication*, London, Routledge.

Barrell, J. (1980) *The Dark Side of the Landscape: The Rural Poor in English Painting 1730–1840*, Cambridge, Cambridge University Press.

Barrow, J. D. (1995) *The Artful Universe*, Oxford: Oxford University Press.

Baudrillard, J. (1981) *For a Critique of the Political Economy of the Sign*, St Louis, Telos Press.

—— (1993) *Symbolic Exchange and Death*, London, Sage.

Baxandall, M. (1972) *Painting and Experience in Fifteenth Century Italy*, Oxford, Oxford University Press.

Becker, H. S. (1982) *Art Worlds*, Berkeley, University of California Press.

Bell, C. (1982) 'The aesthetic hypothesis', in Frascina, F. and Harrison, C. (eds) (1982).

Berger, J. (1972) *Ways of Seeing*, London, BBC Books, Harmondsworth, Penguin.

Bermingham, A. (1984) *Landscape and Ideology*, London, Thames & Hudson.

Blume, M. (1985) *After the War Was Over*, London, Thames & Hudson.

Bocock, R. (1993) *Consumption*, London, Routledge.

Boschloo, A. W. *et al.* (eds) (1989) *Academies of Art Between Renaissance and Romanticism*, The Hague, SDU Uitgeverij.

Bourdieu, P. (1984) *Distinction: A Social Critique of the Judgement of Taste*, London, RKP.

201

Bowlt, J. E. (1988) *Russian Art of the Avant Garde*, London, Thames & Hudson.

Braun, E. (1995) 'Futurist fashion: three manifestoes', *Art Journal*, vol. 54, no. 1 (Spring), pp. 34–41.

Brown, M. (1996) 'A star comes back to earth', *Telegraph Magazine*, 14 December, pp. 22–8.

Bryson, N. (1981) *Word and Image: French Painting of the Ancien Régime*, Cambridge, Cambridge University Press.

Buck, L. and Dodd, P. (1991) *Relative Values, or What's Art Worth?*, London, BBC Books.

Buckley, C. (1989) 'Pottery Women: A Comparative Study of Susan Vera Cooper and Millicent Jane Taplin', in Attfield, J. and Kirkham, P. (eds), *A View from the Interior*, London: The Women's Press.

Bugs! (1994) no. 6, Peterborough, Orbis Publishing.

Burchfield, R. (1988) 'Words and meanings', *The Sunday Times*, 6 November.

Caiger-Smith, M. (1987) 'Introduction' to Osman (ed.) (1987).

Chaney, D. (1994) *The Cultural Turn: Scene-setting Essays on Contemporary Cultural History*, London, Routledge.

Chaplin, E. (1994) *Sociology and Visual Representation*, London, Routledge.

Clark, K. (1969) *Civilisation*, London, BBC Books and John Murray.

Clark, L. (1993) *The Perfect Childhood*, LCB, in association with Thea Westreich.

Clark, T. J. (1980) 'Preliminaries to a possible treatment of "Olympia" in 1865', *Screen*, vol. 21, no. 1 (Spring) pp. 18–41. Also in Frascina, F. and Harrison, C. (eds) (1982).

—— (1982) 'On the social history of art', in Frascina, F. and Harrison, C. (eds) (1982).

Clayson, H. and Leja, M. (1995) ' "Quaecumque sunt vera"?', *Art Journal*, (Fall) pp. 47–51.

Clifton-Taylor, A. (1972) *The Pattern of English Building*, London, Faber & Faber.

Corner, J. and Hawthorn, J. (1980) *Communication Studies: An Introductory Reader*, 3rd edn, London, Edward Arnold.

Cranshaw, R. (1983) 'The object of the centrefold', *Block*, no. 9, pp. 26–33.

Cross, J. (1988) 'Top draw', *Guardian*, 6 September.

Cullerne Bown, M. (1989) *Contemporary Russian Art*, Oxford, Phaidon Press.

Cullerne Bown, M. and Taylor, B. (eds) (1993) *Art of the Soviets: Painting, Sculpture and Architecture in a One-Party State, 1917–1992*, Manchester, Manchester University Press.

Debord, G. (1977) *The Society of The Spectacle*, Detroit: Black & Red.

Doordan, D. P. (ed.) (1995a) *Design History: An Anthology*, Cambridge, Mass., MIT Press.

—— (1995b) 'Design at CBS', in Doordan (ed.) (1995a).

Douglas, C. (1995) 'Suprematist embroidered ornament', in *Art Journal*, vol. 54, no. 1 (Spring).

Elderfield, J. (1984) 'The drawings of Henri Matisse', in *The Drawings of Henri Matisse*, London Arts Council.

Featherstone, M. (1991) *Consumer Culture and Postmodernism*, London, Sage.

Fernie, E. (ed.) (1995) *Art History and its Methods: A Critical Anthology*, London, Phaidon Press.

Fleming, G. H. (1967) *Rossetti and the Pre-Raphaelite Botherhood*, London, Hart Davis.

Ford, S. (1995) *The Realisation and Suppression of the Situationist International*, Edinburgh, AK Press.

Forty, A. (1986) *Objects of Desire: Design and Society 1750–1980*, London, Thames & Hudson.

Foster, A. W. and Blau, J. R. (eds) (1989) *Art and Society: Readings in the Sociology of the Arts*, Albany, State University of New York Press.

Foucault, M. (1977) *Discipline and Punish: The Birth of the Prison*, Harmondsworth, Penguin.

Frascina, F. and Harrison, C. (eds) (1982) *Modern Art and Modernism: A Critical Anthology*, London, Harper & Row.

Freand-Jones, N. (Producer) (1997) 'Forbidden: David Cronenberg and the cinema of the extreme', BBC2, 19 January.

Fuller, R. B. (1970) *Utopia or Oblivion*, Harmondsworth, Penguin.

Gans, H. J. (1974) *Popular Culture and High Culture: An Analysis and Evaluation of Taste*, New York, Basic Books.

Gascoigne, B. (1968) *World Theatre: An Illustrated History*, London, Ebury Press.

Geidion, S. (1948) *Mechanization Takes Command: A Contribution to Anonymous History*, New York: Oxford University Press.

Giddens, A. (1980) *The Class Structure of the Advanced Societies*, London, Hutchinson.

Gombrich, E. (1950 *The Story of Art*, 11th edn, London, Phaidon Press.

—— (1971) *Meditations on a Hobby Horse*, London, Phaidon Press.

—— (1979) *Ideals and Idols*, London, Phaidon Press.

—— (1982) 'Expression and communication', in Frascina, F. and Harrison, C. (eds) (1982).

Gott, R. (1997) 'Pound of sprouts and a Hirst, please', *Guardian*, 6 January, p. 13.

Greenberg, C. (1982) 'Modernist painting', in Frascina, F. and Harrison, C. (eds) (1982).

—— (1986) 'Avant-garde and Kitsch', in O'Brien, J. (ed.), *Clement Greenberg: The Collected Essays and Criticism – Perceptions and Judgements, 1939–1944*, Chicago, University of Chicago Press.

Grossberg, L., Nelson, C., and Treichler, P. (eds) (1992) *Cultural Studies*, London, Routledge.

Hall, S. (1988) 'Brave new world', *Marxism Today*, vol. 32, no. 10 (October).

Hall, S. and Jefferson, T. (1976) *Resistance Through Rituals: Youth Subcultures in Post-war Britain*, London, Routledge.

Hanhardt, J. G. (1982) *Nam June Paik*, Whitney Museum of American Art, in association with W. W. Norton & Co., New York and London.

Harris, J. (1995) *Federal Art and National Culture: The Politics of Identity in New Deal America*, Cambridge, Cambridge University Press.

Hartley, J. (1992) *The Politics of Pictures*, London, Routledge.

Haskell, F. (1972) Entry on 'Patronage', in *The Encyclopedia of World Art*, ed. in chief M. Pallottino, Toronto, McGraw-Hill.

Hebdige, D. (1979) *Subculture: The Meaning of Style*, London, Routledge.

Heskett, J. (1980) *Industrial Design*, London, Thames & Hudson.

Hine, T. (1995) *The Total Package*, Boston, Mass., Little, Brown.

Horkheimer, M. and Adorno, T. W. (1972) *Dialectic of Enlightenment*, New York, Herder & Herder.

Hutchison, S. C. (1986) *The History of the Royal Academy*, London, Westminster Art Galleries.

Jacobson, L. (ed.) (1992) *Cyberarts: Exploring Art and Technology*, San Francisco, Miller Freeman Inc.

Jameson, F. (1971) *Marxism and Form*, Princeton, NJ, Princeton University Press.

Jay, M. (1989) 'In the empire of the gaze', in Appignanesi, L. (ed.) (1989).

—— (1993) *Downcast Eyes: The Denigration of Vision in Twentieth Century French Thought*, Berkeley, University of California Press.

Jenks, C. (ed.) (1993) *Cultural Reproduction*, London, Routledge.

—— (ed.) (1995) *Visual Culture*, London, Routledge.

Jobling, P. and Crowley, D. (1996) *Graphic Design: Reproduction and Representation*, Manchester, Manchester University Press.

Kinross, R. (1992) *Modern Typography: An Essay in Critical History*, London, Hyphen Press.

Kipnis, L. (1992) '(Male) desire and (female) disgust: reading "*Hustler*"', in Grossberg, L. *et al.* (eds) (1992).

Kirkham, P. (1989) ' "If you have no sons": furniture making in Britain', in Attfield, J. and Kirkham, P. (eds) (1989).

Klerk, E. A. de (1989) ' "Academy-beelden" and "teeken-schoolen" in Dutch seventeenth-century treatises on art', in Boschloo *et al.* (eds) (1989).

Lavin, I. (ed.) (1995) *Meaning in the Visual Arts: Views from the Outside*, Princeton, NJ, Institute for Advanced Study.

Lee, D. (trans.) (1955) *Plato: The Republic*, Harmondsworth, Penguin.

Leiss, W., Klein, S. and Jhally, S. (1990) *Social Communication in Advertising*, London: Routledge.

Lister, M. (ed.) (1995) *The Photographic Image in Digital Culture*, London, Routledge.

Llewellyn-Smith, J. (1996) 'Pets turn noses up at animal perfume', *Sunday Telegraph*, 13 October.

Luria, A. R. (1980) 'Cultural factors in human perception', in Corner, J. and Hawthorn, J. (eds) (1980).

Margolin, V. (1995) 'Design history or design studies: subject matter and methods', *Design Issues*, vol. 11, no. 1 (Spring).

Marx, K. (1959) *Capital*, Vol. 3, London, Lawrence & Wishart.

Marx, K. and Engels, F. (1968) *Selected Works in One Volume*, London, Lawrence & Wishart.

—— (1970) *The German Ideology*, London, Lawrence & Wishart.

—— (1992) *The Communist Manifesto*, Oxford, Oxford University Press.

Massey, A. (1990) *Interior Design of the Twentieth Century*, London, Thames & Hudson.

McDermott, C. (1992) *Essential Design*, London, Bloomsbury.

Melville, S. and Readings, B. (1995) *Vision and Textuality*, London, Macmillan.

Miles, M. (1989) *Art for Public Places: Critical Essays*, Winchester, Winchester School of Art Press.

Mitchell, W. J. T. (1986) *Iconology: Image, Text, Ideology*, Chicago, Ill., University of Chicago Press.

—— (1994) *Picture Theory*, Chicago, University of Chicago Press.

—— (1995a) 'Interdisciplinarity and visual culture', *Art Bulletin*, vol. LXXVII, no. 4 (December) pp. 540–4.

—— (1995b) 'What is visual culture?', in Lavin, I. (ed.) (1995).

Morath, I. (1981) 'Introduction' to Shaw, I. (1981).

Morgan, J. and Welton, P. (1986) *See What I Mean*, London, Edward Arnold.

Morley, D. (1995) 'Television: not so much a visual medium, more a visible object', in Jenks, C. (ed.) (1995).

Mulvey, L. (1989) *Visual and Other Pleasures*, London, Macmillan.

Nairn, S. (1990) *The State of the Art: Ideas and Images in the 1980s*, London, Chatto & Windus in collaboration with Channel Four Television Company Limited.

Naylor, G. (1968) *The Bauhaus*, London, Studio Vista.

Neustatter, A. (1992) 'Young love, first love', *Guardian*, 6 January.

Osman, C. (ed.) (1987) *George Rodger: Magnum Opus*, London, Nishen Publishing.

Packard, V. (1961) *The Waste Makers*, London, Longman.

Paglia, C. (1990) *Sexual Personae: Art and Decadence from Nefertiti to Emily Dickinson*, Harmondsworth: Penguin.

Panofsky, E. (1955) *Meaning in the Visual Arts*, Harmondsworth, Penguin.

Papanek, V. (1972) *Design for the Real World: Making to Measure*, London, Thames & Hudson.

Partington, A. (1992) 'Popular fashion and working class affluence', in Ash, J. and Wilson, E. (eds) (1992).

Pearson, N. (1982) *The State and the Visual Arts*, Milton Keynes, Open University Press.

Pevsner, N. (1936) *Pioneers of the Modern Movement*, London, Faber. Revised edition published in 1960 as *Pioneers of Modern Design*, Harmondsworth, Penguin.

Plant, S. (1992) *The Most Radical Gesture: The Situationist International in a Postmodern Age*, London, Routledge.

Plato (1961) *Collected Dialogues*, edited by Edith Hamilton and Huntington Cairns, Princeton, Princeton University Press.

Pointon, M. (1994) *History of Art: A Students' Handbook*, 3rd edn, London, Routledge.

Polhemus, T. (1994) *Streetstyle: From Sidewalk to Catwalk*, London, Thames & Hudson.

Pollock, G. and Parker, R. (1981) *Old Mistresses: Women, Art and Ideology*, London, Routledge.

Presbrey, F. (1929) *The History and Development of Advertising*, New York, Doubleday, Doran & Co.

Radice, B. (1984) *Memphis: Research, Experiences, Results, Failures and Successes of New Design*, London, Thames & Hudson.

—— (1981) *Memphis: The New International Style*, Milan, Electra.

Roberts, J. (1992) *Selected Errors*, London, Pluto.

Roethel, H.K. (1971) *The Blue Rider: With a Catalogue of the Works of Kandinsky, Klee, Macke, Marc*, New York, Praeger.

Rorty, R. (1980) *Philosophy and the Mirror of Nature*, Oxford, Blackwell.

Ruppert, J. (1997) 'The bloke's car is back', *Independent*, 5 July.

Ryle, G. (1976) *The Concept of Mind*, Harmondsworth, Penguin.

Sennett, R. (1990) *The Conscience of the Eye*, London, Faber & Faber.

Shaw, I. (1981) *Paris Magnum: Photographs 1935–1981*, New York, Aperture.

Simmel, G. (1971) 'Fashion', in *On Individuality and Social Form*, Chicago, Ill., University of Chicago.

Solomon, M.R. (ed.) (1985) *The Psychology of Fashion*, Lexington, Massachusetts, Lexington Books.

Sparke, P. (1986) *An Introduction to Design and Culture in the Twentieth Century*, London, Allen & Unwin.

—— (1995) *As Long as It's Pink: The Sexual Politics of Taste*, London, Pandora.

Sudjic, D. (1985) *Cult Objects: The Complete Guide to Having It All*, London, Paladin Grafton Books.

Vasari, G. (1987) *The Lives of the Artists*, Harmondsworth, Penguin.

Veblen, T. (1992, first published 1899) *The Theory of the Leisure Class*, New Brunswick, NJ, Transaction Publishers.

Viola, B. (1992) 'On transcending the water glass', in Jacobson, L. (ed.) (1992).

Walker, J.A. (1983) *Art in the Age of Mass Media*, London, Pluto Press.

—— (1989) *Design History and the History of Design*, London, Pluto Press.

Walsh, D. (1993) 'The role of ideology in cultural reproduction', in Jenks, C. (ed.) (1993).

Warnke, M. (1993) *The Court Artist: On the Ancestry of the Modern Artist*, Cambridge, Cambridge University Press.

Weber, M. (1948) *From Max Weber: Essays in Sociology*, London, Routledge.

—— (1978) *Economy and Society*, Berkeley, University of California Press.

Wildlife (1994) vol. 12, no. 4 (April) Bristol, BBC.

Williams, R. (1958) *Culture and Society 1780–1950*, Harmondsworth, Penguin.

—— (1976) *Keywords*, Glasgow, Fontana.

—— (1980) 'Advertising: The magic system', in *Problems in Materialism and Culture*, London, Verso.

—— (1981) *Culture*, Glasgow, Fontana.

Williamson, J. (1985) 'Royalty and representation' *Ten.* 8, no. 18, pp. 4–9.

—— (1986) *Consuming Passions*, London, Marion Boyars.

Wine, H. (1996) Entry on 'Academy', in *The Dictionary of Art*, (ed.) J. Turner, London, Macmillan.

Winter, I. J. and Zerner, H. (1995) 'Art and visual culture', *Art Journal*, pp. 42–3 (Fall).

Wittgenstein, L. (1961) *Tractatus Logico-philosophicus*, London, Routledge & Kegan Paul.

—— (1974) *Philosophical Investigations*, Oxford, Basil Blackwell.

Wolff, J. (1992a) *The Social Production of Art*, 2nd edn, London, Macmillan.

—— (1992b) 'Excess and inhibition: interdisciplinarity in the study of art', in Grossberg, L. *et al.* (eds).

Wölfflin, H. (1960) *Principles of Art History*, London, Bell and Hyman in association with Dover Publications.

Index

italic = illustration.